LAND GRAB

Books by John Upton Terrell

LAND GRAB

APACHE CHRONICLE

BUNKHOUSE PAPERS

AMERICAN INDIAN ALMANAC

THE NAVAJO

THE MAN WHO REDISCOVERED AMERICA

TRADERS OF THE WESTERN MORNING

THE SIX TURNINGS

JOURNEY INTO DARKNESS

LA SALLE

BLACK ROBE

ZEBULON PIKE

FURS BY ASTOR

ESTEVANICO THE BLACK

WAR FOR THE COLORADO RIVER

FAINT THE TRUMPET SOUNDS

PUEBLO DE LOS CORAZONES

PLUME ROUGE

SUNDAY IS THE DAY YOU REST

ADAM CARGO

THE LITTLE DARK MAN

John Upton Terrell

LAND GRAB

The Truth About
"The Winning of the West"

The Dial Press, New York, 1972

Library of Congress Cataloging in Publication Data

Terrell, John Upton, 1900–
Land grab.

Bibliography: p.
1. Indians, Treatment of–The West. 2. Fur trade–The West. 3. Cattle trade–The West. 4. Land tenure–The West. I. Title.
F591.T45 970.5 72–4335

Printed in the United States of America
First Printing

Book design by Margaret McCutcheon

Author's Note

This is a polemical notebook. A friend who was formerly editor-in-chief of a large publishing house advised me not to compile it.

"It's *the West that Americans would like to forget,*" he said.

Obviously I did not heed his counsel. It is incomprehensible to me how a people can benefit by deliberately suppressing and ignoring opprobrious episodes of their past. By what means can they measure their social, economic and cultural progress without taking into account the mistakes, faults and crimes of their ancestors? Persons whose minds are open only to pleasant legends of bygone years are, in effect, condoning the half-truths customarily disseminated by chambers of commerce and advertising agencies and abetting the immoral practices of pseudopatriots and political demagogues.

In this collection I present in brief form some facets of three important parts of western history. There is nothing in it that cannot easily be substantiated in a good library. I, therefore, thought it unnecessary to burden the pages with copious references to source material. In deference, however, to readers who might wish to delve further into the subject matter, I have inserted occasional numbers which refer to notes at the end of the volume, and these in turn serve as guides to a selected bibliography.

Truly, as my editor friend remarked, this compendium illuminates a side of western history that Americans might wish to forget. Indeed, I am constrained to believe that many of them already have forgotten it. Perhaps those who have done so will be benefitted by the reminders contained in these pages. At least, that is my hope.

John Upton Terrell

Contents

Part One

THE RED AND THE WHITE

The inhumane treatment consciously inflicted upon the Indians by the United States, by both the Government and society in general, is unsurpassed in the annals of any major power which has overwhelmed a weaker and less advanced people.

1

Bold headlines sickened us as they told of the bestial slaughter of helpless men, women and children at My Lai in South Vietnam. During World War II, we were equally horrified by the savagery of Nazis in the town of Lidice, which was razed, all its male inhabitants shot to death, and its women and children sent to starve in a concentration camp.

These outrages, only two of many that occurred in recent years, were not without numerous precedents much closer to the American scene than Europe and Southeast Asia. There were in the western United States scores of *My Lais* and *Lidices*, some of them perpetrated almost within the memory of the living.

They were carried out by uniformed American troops under the guise of "civilizing actions," by lawless bands of settlers and tradesmen who advocated extermination of the Indians as the simplest means by which they could confiscate land and other natural resources for their own enrichment. Each of the massacres was acclaimed by corrupt politicians. Indians, of course, could not vote, but the vilest, most ignorant and debased white man was entitled to place his X on a ballot.

To their credit, many Americans vigorously condemned the injustices and atrocities, but a far greater number approved and applauded them. As late as the eighteen seventies and eighties, numerous newspapers, and especially those in the West, called the fiendish acts commendable and justified, and hailed the perpetrators of them as worthy citizens and heroes.

2

A group of prominent men in Tucson, assisted by some Papago mercenaries (traditional enemies of the Apache) spent an hour or two one Sunday morning in the spring of 1871 killing one hundred and twenty-five unarmed Apaches who had been given sanctuary on a military reservation near Camp Grant, Arizona.

The leader of the mob was William Sanders Oury, a lawyer, cattle rancher and former Tucson mayor. The weapons and ammunition used were furnished by the Adjutant General of Arizona, Samuel Hughes, and were the property of the Territory of Arizona, paid for by taxpayers.

Only seven or eight of the Indians murdered were men, the others were women and children. About thirty small Apache boys and girls were carried off and sold into slavery in Mexico. A number of the squaws were mass-raped before being shot or clubbed to death.

The officer in command at Camp Grant was First Lieutenant Royal E. Whitman. He had served with distinction in the Civil War. When he was transferred to Arizona he was thirty-seven. A man of unquestionable integrity, highly intelligent, conscientious, humane and dedicated to his career, he was considered one of the most promising officers in the regular service.

Camp Grant was a bleak military post, ten square miles in extent, at the confluence of Aravapa Creek and the San Pedro River. When they were attacked, the victims of the slaughter were camped several miles distant from the post headquarters.

In an official report, Lieutenant Whitman stated:

". . . Sometime in February a party of five old [Apache] women came in under a flag of truce . . . saying they were in search of a boy, the son of one of the number, taken prisoner near Salt River some months before. This boy had been well cared for, and had become attached to his new mode of life, and did not wish to return. The party was kindly treated, rationed while here, and after two days went away, asking permission to return again. They came in about eight days, I think, with a still larger number, with some articles for sale to purchase *manta* [a cheap cotton cloth], as they were nearly naked. Before going away they said a young chief would like to come in with a party to have a talk. This I encouraged, and in a few days he came with about twenty-five of his band.

[The young chief was Eskiminsin, called Skimmy by soldiers, and well known as a daring and dangerous fighter.]

"He stated in brief that he was a chief of a band of about 150 of what was originally the Aravapa Apaches; that he wanted peace; that he and his people had no home, and could make none, as they were at all times apprehensive of the approach of cavalry. . . .

"I told him that I had no authority to make any treaty with him or to promise him that he could be allowed a permanent home here, but that he could bring in his band and I would feed them, and report his wishes to the department commander."

Whitman kept his word, and wrote to General Stoneman. For six weeks he waited for a reply. Then his letter was returned to him with a note from some clerk that it had not been prepared in proper form. It is not known whether the Department Commander ever saw it.

Whitman continued in his report:

"He [Skimmy] went out and returned about the first of March with his whole band. In the meantime rumors had been in from two other small bands, asking the same privileges, and giving the same reasons. I made the same reply to all, and by about the 5th of March I had over three hundred here. I wrote a detailed account of the whole matter . . . to department headquarters, asking for instructions. . . .

"At first I put them in camp about half a mile from the post, and counted them, and issued them rations every second day. The number steadily increased until it reached the number of five hundred and ten. Knowing as I did that the responsibility of the whole movement rested with me, and that in case of any loss to the Government coming of it I should be the sufferer, I kept them continually under observation, and I not only came to know the faces of all the men, but also the women and children. They were nearly naked and needed everything in the way of clothing. I stopped the Indians from bringing in hay [without pay] that I might buy from them. I arranged a system of tickets with which to pay them and to encourage them; and to be sure they were properly treated, I personally attended to all the weighing. I also made inquiries as to the kind of goods sold them [by the post trader and others] and prices. This proved a perfect success; not only the women and children engaged in the work, but many of the men. The amount [of hay] furnished by them in about two months was nearly 300,000 pounds.

"During this time many small parties had been out with passes for a certain number of days to burn mescal. . . . I made myself sure by noting the size of the party, and from the amount of mescal brought in, that no treachery was intended. . . . I spent hours each day with them in explaining to them the relations they should sustain to the Government, and their prospects for the future in case of either obedience or disobedience. . . . I made it a point to tell them all they wished to know. They were readily obedient and remarkably quick of comprehension. They were happy and contented and took every opportunity to show it. They had sent out runners to two other bands which were connected with them by intermarriages, and had received promises from them that they would come in . . . I am confident . . . we would have had one thousand persons, and at least two hundred and fifty able-bodied men. As their number increased, and the weather grew warmer, they asked and obtained permission to move farther up the Aravapa to higher ground and plenty of water . . . they were proposing to plant . . .

"Captain Stanwood arrived about the first of April and took command of the post. He had received while en route verbal instructions from General Stoneman to recognize and feed any Indians he might find at the post as 'prisoners of war.' After he had carefully inspected all things pertaining to their conduct and treatment, he concluded to make no changes, but had become so well satisfied of the integrity of their intentions that he left on the 24th with his whole troop for a long scout in the lower part of the Territory. The ranchmen in this vicinity were friendly and kind to them and felt perfectly secure, and had agreed with me to employ them at a fair rate of pay to harvest their barley. The Indians seem[ed] to have lost their characteristic anxiety to purchase ammunition, and had, in many instances, sold their best bows and arrows. I made frequent visits to their camp, and if any were absent from count made it my business to know why.

"Such was the condition of things up to the morning of the 30th of April. They had so won on me, that from my first idea of treating them justly and honestly as an officer of the Army, I had come to feel a strong personal interest in helping to show them the way to a higher civilization. I had come to feel respect for men who, ignorant and naked, were still ashamed to lie or steal, and for women who would work cheerfully like slaves to clothe themselves and children, but, untaught, held their virtue above price. Aware of the lies and hints industriously circulated by the puerile press of the Territory, I was content to *know* I had positive proof they were so.

"I had ceased to have any fears of their leaving here, and only dreaded for them that they might at any time be ordered to do so. They frequently expressed anxiety to hear from the general, that they might have confidence to build for themselves better houses, but would always say, 'You know what we want, and if you can't see him you can write and do for us what you can.'

"It is possible that during this time individuals from here had visited other bands, but that any number had ever been out to assist in any marauding expedition I know is false.

"On the morning of April [30th], I was at breakfast at 7:30 o'clock, when a dispatch was brought to me by a sergeant of Company P, Twenty-first Infantry, from Captain Penn, commanding Fort Lowell, informing me that a large party had left Tucson on the 28th, with the avowed purpose of killing all the Indians at this post. I immediately sent the two interpreters, mounted, to the Indian camp, with orders to tell the chiefs the exact state of things, and for them to bring their entire party inside the post. As I had no cavalry, and but about fifty infantry (all recruits), and no other officer,* I could not leave the post to go to their defense.

"My messengers returned in about an hour, with intelligence that they could find no living Indians.

"The camp was burning and the ground strewed with their dead and mutilated women and children. I immediately mounted a party of about twenty soldiers and citizens, and sent them with the post surgeon, with a wagon to bring in the wounded, if any could be found. The party returned late in the p.m., having found no wounded and without having been able to communicate with any of the survivors. Early the next morning I took a similar party, with spades and shovels, and went out and buried all the dead in and immediately about the camp. . . . While at the work many of them came to the spot and indulged in their expressions of grief, too wild and terrible to be described.

". . . Many of the men, whose families had all been killed, when I spoke to them and expressed sympathy for them, were obliged to turn away, unable to speak, and too proud to show their grief. The women whose children had been killed or stolen were convulsed with grief, and looked at me appealingly, as though I was their last hope on earth. Children who two days before had been full of fun and frolic kept at a distance, expressing wondering horror. I did what I could. . . ."

Under a headline, "Victory for Peace," a Denver news-

* Second in command, Second Lieutenant W. W. Robinson, Jr., was on furlough.

paper declared: "We give this act of the citizens of Arizona most hearty and unqualified endorsement. We congratulate them on the fact that permanent peace arrangements have been made with so many, and we only regret that the number was not double. Camp Grant is the last of those victories for civilization and progress which have made Sand Creek, Washita . . . and other similar occurrences famous in western history. It is just and right and was fully demanded by circumstances of the times."

Arizona papers claimed that the Camp Grant Indians had been conducting raids, but no evidence was proffered to substantiate the charge. On the contrary, abundant evidence was produced to show that the victims had been living in peace and working hard to develop farms of their own.

A Tucson newspaper reported that "the California papers quite generally approve of the Camp Grant massacres," adding that one in San Francisco recited "at considerable length good reasons why such massacres are made necessary in self-defense;" one in Sacramento "heartily endorses the slaughter. . . ." and "San Diego papers speak of it as 'the joyful news.' "

Terming the tragedy as "outrage" and "purely murder," President U. S. Grant warned the Arizona governor that unless the participants were indicted and tried in court he would place Arizona Territory under martial law. The trial was held. It was a farce. The presiding judge instructed a Tucson jury that killing Indians who were "believed" to be a menace to peace was not murder. The jurors deliberated about twenty minutes. All defendants, although they had admitted taking part in the carnage, were found not guilty.[1]

3

At nightfall on Thanksgiving Day, 1868, General George Armstrong Custer, commanding several companies of cavalry, came upon a quiet Indian village on the Washita River in Oklahoma. He made no effort to determine the identity of the inhabitants, or to learn whether they were the hostile Indians for whom he was looking, which he might easily have done through his scouts. Dispersing contingents into battle stations, he went to bed.

As the sun appeared on the horizon of the wintry plain, he ordered the band to play "Garry Owen," his favorite song, and launched an attack. He met no organized resistance. A few Indians, roused from their blankets, fired at the cavalcade sweeping down on them. The people of the village had been unaware that the troops were in the vicinity. They had no reason to fear a surprise attack, for they were peaceable, and a party to the Treaty of Medicine Lodge.

Although they had affixed their marks to this worthless instrument, which the United States had sworn to honor, one hundred and three men of the band were murdered. Custer, one of the most degraded and unconscionable officers who ever wore an Army uniform, did not trouble to count the number of women and children killed without mercy in that November dawn. A report that he was responsible for the slaughter of nearly two hundred Indians who had placed their faith in the integrity of the Federal Government disturbed him not at all.

Captain Frederick W. Benteen, indignant and heartsick at Custer's monstrous actions, would write a letter about the massacre to a friend. It would be printed in St. Louis and New

York City newspapers. Recounting how Custer sat by a campfire after the "victory" and amused himself by shooting Indian ponies, the letter said in part:

"That which cannot be taken away must be destroyed. Eight hundred ponies are to be put to death. Our chief exhibits his close sharpshooting and terrifies the crowd of frightened, captured squaws and papooses by dropping the straggling ponies in death near them. Ah! he is a clever marksman. Not even do the poor dogs of the Indians escape his eye and aim, as they drop dead or limp howling away. . . . The plunder having been culled over is hastily piled; the wigwams are pulled down and throw on it, and soon the whole is one blazing mass. . . . The last pony is killed. The huge fire dies out, and as the brave band of the Seventh Cavalry strikes up the air, 'Ain't I Glad To Get Out of the Wilderness,' we slowly pick our way across the creek over which we charged so gallantly in the early morn. Take care! Do not trample on the dead bodies of that woman and child lying there!"

Western newspapers called the Washita massacre a glorious triumph. Custer was publicly acclaimed as a brilliant and daring Indian fighter. He reveled in the accolades bestowed upon him, for he was planning to become a candidate for the presidency of the United States.

The Sioux spoiled that dream on the Little Big Horn.[2]

4

On a fall day in 1874, a large band of Cheyenne and Arapaho appeared at Fort Lyon, Colorado, to sign a treaty of peace. The pact was negotiated, and they were given supplies and permission by the commanding officer to establish a winter hunting camp on Sand Creek, some forty miles distant from the military post.

Shortly afterward, early on a November morning, they were attacked by a strong force of Colorado Volunteers commanded by Colonel John M. Chivington, a former minister. In the surprise assault on the peaceful Indians asleep in their tepees, Chivington and his soldiers:

1. Murdered at least two hundred men, women and children. The number may have been much greater, for reports were conflicting. Investigators sent to the scene expressed the opinion that as many as four hundred had been slain.

2. Raped wounded squaws before killing them, then amputated their fingers, arms and ears to obtain rings, necklaces and other souvenirs.

3. Knocked out the brains of little children.

4. Cut out the private parts of both men and women and took them to Denver to be exhibited to the public.

5. Under an order from Chivington, scalped nearly all victims.

The colonel boasted that no prisoners had been taken. He was fully aware of the identity of the Indians, knew that they had signed a treaty of peace and that they had been promised protection by military authorities.

In Denver, Chivington and his troopers were toasted as conquering heroes. Said a leading newspaper, "Among the brilliant feats of arms in Indian warfare, the recent campaign of our Colorado Volunteers will stand in history with few rivals, and none to exceed it in final results. . . . All acquited themselves well, and Colorado soldiers have again covered themselves with glory."*[3]

* The Camp Grant, Washita and Sand Creek massacres were typical of many others that took place in the West. A large volume would be required to record descriptions of all of them.

5

The statutory premise that an Indian tribe had a just claim of ownership to the lands its members occupied was totally unacceptable to Americans gazing covetously toward the western plains and mountains. It was a legal decision as incomprehensible to them as Indian culture, as mysterious as Indian ritual, as unintelligible as Indian language.

Their reasoning, or at least what passed for their reasoning, was predicated on the unshakable belief that inasmuch as the economy of the Indians was simple the Indians themselves were stupid.

The westering Americans harbored other conclusions in addition:

Indians were red. They, therefore, ranked far below the white on the human social scale, and must be classed with the black and yellow.

The West was American territory. Americans had fought to acquire it or had legally purchased it. Indians, therefore, were foreigners, intruders, squatters.

Indians had no organized religion, and even the dumb Mexicans had permanent churches in which bells rang.

Indians went about half-naked, and some of them wore only a G-string, and some of the women didn't trouble to cover their breasts. Therefore, Indians were indecent, immoral and depraved.

Indians were attracted by worthless things, such as feathers and horseshoe nails, bright pieces of worn-out cloth and shiny bits of tin. They cared nothing for gold or silver. Therefore, Indians were naive and had no knowledge of values.

Indians didn't have wagons, carriages, plows, good barns and houses, iron stoves or even wooden beds. Indians were, therefore, ignorant and backward.

Understanding has not entirely supplanted these concepts. Only a short time before I wrote these words a white official of the Bureau of Indian Affairs stationed on the Apache Reservation at San Carlos, Arizona, said to me, "Hellfire, when we conquered the West, the Indians didn't even have the wheel. Archaeologists and ethnologists and all the other nutty scientists who study and write about Indians make me sick. Why should we bother our heads about such ignorant, low-type people? Why should we spend millions trying to educate them when they got nothing between their ears but bone? The whole country would have been better off if they had been wiped off the earth."

Well, genocide was advocated by State and Territorial governments, town councils and countless pioneer settlers and merchants throughout the entire period of western conquest. If its popularity as a solution for the Indian problems has generally diminished, it still finds favor in some minds.

6

The ideas that dominated the thinking, if it may be termed that, of Americans who flooded the West during the nineteenth century are not beyond explanation. To achieve an understanding of them one need only remember that by far the larger number of persons, both male and female, who crossed the Missouri as emigrants were not blessed with great intellects. They were people of the backwoods, of the city slums, unlettered common laborers and farmers and hunters and trappers, a vast proportion of them the dregs of American society. They were, with some notable exceptions, uncouth, ill-mannered, crude, ignorant and greedy. They were religious and racial bigots. All of them were looking for something for nothing.

A great fallacy still harbored by a regrettably large number of Americans and still promoted by hypocritical patriots and politicians is that every man and woman who chose to enter Indian Country beyond the Missouri was a hero or heroine. Paeans still ring throughout the land for the brave souls who set out for the unknown, facing the great perils of the wilderness with a burning dream of building a greater America.

They didn't do any such thing. They thought least of all, and most likely not at all, of their country's future. The only dreams they had—except nightmares caused by fear—were of free land and free gold, of becoming rich and secure, with a minimum of exertion and little expense.

It could hardly be expected that people afflicted with such deficiencies, of such low levels and backgrounds, could be expected to display intelligence in their relations with Indians. Obviously they could not make use of qualities they did not possess. Thus, they were governed entirely by animalistic and materialistic instincts, and the purity of these characteristics was seldom adulterated even by small portions of compassion, consideration or justice. As they were unable to understand Indians, they treated them with disdain, hatred and contempt, all thoroughly normal reactions.

The colorful euphemisms that newspapers, books and periodicals showered on the settlers who crossed the western plains enhanced the public's overall picture of the Golden West, but they concealed the ingredients of depravity and viciousness that existed. Most of the frontiersmen, pioneers and conquerors of the wild western domain, were, and still are, highly lauded and eulogized for courage that did not exist in them, and praised for moral principles they did not possess.

God-fearing was a term generously applied to them. True, they attended church and listened to sermons and sang hymns on Sunday, but it was also true that they conveniently forgot all biblical admonitions as soon as they left church services. They turned their religion on and off with an effective mental spigot. They advocated and practiced a method of putting the Indian in touch with Heaven that was more certain and less complicated than that commanded by the doctrines of Christianity. It was, "Shoot them where you find them."

In the unwritten lexicon of the people erroneously called Indians, the words *Christian* and *Christianity* were synonyms for *disaster* and *death*.

The definition found permanency in native parlance and thought as fast as the armored conquistadors and their somberly robed colleagues pushed from the Caribbean islands to the continental mainland. As the invaders drove relentlessly onward through the vast valleys and forests and deserts, over the great plains and plateaus and mountain ranges never before entered by men of the Old World, symbols augmented the clarity of the meaning of the two words: The gun, the sword, the lance and the cross with a tortured, bloody man crucified upon it.

Christianity in all its aspects struck terror into the Indians. If the trauma they suffered no longer endures in its original severity, the confusion it spawned is far from being completely dissipated.

By some curious course of reasoning, the Christian conquerors of the West, including Americans, believed they had a right to force the Indians to accept their religion and to divest themselves of all other spiritual beliefs. Many of their descendants living today proclaim that they hold the same right, and this contention has the support of large church congregations and influential missionary organizations. The premise of their argument is that Indians have no religion. Nothing could be further from the truth. No people more religious than the Indians ever lived on earth.

The myth persists that Indians hastened their own destruction by being reluctant to accept the God of the white invaders and continuing to worship deities representing the natural elements and forces of the cosmos. It should not be forgotten that in the area of the United States the spiritual beliefs of the Indians had prevailed, and their religious ritual had been practiced for countless centuries before the beginning of the Christian era. Yet, they were expected by their white antagonists to abandon overnight their ancient faith and to adopt without question, not to mention comprehend, totally strange beliefs that were based on tenets in sharp conflict with those so deeply instilled in them.

Religious groups and individuals dedicated to "saving the souls of Indians," even if they destroyed them in the process, steadfastly adhered to the theory that all problems involving the "heathens" would be resolved if they could build chapels and missions and force the Indians to affiliate with them. These misguided, fanatical lackeys of numerous denominations were unable to understand—and some of them still are—that a man whose means of living had been taken from him, whose wife and children were sick and starving, whose own belly was empty, could not be inspired to show intense interest in absorbing the Gospel, and could not be made content with the single thought that the Lord would provide.

Indians recognize a supreme power of creation, but not an individual supreme being. In their pantheon, there are many supernatural beings. The prominence of the positions of these deities varies from people to people. There is no clearly defined divine hierarchy. There are holy places but no permanent temples and no established cults associated with religious practice. Nor are there priestly administrative orders under which religion is organized for practical purposes.

While white society tends to turn religion on and off as needs demand or moods please, the Indian is never detached from it, day or night. It is improbable that any people are, or ever were, more influenced by the supernatural or guided to a greater extent by spiritual beliefs. Religion affects very nearly everything the Indian does or thinks.

The Indian has no conception of a hereafter, such as the Christian Heaven or Hell. Their religion, generally speaking, is a system of imitative and sympathetic magic aimed ritually at fulfillment of the requirements of life and living. It is not concerned with preparation for death and afterlife. Although, like any sane human being, the Indian struggles to prolong his life, he does not live in morbid fear of dying. Death is looked upon as the normal end of a cycle for man, just as it is for plants and animals. When death comes, an Indian becomes one with the cosmos, a condition in which he is neither punished nor rewarded; water poured into a river is no longer identifiable in itself.

Every Indian ceremony is designed to accomplish a specific purpose. Some are prophylactic in nature, constructed to ward off evil or attract goodness. Some are meant to exorcise evil and restore the health and strength of an afflicted person. Some are pleas to individual deities for success in hunting or in warfare, for rain, for bountiful harvests, for development of strong character, for wisdom. Invariably the legends, prayers, poems and songs that compose the immense body of Indian sacred literature exhibit great beauty and imagination.

"They are," states the noted Indian scholar, Robert W. Young, "in no wise less worthy of literary rank than the Homeric poems, Hymns of the Rig-Veda and many other heritages from our past. They are stories of adventure and magic, hero-myths and travels. There is humor and suspense in tales told with mimicry and great beauty. . . . The poems form parts of chants, beautiful in content and chanted in a peculiar rhythm with vowel lengths and tones of the words altered in a characteristic manner."*

The picture of a God that is all good always has been and still remains incomprehensible to the Indians.

8

Thousands of Americans visit the old California missions each year, but few of them realize that what they are seeing was the first organized penal system on soil that would become a part of the United States.

* Although in this statement Young was speaking of the Navajo, his words may be applied generally to the religious ritual of most Indian peoples.

Probably sixty thousand Indians, who were no more than a step out of the Stone Age, were forced into these concentration camps during the sixty-five years of their operation. Not only adults were made slaves. Children were taken from their families to be reared behind mission bars. They were permitted to leave locked dormitories only to attend services and to perform assigned duties. When grown enough they were put to work in the expansive vineyards and orchards with older Indians.

All of the so-called mission Indians were prisoners. They not only labored in the fields and tended the herds, but they were also compelled to work at constructing the buildings now so greatly admired for their architecture and beauty. The blood of the builders stained the adobe walls.

Discipline in the missions was rigid. For failure to perform their labors adequately and for minor infractions, the Indians were denied food. For being absent from church, or even for tardiness, they suffered corporal punishment and solitary confinement. Women as well as men were suspended by their hands and flogged by priests. Attempts to escape—and there were many—were usually futile. The runaways were pursued by soldiers and brought back to suffer severe penalties, which included beatings and days of starvation. How many thousand mission Indians perished in bondage cannot be determined, but there were a great many, and it can be said that they perished under the banner of Christianity.

American settlers and gold-seekers finished the job of destroying the California Indians. The glitter of romance with which the Gold Rush is traditionally painted becomes tarnished by corrosive facts. The riffraff of America poured westward to the land of promise. In a few years they murdered some thirty-five thousand Indian men, women and children.[4]

9

All Indian peoples have creation myths, and in their fundamental elements, they are no less miraculous or imaginative than the fables in the Christian bible.

The origin myth of the Navajo serves as an excellent example.

In the Navajo genesis man evolved through four underworlds before reaching the surface of the earth. The four underworlds and the surface world are portrayed as superimposed hemispheres, the skies of which are supported by deities. All events that occurred in the four underworlds were evolutionary steps toward the birth of mankind in the surface world.

In the first underworld there were four clouds, which embodied the prototypes of males and females. First Man was created along with an ear of white corn, when two of the clouds met in the east. In the west two clouds met and created First Woman and an ear of yellow corn. Although First Man and First Woman lived together, they did not produce mankind. They were merely prototypes, not in themselves human beings. But in this darkness it was predestined that man would be, for First Man and First Woman planned his creation and, with the help of Coyote Beings, Spider Beings and other animate creatures among whom they dwelt, also planned all other developments for the surface world of man.

In the second underworld the prototypes fought with Bird Beings, and moved up to the third underworld. There they encountered Holy People and various other kinds of beings. In the third underworld many miraculous things came to pass. There the emerging people, who would call themselves Dineh, found the prototype of Changing Woman, who represented fertility and life—the seasons. There agricultural seeds were obtained. There were found the prototypes of the four sacred mountains that would mark the boundaries of the Dineh's world on earth.

But the third underworld was not without misfortunes. There the sexes were temporarily separated, with the result that monsters were born. The Water Monster produced a great flood that drove all beings upward to the fourth underworld. At last the sexes were reunited, but the monsters made the fourth underworld a fearful place, and First Man and First Woman led everyone up to the fifth world, the surface.

All the prototypes of mountains, rivers, and other geographical features, which were both male and female, were also brought up to the fifth world, and there the animate and the inanimate took the forms in which they would forever remain. According to the cosmic plan formulated in the lower worlds, the sun, the moon, and the stars were assigned their places, and so night and day and the seasons were established. The Holy People, the spiritual deities, went to live on the four sacred mountains, which were adorned, each in its turn, with jet, turquoise, abalone shells and white shells. Ever since, when the Holy People wish to make a journey, they have traveled on sunbeams, rainbows and lightning. And Changing Woman, who is blessed with eternal youth, lives in a great house beside the western ocean.[5]

10

Indians regard themselves not as owners of the physical earth but part of it. They think of themselves as being inextricably woven into its scheme, and, actually, into the natural scheme of the entire universe as they conceive it. They do not look upon themselves as simply pieces of bone and flesh, not simply as possessors of certain faculties. They know they are those things, but they also believe that they are of the soil, the winds, the stars, the plants and grasses, the thunder and lightning and rain—everything that is born and lives and dies in the eternal cycle of life.

The white man, of course, has no such conception. He thinks of natural resources only as products to be exploited. He attaches no spiritual significance to the land or any of its treasures. His program is take, rape, destroy and look elsewhere for opportunities to repeat the process. In the belief of the white man, there is no relationship between religion and the physical world.

After more than four centuries of trying to destroy the spiritual beliefs of the Indians, the emissaries of Christianity have made little progress. The only success they are justified in claiming is that they have created in the Indians an intense distrust of Christian doctrines.

Why should the Indian adopt Christianity? Men calling themselves Christians, since the discovery of America, have demonstrated to the Indians that the Christian credo has no influence on Christian actions. The white man preaches goodness and practices badness.[6]

11

When the United States Government was organized, it recognized the right of Indian tribes to occupy their respective homelands. The *right to occupy*, not the right of ownership. This, of course, would have been a totally meaningless concession had it been permitted to stand alone within such narrow and impervious confines. But it was implemented by the decree that only by treaty or purchase, and in either case only with just compensation, could land be taken from a tribe claiming it.

The qualifications, however, did not mean that ultimate sovereignty did not belong to the Government. This was the greater right, but in claiming it the Government at the same time recognized the inherent lesser right, the Indians' *right of occupancy*. Basic United States statutes, innumerable interpretations by eminent jurists and rulings of the Supreme Court have made this contention indisputable.[7]

Some examples follow:

"By the treaty which concluded the War of our Revolution, Great Britain relinquished all claims not only to the government, but to the proprietary and territorial rights of the United States. . . . By this treaty the powers of the government and the right to soil which had previously been in Great Britain passed definitely to these States. We had before taken possession of them by declaring independence, but neither the declaration of independence nor the treaty confirming it could give us more than that which we before possessed, or to which Great Britain was before entitled. It has never been doubted that either the United States or the several States had a clear title to all the lands within the boundary lines described in the treaty, *subject only to the Indian right of occupancy*, and that the exclusive right to extinguish that right was vested in that government which might constitutionally exercise it.

"The title by conquest is acquired and maintained by force. The conquerer prescribes its limits. Humanity, however, acting on public opinion, has established as a general rule that the conquered shall not be wantonly oppressed, and that their condition shall remain as eligible as is compatible with the objects of the conquest. Usually they are incorporated with the victorious nation. . . . When this incorporation is practicable, humanity demands, and a wise policy requires, that the rights of the conquered to property should remain unimpaired. . . . When the conquest is complete, and the conquered inhabitants can be blended with the conquerors, or safely governed as a distinct people, public opinion, which not even the conqueror can disregard, imposes these restraints upon him, and he cannot neglect them without injury to his fame, and hazard to his power."[8]

"In our Union the aborigines had only a possessory title, and in the original thirteen States each owned in fee, *subject to the Indian right*, all ungranted lands within their respective limits; and beyond the States the residue of the ungranted lands were vested in fee in the United States, *subject to the Indian possessory right*, to the extent of the national limits."[9]

"The Indians have no fee in the lands they occupy. The fee is in the Government. They cannot, of course, aliene [sic] them either to nations or individuals, the exclusive right of pre-emption being in the Government. Yet they have a *qualified right of occupancy which can only be extinguished by treaty, and upon fair compensation;* until which they are entitled to be *protected in their possession.*"[10]

"It has never been contended that the Indian title amounted to nothing. Their right of possession has never been questioned."[11]

"Indians are acknowledged to have an unquestionable, and heretofore unquestioned, right to the lands they occupy until that right shall be extinguished by a voluntary cession to the Government.

"The Indian nations have always been considered as distinct

independent political communities, retaining their original national rights as the undisputed possessors of the soil, from time immemorial, with the single exception of that imposed by irresistible power, which excluded them from intercourse with any other European potentate than the first discoverer of the coast of the particular region claimed; and this was a restriction which those European potentates imposed on themselves as well as on the Indians. The very term 'nation,' so generally applied to them, means 'a people distinct from others.' The Constitution, by declaring treaties already made, to be the supreme law of the land, has adopted and sanctioned the previous treaties with the Indian nations, and consequently admits their rank among those powers who are capable of making treaties. The words 'treaty' and 'nation' are words of our own language, selected in our diplomatic and legislative proceedings by ourselves, having each a definite and well understood meaning. We have applied them to the Indians as we have applied them to other nations of the earth. They are applied to all in the same sense."[12]

Stating that Indian tribes were nations, President John Quincy Adams told Congress, "At the establishment of the Federal Government the principle was adopted of considering them as foreign and independent powers, and also as proprietors of lands. As independent powers, we negotiated with them by treaties; as proprietors, we purchased of them all the land which we could prevail on them to sell; as brethren of the human race, rude and ignorant, we endeavored to bring them to the knowledge of religion and letters."[13]

How did we do these things? This was the procedure:

1. Invade Indian lands.
2. Confiscate their resources.
3. After they were stricken, desperate and destitute, offer

them a treaty under which the lands they had already lost would be surrendered to the Government.

4. Tell them to move west and find other lands unoccupied by white settlers.

5. Offer to pay them something for the territory and resources of which they had been deprived, but withhold the promised funds under one pretext or another.

Thus, the Federal Government failed to comply with the laws decreeing that only by treaty and with just compensation could Indian lands be acquired.

The policy upon which those laws were based had been proclaimed by Congress while still acting under the Articles of Confederation, when the rumble of guns still echoed in the ears of the men who had fought at Valley Forge and Yorktown. Said a Congressional Resolution in 1783: ". . . it is essential to the welfare of the United States, as well as necessary for the maintenance of harmony and friendship with the Indians, not members of any of the States, that all cause of quarrel or complaint between them and the United States or any of them, should be removed and prevented; therefore, the United States in Congress assembled, have thought proper to issue their proclamation, *and they do hereby prohibit and forbid all persons from making settlements on lands inhabited or claimed by Indians, without the limits or jurisdiction of any particular State, and from purchasing or receiving any gift or cession of such lands or claims without the express authority and direction of the United States in Congress assembled.*"[14]

On paper it was a just and equitable policy. The basic statutes that were written embodied and supported it, providing it with the guise of clear and unequivocal law. In reality those legal rulings were worthless, for neither the Executive nor the Legislative Branches of the Government enforced them; indeed both were guilty of repeatedly violating them, and society in general ignored them. Of course, they could have been enforced only with guns. Force of arms was the only means by which Americans could have been halted in their stealing of Indian resources and their slaughtering of Indians who sought to defend themselves and retain the rights which the laws of the United States gave them. Laws meant nothing to the thieves who "won the West."

12

For more than half a century, the Bureau of Indian Affairs, a division of the Department of the Interior, reigned as the outstanding cesspool of the Federal Government. Its distinction in this respect becomes all the more notable when one takes into account the fact that in the latter half of the nineteenth century cesspools were a commonplace in Washington.

It has been estimated by highly qualified authorities that less than 20 per cent of the goods purchased for Indians of the West between the years 1830 and 1885 reached them.

These goods, paid for with public money, included food, clothing, building materials, tools, farming implements, livestock and medical supplies. Contractors received payment for articles that were never shipped.

Entire wagon trains of supplies vanished. Railroad cars loaded when they left the East were empty when they reached the West.

Some Indian agents, of course, were honest and dedicated to

their work, but they were a small minority. There were many more who were talented thieves, and belonged to rings of contractors and Indian Bureau officials who conspired to defraud the Indians of necessities they needed to survive.

As a result thousands of American Indians died of malnutrition and neglect while being helplessly confined on reservations or in concentration camps.

There are countless official reports of individual agents who left their posts after short tenure, perhaps no more than two or three years, with fifty to a hundred thousand dollars, acquired by selling to merchants goods purchased for Indians.

If the Bureau of Indian Affairs (BIA) ceased to be a thieves' market some years ago, it has now become a political and administrative jungle. Employees crowd its main and all its branch offices, confused, frustrated, inept and wandering helplessly in a red tape wilderness.

The BIA is not its own master in handling Indian affairs. It must coordinate its activities with those of a dozen other departments—Agriculture, Forest Service, Bureau of Land Management, Health, Education, and Welfare, Bureau of Reclamation, to name a few, all of which have their fingers in the Indian pie. It would be extremely difficult for an expert accountant to determine how many millions are spent each year on Indian projects by these various agencies and the BIA. Certainly the total would approximate a billion dollars.

Thus, having failed to annihilate the Indians by warfare, murder and starvation, American society is now attempting to shape their destiny at an annual cost of six or seven thousand dollars a year for every Indian family living on a reservation. It is not impossible to destroy a people with excessive interference in their daily lives, proclaimed concern that is false and the poisonous fruit of political patronage.

13

There never was, and there is not today, an official Indian policy. If there always was an underlying legal policy, as stated by laws and courts, there never was a basic administrative policy. A new one was contrived by each succeeding administration, and invariably its vagueness made futile any attempt to obtain a clear and binding interpretation. The result was that each of the several Federal departments involved in relations with the Indians had what it termed its Indian policy. State and Territorial Governments, also had their own peculiar policies. None of them conformed in specific details with any of the others.

Even if reconciliations of the differences had been possible, which they were not, they would have brought little or no progress toward a solution of the dilemma. Direction, honest, forceful, competent direction, was mandatory. Within the established structure of the government, this was not attainable. Corruption and political machinations, if not diverse social and economic theories, placed such a goal beyond human reach. Under such a system, not even a President could have formulated and enforced a definitive policy.

14

The many groups outside the government that concerned themselves with Indian affairs were precluded by conflicting philosophies and convictions from organizing a united front. If the starry-eyed idealists, the missionary societies, the tub-thumpers for moral excellence in legislative and administrative practices, the crusaders for the brotherhood of man, had anything in common it was indicated only in their proclaimed hope of improving the lot of the unfortunate Indians. But even the texture of the banner symbolizing this noble objective was discolored and raveled by the hodgepodge of threads with which it had been woven. By comparison, the grafters, swindlers and unconscionable bureaucrats entrenched in the Washington offices of the Interior Department, its satellite, the Indian Bureau, and their cohorts in the field, although fewer in number, enjoyed far more power to influence the course of any western project. Their operations, conspiratorial in structure, bonded by unity of purpose, and menaced only by occasional incidents involving extreme individual greed, for the most part were highly successful.

Practicality seldom, and reality never, influenced the reasoning of either the secular or ecclesiastical clans dedicated to saving the Indians. If they wanted justice for them, they wanted peace more. They stumped for gigantic federal appropriations to pay the cost of furnishing the Indians with all the necessities of life. Only through unqualified subsidization, they argued, could the way be cleared for civilizing and Christianizing the ignorant aborigines. Only by this means could Indians be transformed into Americans. While they expressed the opinion that in the end such a program, immense as it might be, would prove to be cheaper than warfare, they insisted in the same breath that expense was not the paramount factor. The most important thing was to establish a lasting peace . . . at any price.

The thieves in the Indian Bureau had every reason to give such a policy their support. It was made to order for them, for peace in the West meant a larger pork barrel. You couldn't furnish Indians with the necessities of life while fighting them.

No one had devised a scheme for furnishing dead Indians with anything but graves. With Indians confined in concentration camps even a mildly enterprising agent could accumulate ten to twenty thousand dollars a year on an annual salary of twelve hundred, and comparable thriftiness could bring a cooperative manufacturer or merchant even greater returns. These were not insignificant rewards, but they would be small by comparison with those to be gained if all Indians could be forced to abandon their traditional ways and agree to live in permanent establishments. Under such conditions the number of wards to whom the Government would be obligated to furnish the necessities of life would be immeasurably increased, and so thereby would opportunities to steal from both the Indians and the Government.

Thus, for entirely different reasons both factions urged a cessation of hostilities. Actually, however, ensuing events showed that the disparity of their private goals was not a matter of great significance. Each party was too strong, too well fortified, to be summarily eliminated. When politicians saw an advantage in approving certain recommendations of missionary and other groups, no curtailment of the stealing followed. Indeed, in some areas of the West it increased. Almost every remedial measure attempted was a failure. The few that succeeded were inconsequential, of no overall benefit. Eventually a plan which categorically divided authority and specified responsibilities was initiated. The result was chaos. The religious fanatics concentrated on destroying Indian culture and spiritual beliefs. The reformers and do-gooders sought to impose on Indians overnight economic systems and juridical codes that were not only incomprehensible to them but were the antithesis of tenets and habits to which they had adhered for countless generations. Seeing no profits to be gained by any of these exertions, the swindling rings directed their attention to devising means by which they could enlarge their nefarious operations.

In the center of the turmoil, pressured from all sides, was the Army. Essentially its responsibilities added up to the single duty of keeping order on the frontier.

In fairness, it must be said that field commanders striving to carry out this immense and complicated assignment were harrassed by self-serving politicians, exploited by corruptors, often given inadequate forces for a specific campaign, and frequently thwarted by conflicting orders from brass far distant from the scenes of action.

On numerous occasions the Army was undeservedly blamed for the reverses and hardships it suffered; as if it should have been able to control weather, prevent droughts, sandstorms, blizzards, heat and grass fires; as if it were responsible for the schemes of thieves who consorted with members of Congress and high Federal officials; as if it stole the supplies needed for grueling marches; indeed, as if it were responsible for the characters and complexities of the Indians it had to fight.

If the Army caught and punished white criminals it was accused of being prejudiced against civilians. If commanding officers showed compassion and attempted to carry on with an understanding of Indian problems, they were branded weaklings and charged with betraying their own people for bloody savages. If the Army shot raiders in the act of carrying off white women and children, it was a ruthless force determined to wipe out the helpless Indians.

Some settlers and merchants of little western towns had a good word for the Army because it protected them, but more often than not the praise was qualified with the criticism that the Army was too stringent in the enforcement of laws on white people. Members of Congress frothed in fury at reports reaching them through the War Department, prepared from the testimony of intelligent and fairminded officers, that most of the troubles and tragedies of the West were brought about by the avarice and lawlessness of white farmers, storekeepers and businessmen who coveted the land and the resources of the Indians. Congress simply would not tolerate the assertion that voters cheated, robbed, maimed and murdered Indians without good cause, not those good voters who attended services in little clapboard churches on Sunday mornings. More than one Army officer was removed from command for no more than intimating that western settlers, the backbone of American society, the finest people on God's green earth, were guilty of such crimes.

It is an unavoidable fact, however, that many of the Army's worst troubles were caused by its own unbelievable red tape, its gross remissness and bungling. Moreover, the Army contained officers, some in the highest ranks, and countless soldiers, who were hardly qualified for inclusion in the lowest order of *Homo sapiens*. They were men without a redeeming quality, who had no more compunction about murdering an Indian than about shooting a rabbit. They left a record for barbarism that outshone any savagery displayed by their red adversaries. The Army's job in the West would have been difficult enough without these psychopaths in uniform.

The prowess of the Indians as fighters, their courage and spirit, may not be exaggerated. This is amply manifested by the length of time required to subjugate them. It is even more graphically and vividly demonstrated by consideration of the conditions under which they defended themselves, the disadvantages burdening them, their tools of warfare and their inability to comprehend the motivations of their antagonists. With almost incredible constancy, the Army underestimated the intelligence, fortitude and skills of the Indians.

From the time of the invasion of the Seven Cities of Cibola to the battles of the Little Big Horn and Wounded Knee, white men, both soldiers and civilians, thought of themselves as superior in every way to red men. It was an expensive mistake, but as costly and as tragic was the conception that because Indians sought to preserve the wilderness instead of destroying it, because they had little or nothing in the way of intrinsic resources, they were also animals, undeserving of either compassion or consideration.

Not only the Indians suffered under such mistaken and unintelligent beliefs. Those who harbored them were also victims, and they left to posterity a dishonorable historical image. At least, the Indian did not do that.

15

In acquiring territory, either by cession or purchase, the United States assumed and recognized all treaties made with Indian tribes by the previous occupying powers. Here again the Indians' *right of occupancy* was not questioned, and here again the principle was accepted and supported by court rulings that only by treaty and just compensation could title to lands claimed by Indians be obtained by the Government.

". . . the treaties which had been made with the Indian tribes . . . by Spain and Great Britain," declared the Supreme Court, "remained in force over all the ceded territory, as the law which regulated the relations with all the Indians who were parties to them, and were binding on the United States by the obligation they had assumed by the Louisiana treaty as a supreme law of the land."[15]

In Article Six of the treaty of April, 1803, by which France ceded Louisiana, the United States promised "to execute such treaties and articles as may have been agreed between Spain and the tribes and nations of the Indians, until by mutual consent of the United States and the said tribes or nations, other suitable articles may have been agreed upon."

The acquisition of Louisiana Territory, an enormous region with poorly defined boundaries, the contents of which were not known, gave birth to the idea of making it the home of all Indians. A year after the purchase, before any explorations had been made, Congress had this to say:

"The President of the United States is hereby authorized to stipulate with any Indian tribes owning lands on the East side of the Mississippi, and residing thereon, for an exchange of lands the property of the United States, on the West side of the Mississippi, in case the said tribe shall remove and settle thereon; but, in such stipulation the said tribes shall acknowledge themselves to be under the protection of the United States, and shall agree that they will not hold any treaty with any foreign Power, individual State, or with the individuals of any State or Power; and that they will not sell and dispose of the said lands, or any part thereof, to any sovereign Power, except the United States, nor to the subjects or citizens of any other sovereign Power, nor to the citizens of the United States.

"And in order to maintain peace and tranquility with the Indian tribes who reside within the limits of Louisiana, as ceded by France to the United States, the act of Congress, passed on the thirtieth day of March, one thousand eight hundred and two, entitled 'An Act to regulate trade and intercourse with the Indian tribes, and to preserve peace on the frontiers,' is hereby extended to the territories erected and established by this act; and the sum of fifteen thousand dollars, of any money in the Treasury, not otherwise appropriated by law, is hereby appropriated, to enable the President of the United States to effect the object expressed in this section."[16]

The seed of the official policy under which eastern Indians would be uprooted from their homelands and driven into a country totally different from any they had ever known had been planted. It would germinate slowly over a period of nearly three decades before it would achieve the status of a fully matured statute.

It is improbable that any people in world history were driven by a conqueror down the road to disaster and destruction with more injustice and cruelty than Indians whose homelands were in the East. The removal program was not conscientiously executed, nor was it carried out in any of its phases with honesty, decency and understanding.

The Indians were tricked and deceived and swindled out of their lands by agents of the Federal Government, with the approval of Congress. Once they were homeless and helpless, they were driven into the wilderness beyond the great river, left to starve, driven in winter as well as summer. Children died of cold and hunger. The emigrating bands were herded like cattle, given neither sustenance nor shelter nor proper clothing nor equipment, in many cases not even transportation.

All prior commitments made by the United States to the eastern tribes were broken, all treaties were abrogated, all rights of the Indians, held under law, were ignored. White settlers swarmed onto Indian lands. The United States Government failed to enforce Federal statutes and left the Indians at the mercy of State laws, unscrupulous and greedy State officials and State militia.

Some members of the Congress vehemently protested the illegal actions of the Government. Among many others, these arguments were voiced:

1. By immemorial possession, as the original tenants of the American soil, the Indians held a title superior to any other.

2. God, in His providence, planted these tribes on the North American continent long before any European power had a political existence.

3. Indians are men, endowed with kindred faculties and powers.

4. By what code in the laws of civilized nations, or by what process of abstract deduction, have the rights of Indians been extinguished?

5. Is it one of the prerogatives of the white man, that he may disregard the dictates of moral principles when an Indian shall be concerned?

6. The pious declaration that the Government was executing a plan designed to help the Indians was a fallacy. The truth was that Indians were being forced out of communities in which they had built pleasant homes, churches, schools and in which they had productive farms. Was it helping them to drive them into a wilderness in which wilder tribes would be their neighbors and would prey on them?

The voices of these men of conscience were drowned in the roar of the political hurricane.

The question of moral principles did not enter the thinking of Washington officials, State officials, or the swarms of human locusts who invaded Indian lands. The highest government executives violated the Constitution, which gave to Congress the right to regulate commerce with foreign nations and among the several States "and with the Indian tribes." They violated the Act of 1796 to regulate trade and intercourse with the Indians. They violated the Act of March, 1802, which reaffirmed the rights of Indians. It did not matter in the end, for Congress itself ignored and violated not only the Constitution but the statutes it had prepared and enacted.

President Andrew Jackson, who possessed a consuming hatred of Indians and ignored all laws designed to protect their rights, sent agents among the eastern and southern tribes with instructions to appeal to them "to listen to the voice of their father, and their friend. Where they are now, they and my white children are too near to each other to live in harmony and peace. Beyond the great river Mississippi . . . their father has provided a country, large enough for them all, and he advises them to remove to it. There their white brethren will not trouble them, they [the white brethren] will have no claim to the land, and they can live upon it, they and all their children, *as long as grass grows or waters run*, in peace and plenty."[17]

The hypocritical, dishonest statement remains unsurpassed as an example of a white man talking with a forked tongue.

But if President Jackson thought he was actually talking to children he soon learned that he was not. Eastern and southern Indian leaders quickly made these points clear to him:

1. They had no expectation that if they should agree to move west of the Mississippi, treaties would be made with them that would give them greater benefits than those already promised them under existing treaties.

2. Why should they expect the white man to be more honest and more generous west of the Mississippi than east of it?

3. They believed that in a few years Americans also would desire to possess the lands awarded to Indians west of the river.

4. They had no wish to sell their country or their holdings.
5. All they wanted was to stay in their homelands and continue to improve themselves and develop their economy.

With weapons pointing at them, the Indians were forced to sell for pittances to white men. Settlers continued to intrude on their lands, to defraud them, to deny them any right, legal or moral, to drive them out of their homes, to murder them. Indian agents—and there were some sincere and honest men in this service, although their number was small—who arrested white men for illegally appropriating or deliberately confiscating Indian property were dismissed in disgrace.

Nine missionaries working among the Cherokee in Georgia were used by the Federal Government to distribute money awarded under a treaty. In this capacity they served as agents of the Federal Treasury. When they protested in a resolution that the forceful removal of the tribe to the West would inflict great hardships, they were ordered by the State Government to leave the area. When they refused to leave, they were arrested.

The Secretary of War ruled that eight of them could not be considered as Government agents. The ninth, however, was also a postmaster. The President of the United States took it upon himself to fire the missionary-postmaster. That solved the matter, and it also left all the missionaries at the mercy of State law. Once again the State invited them to leave. Seven went, but two still refused to abandon their posts. They were sentenced to four years at hard labor. One of the cases was appealed to the Supreme Court of the United States, which ruled that a State Government could not extend its authority over Indian land, and declared the sentence null and void.[18]

Georgia refused to honor the decision, and continued to imprison the missionary. President Jackson shrugged off the matter with the statement: "Well, Chief Justice Marshall has made his ruling. Now let him enforce it."

16

The record of the State of Georgia's treatment of the Creeks and Cherokees serves as a forceful example of the depths to which American society sank in its fiendish efforts to swindle Indians out of their lands and drive them to the unsettled West. In these cases the actions of the Federal Government revealed its weakness and corruption and in the end equaled those of Georgia in infamy.[19]

Georgia demanded that these Indians be removed to the West, and in 1825 an agent of President James Monroe bribed a small faction of the Creeks into signing an agreement to relinquish their lands and depart for the West by the fall of 1826. Ninety per cent of the Creeks were opposed to selling, and when they learned of the illegal treaty, they promptly executed the leader and two other men of the small faction which had signed it for money. This brought the whole matter out into the open. President Jackson took office, and he summoned the Creek chieftains to Washington. The illegal treaty was destroyed, and a new one was signed. The result was the same: the Creeks were forced to abandon their homes but were promised more ample awards and just and proper treatment and were permitted until 1827 to depart.

This did not suit officials of Georgia. They refused to honor the new treaty, and announced that white men, residents of Georgia, of course, would begin to occupy Creek lands in 1826. The President urged the Creeks to leave as fast as possible. Georgians overran Creek lands. Swindlers and landgrabbers cheated the Creeks by paying them for their lands in worthless bank notes. Some were whipped until they agreed to sell. Others were induced to sign away their farms after being made drunk. No Federal officers sought to help them. The Government remained inactive, refusing to step in to halt the swindling or to bring the perpetrators to justice.

But the Federal Government finally did step in, after the Creeks were driven by hunger to stealing food. This was an excuse for President Jackson to halt "Indian depredations" which were endangering the peace. He sent soldiers to drive the Creeks westward with bayonets; after all, white people had to be protected from the savages. In the migration, many Creek men, women and children perished of hunger, disease and mistreatment.

Next Georgia set out to drive the Cherokees across its borders. No regard whatsoever was given to Federal laws.

The Cherokees, numbering some fifteen thousand, were well adjusted to the ways of civilization and were progressive, peaceful and highly intelligent. They owned 22,000 cattle; 1,300 slaves; 2,000 spinning wheels; 700 looms; 31 grist mills, 10 sawmills; 8 cotton gins and 18 schools. They had a written language and published a newspaper.

The Cherokees, said an Indian Department report, "carry on considerable trade with the adjoining States; some of them export cotton in boats down the Tennessee to the Mississippi, and down that river to New Orleans. Apple and peach orchards are quite common. . . . Butter and cheese are seen on Cherokee tables. There are many public roads in the nation. . . . Numerous and flourishing villages are seen in every section. . . . Cotton and woollen cloths are manufactured. . . . Industry and commercial enterprise are extending themselves in every part. . . . The Christian religion is the religion of the nation. . . ."

The State of Georgia found that it was not easy to dispossess and destroy such an advanced people. The Cherokees were neither savages, nor barbarians.

In 1827, Cherokee leaders drafted a constitution for the tribe, which was approved by their people. This was the opportunity for which the State of Georgia had been waiting. Under the United States Constitution, no new State could be created without the consent of the established State in which it would be located. Georgia claimed that the Cherokee constitution violated this provision, and demanded that the Federal Government punish the Cherokees by removing all of them west of the Mississippi.

Congress agreed, and appropriated $50,000 to pay for the removal. War Department agents went among the Cherokees requesting them to move peacefully. They were promised all the land in the West they required, all transportation, a blanket and rifle each, cooking utensils, tobacco, a year's supply of foodstuffs, and $50 per person in cash.

The Cherokees turned down the offer. They loved their lands, their farms, their homes, their businesses, their schools, and they were proud of their development. Their only wish was to remain where they were and make further progress.

The Georgia Legislature responded to this adamant attitude by passing a resolution which provided that after January 1, 1830, all State laws applied to Indians. This was a clear violation of Federal statutes. The State Legislature also denied Indians the right to be either a witness or a party to any legal suit in which a white man was involved.

White men immediately began to take over Cherokee lands without fear of legal intervention from the State. The

Cherokees appealed to Washington to protect their rights. The reply by Congress was an infamous bill that authorized the President to uproot any tribe and move it to the West, *by force if necessary*.

The Cherokees were broken. President Jackson ordered them to leave Georgia. Their annuities were stopped, all debts owed to them were declared cancelled. They were driven from their lands. Their homes were taken over by batches of Crackers whose qualities and intelligence were grossly inferior to the residents they had ousted.

Desperate, the Cherokees appealed to the Supreme Court, and it found for them, declaring that they were a "distinct community, occupying its own territory, within boundaries accurately described, in which the laws of Georgia can have no force, and which the citizens of Georgia have no right to enter, but with the consent of the Cherokees themselves, or in conformity with treaties, and with the acts of Congress."

Again President Jackson ignored the Supreme Court. He sent agents among the Cherokees to find some that might be bribed into deeding all the tribe's land to the United States. The agents were successful. Late in 1835, a few weak Cherokees sold out, ceding all the tribal lands for $5,600,000, reimbursements of all Indian physical improvements, and free transportation to some new home in the West.

The Cherokees were doomed. Proof that the majority of the tribe had not approved the treaty was ignored. When, after two years, most of them still refused to leave, although they were starving and homeless, the United States Army was sent to drive them out.

Proclaimed General Winfield Scott:

"Cherokees, the President of the United States has sent me with a powerful army to cause you, in obedience to the treaty of 1835, to join that part of your people who are already established on the other side of the Mississippi. . . . The full moon of May is already on the wane, and before another shall have passed away every Cherokee man, woman and child must be in motion to joining their brethren in the West."

The Cherokees estimated the cost of their removal at $65,000 per thousand persons. Too high, said the general, adding that he was confident that out of every thousand there would be "at least five hundred strong men, women, boys and girls not only capable of marching twelve or fifteen miles a day, but to whom the *exercise would be beneficial.*" The general also protested that an estimated sixteen cents per day for rations for each person was exorbitant.

The Cherokees astounded everyone by announcing they would undertake the tremendous task of removal at their own expense! It could be deducted from the money owed them.

The Commissioner of Indian Affairs accepted the offer, expressing the opinion that "as their own fund pays it, and it was insisted on by their own confidential agents, it was thought it could not be rejected."[20]

Noble generosity! The Government forced the Cherokees at bayonet point to abandon their own homes and lands, everything they owned in the world and then agreed to let them use as much of their own money as they wished to pay for the migration.

The Indian Commissioner also approved a request that the Cherokees be allowed as much soap as they needed for the march into the wilderness. "The case of the Cherokees is a striking example of the liberality of the Government in all its branches," he stated.[21]

Lewis Cass, Secretary of War, also had a comment to make:

"The generous and enlightened policy evinced in the measures adopted by Congress toward that people . . . was ably and judiciously carried into effect. . . . Humanity no less than good policy dictated this course toward these children of the forest. . . . It will always be gratifying to reflect that this has been effected not only without violence, but with every proper regard for the feelings and interests of that people."

The Cherokees crossed the Mississippi in the dead of winter. More than a quarter of them perished on the march.

A distinguished French scholar, Alexis de Tocqueville, studying democracy in America, had an opportunity to see with his own eyes the tragedy of the Trail of Tears. He witnessed the crossing of the Mississippi near Memphis of a "numerous band."

"These savages," he wrote, "had left their country, and were endeavoring to gain the right bank of the Mississippi, where they hoped to find an asylum which had been promised them by the American Government. It was then the middle of the winter, and the cold was unusually severe; the snow had frozen hard upon the ground, and the river was drifting huge masses of ice.

"The Indians had their families with them; and they brought in their train the wounded and the sick, with children newly born, and old men upon the verge of death. They possessed neither tents nor wagons, but only their arms and some provisions. I saw them embark to pass the mighty river, and never will that solemn spectacle fade from my remembrances. No cry, no sob, was heard amongst the assembled crowd; all were silent.

"Their calamities were of ancient date, and they knew them to be irremediable. The Indians had all stepped into the bark which was to carry them across, but their dogs remained upon the bank. As soon as these animals perceived that their masters were finally leaving the shore, they set up a dismal howl, and, plunging altogether into the icy waters of the Mississippi, swam after the boat."[22]

This was a brief part of the noted visitor's picture of the "benevolent" United States Government at work in upholding Federal laws and carrying out the promises it had made to Indians driven beyond the frontier.

Many tribes were forced to cross the river, among them the Ottawas, Pottawatomies, Kickapoos, Choctaws, Chickasaws, Seminoles, Wyandottes, Winnebagos, Sacs and Foxes, Delawares, Shawnees, Weas, Peorias and others. The Indian problem became a western problem. How it was resolved there is the blackest, most scandalous and inhumane chapter in western history.

17

Of all the scores of Indian concentration camps, the largest was located at Fort Sumner, New Mexico. To it were sent more than nine thousand Navajo and several hundred Mescalero Apache. For approximately four years, 1864 to 1868, these people were held prisoner under the most revolting and barbarous conditions.*

* After more than two years of terrible privation and suffering most of the Mescalero escaped. In secretly planning their flight they had reasoned that if they left from time to time in small groups, they would be pursued and recaptured by troops, but if they all slipped away at the same time and scattered they would have a chance of succeeding. They did not believe that the military at the post was capable of retaking all of them. Moreover, if the

In 1862, the military commander of New Mexico was General James H. Carleton, a brutal, uncompromising Indian-hater, who would scheme with prospectors and politicians to acquire mines and land in areas occupied by the Navajo. Carleton's Indian policy was comprised of one word: extinction. He condoned the wanton murders of several hundred Indians and was responsible for the death of several hundred more by the expedients of starvation and neglect.

A hundred and seventy-five miles southeast of Santa Fe, the red, muddy Rio Pecos twisted through the western reaches of the vast Llano Estacado, a dry barren land, treeless except for ragged cottonwoods that lifted their tortured limbs along the edge of the alkaline stream. The country suited in almost every particular the plan General Carleton had conceived. It was isolated; far from any white settlement; a part of the public domain and inhabited only by some buffalo, wolves, coyotes, jack rabbits and an occasional wandering band of Indian hunters. To Carleton's way of thinking, no better place could be found in which to confine the Navajo, and, thereby, forever end the grievous troubles between them and white settlers and the Federal Government.

He won official approval of his proposal. A military post, to be called Fort Sumner, would be constructed at a place known as Bosque Redondo, where groves of cottonwoods

---

troops left Fort Sumner, thousands of Navajo would escape. They were right. More than four hundred Mescalero men, women and children vanished one night. Only nine who were too sick or badly crippled to travel were left behind. The Mescalero swiftly scattered to the four winds, some returning to their homeland in the Sierra Blanca, some disappearing into the plains of the Llano Estacado, and joining their ancient enemies, the Comanche, some traveling into southwest Texas, some going west of the Rio Grande and finding havens with other Apache bands.

stretched for several miles along the Rio Pecos, and enough soldiers would be stationed in it to prevent the prisoners from escaping.

A board of Army officers assigned to inspect the site vociferously disagreed with Carleton that it was suitable for the purpose. The inspectors reported that Bosque Redondo was remote from the nearest depot of supplies, Fort Union, and from areas in which forage could be obtained. Building materials would have to be transported great distances. The water of the Pecos contained much unhealthy mineral matter. The surrounding countryside was subject to inundation by spring floods. Much better places for the concentration camp—euphemistically termed a reservation—were available closer to Las Vegas and Fort Union, New Mexico, where adequate water, building timber, firewood and good farming lands were obtainable. Carleton was successful in having the inspectors overruled in Washington.

Carleton proclaimed his intention to make of the Navajo an agricultural people. But that is exactly what they were. Although they conducted raids against New Mexicans who captured their children and young people to be sold into slavery and against white men who coveted their lands, they maintained large herds of livestock and operated irrigated farms in the valleys of their vast homeland.

Facts never bothered Carleton, nor was compassion one of his inherent qualities. He wrote the War Department that at Bosque Redondo "old Navajos would soon die off, and carry with them all the latent longings for murdering and robbing; the young would take their places without these longings; and thus, little by little, the Navajos would become a happy and contented people, and Navajo wars would be remembered only as something that belongs entirely to the past."

He also wrote one of his superiors that he was endeavoring to "brush back the Indians, so that people could get out of the valley of the Rio Grande, and not only possess themselves of the arable lands in other parts of the territory, but, if the country contained veins and deposits of precious metals, that they might be found . . . There is every evidence that a country as rich if not richer in mineral wealth than California, extends from the Rio Grande, northwestwardly, all the way across to Washoe [Nevada]."[23]

Carleton notified the Navajo they had until July 20, 1863, to surrender or be hunted down like animals. Several Navajo leaders informed him of their willingness to capitulate but expressed the fear they would fall into the hands of slavers before they could reach military posts. Carleton made no effort to give them the protection they needed, and New Mexican slave traders swept through the country, preying on groups attempting to surrender.

After July 20, Carleton told Colonel Christopher (Kit) Carson and other officers who would conduct the Navajo roundup, "troops must be kept after the Indians, not in big bodies, with military noises and smokes, and the gleam of arms by day, and fires, and talk, and comfortable sleep at night; but in small parties moving stealthily to their haunts and lying patiently in waiting for them."

Like the tentacles of a great octopus, from July to December, fast moving contingents of cavalry snaked through the canyons and valleys and over the mesas of the Navajo Country. Every field, every hogan, every storehouse they found was burned. Carson reported that in the Bonito Canyon area alone, his troops destroyed more than two million pounds of Navajo grain.

Ravaging the country, however, was easier than capturing

Navajos. By the end of the year, only a few hundred had been taken. Deeply disappointed, Carleton ordered that the campaign be continued through the winter. Troop strength was increased, and bounties were paid for Navajo horses, mules and sheep delivered by soldiers to the Army Quartermaster. Carleton had issued instructions that all prisoners were to be sent directly to Santa Fe, but as bounties were not paid for Navajo children, some soldiers took advantage of the opportunity to sell them to New Mexican slavers. Although these violations were reported, Carleton made no effort to punish the troopers who committed them.

The destruction of Navajo resources had the desired effect. As the winter campaign progressed, Navajos began to surrender, at first in groups of two or three families, but soon larger bands came in under white flags. On February first, more than eight hundred Navajos were prisoners at Forts Canby and Wingate, but before the month ended this number had increased to nearly three thousand men, women and children. Many old people, women and children had already died of hunger and exposure.

Kit Carson and other informed frontiersmen estimated the Navajo population at twelve thousand. Carleton disputed them. Thus, he found himself faced with a desperate situation. He made frantic appeals to the Quartermaster Department for food and clothing. The supplies obtainable were far from adequate. Stores at the various military posts at which Navajo were surrendering by hundreds were soon depleted.

In a single week, 126 Navajos died of dysentery and exposure at Fort Canby, and the death tolls at other establishments were equally high in proportion to the numbers confined in them.

Prisoners were started as rapidly as possible on the "long

walk" to Bosque Redondo, from some posts in the Navajo Country a distance of four hundred miles. A poor grade of flour was the only staple some posts could furnish for their sustenance. It was a food totally strange to most of the Navajo. They mixed it with water and ate the cold paste. The result was that large numbers suffered severe cramps and fell to the roadside. Many more collapsed from weakness and serious afflictions. There were no Army vehicles in which to transport them, for the few available were overloaded with aged and crippled. The military escorts had only one alternative to leaving them to die lingering deaths. It was shoot them and leave their bodies to the wolves and vultures. Scores of helpless Navajos were mercifully slain.

How did General Carleton feel? The answer is contained in a letter he wrote to the Adjutant General of the U. S. Army:

"The exodus of this whole people from the land of their fathers is not only an interesting but a touching sight. They have fought us gallantly for years on years. They have defended their mountains and their stupendous canyons with a heroism which any people might be proud to emulate; but when, at length, they found it was their destiny to give way to the insatiable progress of our race, they threw down their arms and, as brave men entitled to our admiration and respect, have come to us in confidence of our magnanimity, feeling that for having sacrificed to us their beautiful country, their homes, the associations of their lives, their scenes rendered classic in their traditions, we will not dole out to them a miser's pittance in return for what they know to be and what we know to be a princely realm."

18

Conditions at Bosque Redondo:

By the late fall of 1864, a tally showed 8,354 Navajos held prisoner. To make this count they were run like sheep through a pen gate.

The great majority of Navajo were living in holes in the ground. Others had managed to acquire cowhides, pieces of discarded Army tents and brush with which to build small shelters.

During the next two years, more Navajos who had eluded Kit Carson's long rope were captured and brought in. Hundreds were almost naked, and nearly all were without footwear.

Supplies trickled in. Their inadequacy was demonstrated by Carleton's orders. The prisoners were to be "fed at the rate of one pound for each man, woman and child per day of fresh meat, or of corn, or of wheat, or of wheat meal, or of corn meal, or of flour, or of pickles." If none of these commodities was available, the Indians were to be given "half a pound of beans, or of rice, or of peas, or of dried fruit."

Note that the conjunction was "or," never "and."

After they had tried to grow crops for two successive years it was obvious that further efforts would be useless. Cutworms, floods, snow, sleet, burning winds destroyed the plants before they could be harvested.

Foodstuffs and other articles purchased by the Army Quartermaster for the prisoners were systematically stolen en route to Fort Sumner, and some things were stolen after they had arrived. Example: Congress appropriated $100,000 in 1865 "for the subsistence and support of the Navajo." Responsibility for the purchase and delivery of the goods was given to the Indian Bureau, over the vehement protests of the War Department. A long wagon train supposedly carrying the vitally needed goods arrived. A number of the wagons were loaded with nails, iron, blacksmith forges and tools of no use to the Indians. Most of the provisions that did arrive were of such inferior quality that they were worthless. The manifest showed that crooked Indian Bureau buyers had paid $18.50 for blankets of a type regularly purchased by the Army Quartermaster for $5.85, and that other goods had been purchased at similarly exorbitant prices. The entire cargo of the long supply train was estimated to be worth no more than $30,000. Thus, $70,000 of the $100,000 appropriation had been wasted or carried off through the Indian Bureau channels of corruption.

In another instance, two Army captains were caught selling plows, shovels, hoes, cattle and grain, purchased with Federal funds, to an Indian Agent who had established a profitable ranch near Fort Sumner. The officers were dishonorably discharged, but suffered no other punishment.

Reports of the dire situation at Bosque Redondo at last began to reach some members of Congress, and at their urging a commission was appointed to make an investigation. Chairman was Senator James R. Doolittle. His name was not appropriate, for he and his investigators did a great deal, and the report they made shocked the nation.

Still, remedial action followed slowly. Proposals to correct the terrible situation were ensnarled in Washington red tape. The War and Interior Departments quarreled bitterly about who was to blame for the mistreatment and cruelties inflicted on the Navajo.

At last it was agreed that they should be returned to a reservation in their own country. In May, 1868, a treaty was signed at Fort Sumner. Among other things a report disclosed these facts:

Approximately 7,300 Navajo men, women and children were still clinging to life at Bosque Redondo.

More than 2,000 had died while the tribe was confined there of malnutrition, exposure and disease. Another thousand had disappeared, but their fate was unknown.

Many Navajos were suffering from bronchial disorders, tuberculosis and venereal disease. Navajo women had sold themselves for food to the four hundred soldiers stationed at Fort Sumner, with the result that syphilis and gonorrhea had spread rapidly among both the Indians and the troops.

The Fort Sumner hospital provided for the Navajo consisted of nine small rooms, four of which were used as a surgery, kitchen, mess and sleeping quarters for medical attendants. The entire building was on the verge of collapse. The roof leaked. Navajos feared to enter it, for most of those who did were soon in graves.

The water of the Pecos was unfit for human consumption. It was the cause of the dysentery that so weakened the Navajos that they were incapable of throwing off other ailments.

All fuel in the region had been used, and the Navajos were obliged to travel as much as twenty miles on foot for mesquite roots and bear them on galled and lacerated backs that distance to their mud and brush hogans.

Carleton was not there to see the Navajos freed and returned to their homeland. He had charged that the Indian Bureau was attempting to stifle all western progress, to stop the advance of civilization and to frustrate him in his struggle to open the wilderness to development. "By subjugation and colonization of the Navajo tribe," he had declared, "we gain for civilization their whole country, which is much larger in extent than the state of Ohio; and besides being the best pastoral region between the two oceans, it is said to abound in precious as well as useful metals."

If his actions and contentions found favor with some politicians and covetous white cattlemen, they created a tidal wave of adverse public opinion that swept through the marble halls of Washington. Carleton was transferred to Louisiana.

President Andrew Johnson and his advisers approved a plan under which the Navajo would be relocated on a suitable reservation in the territory they had formerly occupied and removed from the control of the military. In view of the unfavorable situation in which Carleton had placed it, the War Department was only too glad to comply. General Sherman was sent to Fort Sumner to sign a treaty with the Navajo and supervise their removal from the concentration camp.

In the early summer of 1868, the Navajo went home. Long columns moved slowly westward from Bosque Redondo. The crippled, the ailing and the old were transported in Army vehicles. Squaws with children clinging to them rode on bony horses. More than seven thousand men, women and children were on the dusty, rutted, hot trail that snaked through the red hills and yellow arroyos. All were undernourished, all were ragged, but their eyes were filled with hope and new courage filled their hearts.

19

The United States signed more than 370 treaties with Indians, approximately three-fourths of them with tribes living west of the Mississippi River, between 1778 and 1871.[24]

It would be difficult to find a case in which the provisions of a treaty were fully honored by the Federal Government. In most cases the ink had no more than dried on the documents before they were violated or relegated to the realm of discarded state papers.

No nation on earth can boast of breaking so many treaties, solemnly executed under oath. This is a position in which the United States stands alone.

After 1871, and until 1887, treaties were supplanted by instruments termed "agreements," and sometimes "conventions." The change of name did not in any way interrupt the long-established custom of dishonoring them.

For nearly a hundred years, the United States conducted its relations with the Indians under the theory that they were foreign nations. The origin of this legal fiction is easily explained.

The United States Constitution delegated to the legislative branch of the Government the power "To regulate commerce with foreign nations and among the several states, and with the Indian tribes." Here we have the words *foreign nations* and *Indian tribes* in a single sentence. Congress considered it apparent that the framers of the Constitution means that Indian tribes were to be dealt with in the manner of foreign nations, that is, with treaties.

It enacted the principle into law in 1793 with "An Act to Regulate Trade and Intercourse with the Indian Tribes," which said in part: "And be it further enacted, That no purchase or grant of lands, or of any title or claim thereto, from any Indians, or nation or tribe of Indians, within the bounds of the United States, shall be of any validity, in law or equity, unless the same be made by a treaty or convention entered into pursuant to the Constitution." The statute was repeated in several later legislative measures having to do with the Indians.

Under this inane and hypocritical procedure, a treaty negotiated with a small band of ragged, hungry and dispirited Indians was written in the same stately verbiage as all important pacts with powerful foreign nations, such as the treaty that gave the United States its independence from Great Britain.

If there was no difference in language, however, there was a difference in attitude on the part of the United States through twenty-five or thirty succeeding administrations. To violate a treaty with a European monarch was to invite retaliation in the form of sanctions or warfare. Violation of a treaty with Indians involved little danger, for they were helpless savages who could be quickly subdued with force of arms or measures by which they could be starved into submission. Moreover, there was always an excuse acceptable to the American people: abrogating, or disregarding in its entirety, a treaty with Indians was invariably explained as steps taken to insure peace, to improve the social and economic positions of the victims, in the interest of the general welfare of both the white and red races.

Throughout the history of international law, legal authorities and noted scholars have disavowed such pretensions. There never was, and there is not now, any dispute between them as to the meaning of a treaty.

Aristotle: "Take away faith, and all human commerce fails. It is, therefore, an execrable thing to break faith on which so many human lives depend."

Emerich de Vattel, famed Swiss jurist: "Treaties are no better than empty words, if nations do not consider them as respectable engagements, as rules which are to be inviolably observed by sovereigns, and held sacred throughout the whole earth. The faith of treaties—that firm and sincere resolution, that invariable constancy in fulfilling our engagements, of which we make profession in a treaty—is therefore to be held sacred and inviolable between the nations of the earth, whose safety and repose it secures; and if mankind be not wilfully deficient in their duty to themselves, infamy must ever be the portion of him who violates his faith.

"He who violates his treaties, violates at the same time the law of nations, for he disregards the faith of treaties, that faith which the law of nations declares sacred. Doubly guilty, he does an injury to his ally, and he does an injury to all nations, and inflicts a wound on the great society of mankind.

"Treaties may be dissolved by mutual consent at the free-will of the contracting powers."[25]

Felix S. Cohen, an outstanding authority on Indian law:

"It is said in defense of the continuous violations by the United States of its treaties with the Indians, that the practice of all nations has been and is to abrogate a treaty whenever it saw good reason for doing so. That is true; but the treaties have been done away with in one of two ways, either by a mutual and peaceful agreement to that effect between the parties who had made it, or by a distinct avowal on the part of one nation of its intention no longer to abide by it, and to take, therefore, its chances of being made war upon in consequence. Neither of these courses has been pursued by the United States Government in its treaty-breaking with the Indians."[26]

James Kent, noted American professor of law: "The violation of any one article of a treaty is a violation of the whole treaty."[27]

Politicians attempting to defend the disgraceful record of

the United States in breaking treaties with Indians have advanced the argument that no Congress can be bound by the acts of a preceding Congress. That is true with regard to some legislative acts. With regard to treaties, every fundamental principle of international law refutes such a contention. Treaties continue to bind a nation no matter what revisions may be made in its constitution, no matter what new laws may be enacted, no matter what internal political changes may take place. New legislators have no power to abrogate arbitrarily a treaty made by their predecessors.

In the thinking of the Indians, the signing of a treaty was a solemn occasion. It represented a pledge of their friendship and faith, and it involved issues bearing upon their welfare. A treaty could be, and generally was to them, a matter of life and death. They entered into a *treaty smoke* in all seriousness, and conducted themselves with gravity and dignity during the ceremonies.

In the thinking of Washington officials sent out to negotiate a treaty, the chore was a damn nuisance. The straight faces and sober demeanor they displayed were false, hiding their true feelings. They understood that the whole procedure was a farce, that the treaty, bearing the thumb prints and the marks and the signatures most likely would go into a Washington pigeonhole and be ignored if not completely forgotten. Behind their poker masks they were laughing at the Indian negotiators, ignorant, dirty men who made stupid speeches about the moon and the sun and the waters running forever.

Of course, the Washington emissaries were fully aware that a treaty did give the Government certain advantages. It was a means of achieving a temporary peace. The Indians usually were naive enough to believe that they had increased their own security and won protection for their hunting grounds. At least, that is what they believed for a time, normally a period long enough to allow the Government to revise its strategy and formulate new plans for resolving the problem; that is, actually, long enough to devise new means of taking more territory away from them for white settlement. If, meanwhile, the Indians threatened to go on the warpath, or even began hostilities, it was usually possible to sign a new treaty, promise them their beloved moon and the stars and the sun and gain a new temporary peace. With each treaty the Indians lost more of their rights, lost more ground in their struggle to defend themselves, in the fight to halt the invasion of their territory. There could be no denying that treaties were handy weapons in dealing with dumb, trusting people.

20

The Treaty of 1851 remains today an outstanding monument to the criminal negligence of the United States in its relations with western Indians.

Within three years after the 1848 discovery of gold in California, more than a hundred thousand persons had crowded into mining camps in the Sierra Nevada. Not all of the emigrants, however, had gone to the West Coast. Many of them had stopped in the Rockies. Many had gone no farther west than the fertile valleys stemming from the lower reaches of the Missouri, the Kansas, the Platte, the Arkansas and other rivers. In these prairie regions towns seemed to appear overnight. Men plowed fields where a day before Indians had hunted and camped.

Many of the tribes which had lived in these areas on the eastern perimeter of the Plains already had been made homeless and destitute. Many were starving, tenaciously clinging to their ancestral homes, precariously existing by begging and stealing, but many had gone away, desperately looking for a means of surviving, for greener pastures, for new hope.

The irresistible human flood was pursuing them. There was no indication that it would abate. The Federal Government was powerless to stem it, or even direct its course. That could have been done only by force of arms, and such drastic action, of course, would have meant interference with progress and development—manifest destiny. No politician in his right mind would have approved measures to prevent white persons from invading Indian lands.

It is hardly necessary to state that the Indians of the Great Plains did not think of the mass movement as development or progress, but only as an invasion swallowing and destroying them. No ears were open to them in Washington. If their protests were heard there, they were swiftly forgotten. The only alternative the Indians saw open to them was violent retaliation. They had begun to adopt it with terrible consequences.

Officials of the Indian Bureau and the War Department realized that some form of action by them was immediately necessary. Intelligence reports from the West left no doubts that a long, bloody and costly war was beginning. The mounted plains Indians had an annoying habit of vanishing into the sky when pursued by soldiers, only to reappear suddenly to kill emigrants and pillage and burn wagon trains. Thousands of troops could not resolve the problem, but perhaps it could be alleviated, at least temporarily, through a treaty.

That course was adopted. Word went out that the Great White Father would send his agents to hold a general and conclusive council with the leaders of all tribes living in the northern Great Plains. The *big smoke* would be held at Fort Laramie in mid-September.

In addition to the official negotiators, the Indian Bureau invited a number of distinguished persons versed in Indian affairs to be guests at the conference. One of these was the famed Black Robe, Father Pierre Jean De Smet, a man blessed with a rare combination of qualities—great intelligence, practicality, physical courage—a true friend of the Indian.

Father De Smet, as realistic as he was devout, had no hesitancy in voicing his skepticism that the proposed treaty would be of benefit to the Indians. He wrote: "Will not the President of the Republic, like some of his predecessors, pluck some plumes from the Indian eagle, once the emblem of their greatness and power, to place them in the crown composed of the trophies of his administration?"[28]

Here was an unprecedented and timely opportunity to provide the plains Indians with a permanent and adequate home, to give them a chance to adjust themselves to the civilization that was destroying them. It was not too late. There still was an almost inconceivably enormous territory that might be set aside in perpetuity for them. Except for trails and trading posts, the map from the upper Missouri to the Rocky Mountains was largely a blank. There was still room for the red people, but it was obvious that their staunch friend, the noted Black Robe, had little hope that it would be preserved for them. He held a vision of the President looking at a map of the northern plains country and seeing there only more stars "of the first magnitude which will enhance the luster of the galaxy of the flag of the Union. This great territory will hold an immense population, destined to form several great and flourishing states." The question of what was to become of the tribes who lived in the seas of grass and the rich valleys awakened "gloomy ideas in the observer's mind, if he has followed the encroaching policy of the states. . . . If they are again repelled and banished further inland, they will perish infallibly. The Indians who refuse to submit or accept the definite arrangement, alone favorable to them . . . would close their sad existence as the bison and other animals on which they live vanish."

Father De Smet travelled with a group of his closest friends to the conference, thirty chiefs of the Assiniboines, Minnetarees and Crows. They started from Fort Union, at the junction of the Missouri and Yellowstone Rivers (in the northwestern corner of the present State of North Dakota). They took with them two four-wheeled wagons and two carts, the first ever driven across "this unoccupied waste. There is not the slightest vestige of a beaten track between Fort Union and the Red Buttes, which are on the route to Oregon [Oregon Trail], and 161 miles west of Fort Laramie [at the confluence of the Laramie and North Platte Rivers in southeastern Wyoming]."

Approaching Fort Laramie early in September, they were surprised to see numerous large campsites which recently had been abandoned. At the fort they found only a small military contingent on guard duty. They were informed that the site of the Great Council had been moved some thirty miles eastward to Horse Creek.

The change had been ordered by the Indian Agent in charge for very good reasons. For more than a month, bands of Ogallala and Brule Sioux, Cheyennes, Arapahoes, Assiniboines, Arikaras, Minnetaries, Crows and other Indians had been arriving and had set up villages near the fort. By September 1, more than ten thousand Indian men, women and children, some twenty thousand horses and uncounted thousands of dogs were crowded on the plain on each side of Fort Laramie. Numerous traders had come in with their wagons heavily loaded with merchandise to take advantage of the unusual opportunity. Soldiers and Indian Agents had made strenuous efforts to prevent the sale of rotgut whiskey, but it was surreptitiously dispensed in small cups at exorbitant prices.

Horse trading went on continuously, as did racing, wild dancing and gambling. The great babble, the neighing, the barking and the drums never ceased. The enormous herds had soon consumed the grass for miles in each direction, leaving a scarred and desolate prairie from which blew great clouds of blinding, choking dust. The foul smell which came from the camps had become more than the two hundred dragoons and the civilians quartered in the fort could endure. No breeze that blew night or day could bring relief, for the filth and refuse spread in an unbroken circle around the post.

A large train of some hundred wagons carrying supplies, foodstuffs and gifts from the Government had been scheduled to arrive before the beginning of the council. It had not appeared. Indian tempers were growing short. Fights and quarrels were increasing in frequency. Two official interpreters expressed the fear that major trouble was brewing. Guard lines were strengthened.

The arrival of the Government negotiators and high officials of the Indian Bureau diminished the danger of uncontrollable violence, but not for long. They were forced to admit that the Army had bungled things, and the wagon train had been several days late in leaving Westport Landing.

The announcement was not well received, but the officials

believed they had succeeded in placating the Indian leaders and had induced them to preserve the truce under which the tribes had come together for at least a few days. It could only be hoped that by that time the gifts would have arrived.

This optimistic outlook was quickly destroyed. Word was received that the Shoshones, enemies of virtually all the tribes present, were approaching in force. Two Shoshone warriors already had been killed en route to the council by some wandering Cheyennes. The Shoshones undoubtedly would seek to avenge their deaths. A slaughter might well take place.

Interpreters, Indian Agents and the military prepared for the worst. When the Shoshones were sighted, a bugle sounded, and the dragoons, augmented by the military escort of the officials, wheeled into line.

This show of armed strength had the desired effect. Taunts and insulting remarks were shouted at the Shoshones by watching Indians, hatchets were brandished and there was some brief scuffling between police and a few individuals who tried to launch an attack. The police won. Not a shot was fired. The Shoshones, all arrayed in their most brilliant trappings, swept by in a colorful parade before the line of soldiers, performing several complicated maneuvers with amázing precision, then rode on to the campground which had been set aside for them. The dangerous situation passed.

Although the wagon train had not arrived, the *treaty smoke* was officially opened on September 12. It was the largest gathering of Indians in the history of the West. Along the plain bordering Horse Creek [virtually on the present Nebraska-Wyoming boundary] stood the lodges of more than ten thousand red people from a dozen major tribes. The smoke of thousands of campfires threw a haze over the area. Following the daily talks, the deepthroated drums sounded throughout each night, and the chants and wild yells of dancers mocked the yapping of coyotes and the howls of wolves under the prairie stars.

At the end of four days of negotiating, the Army wagons still had not appeared. Food was running out, and Fort Laramie had none to send. All game animals had vanished from the surrounding country. The stench from the campgrounds had become so terrible that troops and officials had moved their own camp more than two miles up the creek where, at least at night, they could escape it.

The Indians were slaughtering their dogs to supplement their swiftly vanishing rations. Great hunger seemed imminent.

"No epoch in Indian annals," wrote Father De Smet, "probably shows a greater massacre of the canine race."

It was September 18th when the long-awaited wagon train came in sight. As swiftly as possible the food was distributed. Even though countless lodges were without meat, and many persons had nothing at all to eat, there were no disorders during the distribution. Indians took "the respective places assigned to each particular band, thus forming an immense circle, covering several acres of land."

The gifts were passed out next, and "the great chiefs of the different nations were served first, and received suits of clothes . . . and were for the first time in their lives pantalooned . . . each was arrayed in a general's uniform, a gilt sword hanging at his side. Their long coarse hair floated above the military costume, and the whole was crowned by the burlesque solemnity of their painted faces. The conduct of this vast multitude was calm and respectful."

The treaty presented to the meeting had been prepared in Washington by State Department lawyers who in all probability had never seen a wild Indian or the vast region with which they were treating. The negotiators read it "sentence by sentence, and distinctly explained to the different interpreters, that they might have the exact and legitimate meaning of each article." It appeared at first thought to be highly favorable to the Indians, but in reality it was ambiguous and tricky, full of loopholes that gave the Government every advantage.

The Government got what it wanted: time. Perhaps, Federal negotiators thought, by getting the northern plains Indians to agree not to attack caravans and westward-moving settlers and miners for even a brief period, the whole problem would somehow evaporate into the thin air of the high country. This agreement was obtained by making wild promises, which the Government had no intention of even attempting to fulfill.

Enormous territories embracing some 150,000 to 200,000 square miles were designated as "Indian Country." Various tribes were awarded these immense hunting grounds in *perpetuity*. The Indians interpreted the word to mean *forever*. To the Government it meant *as long as convenient* or *until needed*.

The chiefs wished to be reasonable. If the Government was willing to guarantee them the areas they wanted and needed, they would agree to permit it to lay out transcontinental roads and establish military posts. It was not their wish to stand in the way of white persons who wished to travel peacefully through the country. All they asked was that settlement in their hunting grounds be prohibited. The Government agreed.

The concession was the Indians' undoing. By being cooperative, instead of gaining protection for themselves, they kept the door open for an invasion of the lands which had been awarded to them.

The Indians promised to maintain peace and to pay for

losses that were inflicted on white people by uncontrollable warriors. How these payments were to be collected not even the schemers on the banks of the far-off Potomac knew. It really did not matter, for the condition produced a stalemate. As a sop to justice, the Government acquiesced to an Indian demand that the tribes be indemnified for damage caused to their hunting grounds by "travelers" from the States—"travelers," not settlers who took their lands. One provision cancelled out the other. Moreover, the Indians were to be given $50,000 at once, and that certainly would pay for all the damage white travelers might cause.

The Washington treaty-writers adhered to that erroneous conviction, so firmly embedded in American thought patterns (as it still is today), that an offer of money can ameliorate any problem. Gold is the true miracle medicine. Every man, every government, every people has a price.

With irresponsible generosity the treaty-writers committed the Government to pay the tribes signing the Treaty of Laramie $50,000 annually for fifteen years. They had no authority to make such an offer, for the money was not available, and could only be paid out after a specific appropriation by Congress.

The Treaty of Laramie was probably the most important instrument of its kind ever negotiated between Federal emissaries and the powerful tribes of the West. Had it been honored and enforced by the Government, thousands of lives would have been saved, many of the terrible conflicts which continued for more than thirty years might have been averted.

That, of course, did not happen. Even as they were preparing it, the Washington authors looked upon their work as nothing more than another worthless and meaningless document. They knew that in all probability it would be tossed onto the mounting pile of other pacts which had been made with the people who were an impediment to progress. Integrity and faith were, after all, relative, not to be taken too seriously when dealing with savages, not to be permitted to influence any political program or to interrupt the advancement of the American economy.

The tide of settlement continued unabated to flood over the lands pledged to the Indian signatories. Miners swept by thousands into the Rocky Mountains. The game was destroyed, and the Indians hungered. Supplies promised failed to reach them. The military and the civilian invaders murdered them by hundreds. They struck back in the only way they could—with the force of arms.

On the other hand there was really no way in which the Indian Department and the Army could honor and enforce the treaty, for Congress never bothered to ratify it. The whole thing had been a sham.

21

On the part of the Government, the great majority of the treaties signed with Indian tribes were entered into as delaying tactics. Using this dishonorable system, the United States frequently signed a number of treaties with the same tribe. When trouble arose with certain Indians, a new treaty was used as a means of effecting a temporary truce.

For example, Federal emissaries negotiated and solemnly signed more than fifty treaties with various divisions of the Siouan people. Virtually every promise made to these Indians was broken during a period of more than seventy years.

Treaty violations, the confiscation of Sioux property, brutal treatment and every conceivable form of injustice finally resulted in the Sioux outbreak in Minnesota in 1862. White settlers took over agricultural lands awarded "in perpetuity" to these Indians, and the Government made no attempt to halt the invasion. Hungry, homeless, destitute, the Sioux, after years of cruel treatment, turned to open warfare and inflicted terrible vengeance.

The people of Minnesota got what they asked for, and paid a high price for it.

22

Various excuses and explanations were advanced for the 1871 decision of Congress to abandon the treaty system. Under the act, Indian tribes were no longer to be regarded as foreign nations. Therefore, so-called international treaties could be supplanted by agreements. These pacts would become operative with the approval of Congress.

The change, declared some supporters of the act, would open the way for easier and improved methods of dealing with the complicated Indian problems. It was maintained that self-rule, that is, the existence of independent Indian governments, handicapped and delayed the adjustment of the Indians to civilization.

This was rubbish. The truth was that the legislation put all Indians completely at the mercy of corrupt politicians. It deprived them of any voice in their own affairs.

The result was nothing less than might have been expected. In the following two decades scores of agreements, smelling no better under the new name, were negotiated between Federal agents and Indian leaders, and were wantonly violated by the Government. Tribes were awarded lands, but the moment these lands were coveted by white men they were thrown open to settlement. The Indians occupying them were forced to accept other lands, usually too poor to support any form of agriculture. Rights of ways were granted for roads and railroads, in disregard of agreements which had prohibited them.

One might cite innumerable examples of how the Federal Government used trickery, deceit, coercion and the force of guns to secure "agreements" under which Indians could be deprived of valuable lands which had been awarded to them. The cases would be repetitious, and their monotony would be relieved only by variations in their locales. A single one, that of the Ponca, serves as well as a score to illustrate the appalling crimes committed in the guise of legal actions by the Congress and high Washington officials, not excluding those of cabinet rank and the Presidents themselves.

No more industrious, progressive and peaceful Indians ever lived in the West than the Poncas. The first treaty between them and the United States was signed in 1817. In it the two "powers"—the United States of America and the tiny "nation"—expressed their friendship for each other. In 1825, the Poncas willingly signed another treaty. The Federal Government asked them to admit that they "reside within the territorial limits of the United States, acknowledge their supremacy, and claim their protection." The Poncas saw no reason to deny that they lived on the Niobrara River, or that the United States was more powerful than they, and they were quite willing to have the United States protect them.

They also admitted that the United States had the right to

regulate all trade and intercourse with them. In view of the other provisos, they saw no ground on which to reject this understanding, although it appeared somewhat superfluous. The danger in it was soon made apparent to them.

In return for these concessions, the United States made a gesture that was meaningless as far as the Indians were concerned, and which in reality relieved the Government of all responsibility. The United States agreed to "receive the Poncar [sic] tribe of Indians into their friendship and under their protection, and to extend to them *from time to time such benefits and acts of kindness as may be convenient, and seem just and proper to the President of the United States*."[29]

For more than thirty years, while most other tribes of the Upper Missouri country presented the United States with difficult problems and warred on each other and the military, the Poncas were so peaceful that they scarcely came to notice in official records. Then, in 1856, this bright horizon began to darken. An Indian Agent reported that white settlers were intruding on Ponca lands. In the next year, the Poncas complained that squatters were cutting their trees, building farms and driving away game on which they depended.[30]

The protection which the United States had promised failed to materialize, and President James Buchanan apparently found it *inconvenient* to extend any *benefits* or perform any *acts of kindness*. It was *convenient*, however, for the Government to send foreign relations emissaries to advise the Poncas that they could no longer expect the United States to live up to its promises.

In 1858, the Indian Bureau's annual report announced that new treaties had been entered into "with the Poncas and Yankton Sioux, who reside west of Iowa, for the purpose of extinguishing their title to all the lands occupied and claimed by them, except small portions on which to colonize and domesticate them. This proceeding was deemed necessary in order to obtain such control over these Indians *as to prevent their interference with our settlements*, which are rapidly extending in that direction."

The Senate didn't find it *convenient* to ratify the treaties. Meanwhile, the Poncas having signed them, and believing them to be in effect, proceeded in good faith to carry out their end of the bargain. They complied with the provisions by abandoning their settlements, and moving to the comparatively small area which, presumably, was to be their permanent home. "Being without a crop to rely upon," said an Indian Agent's report, "and having been unsuccessful in their usual summer hunt, they were reduced to a state of desperation and destitution."

Some humane persons in the Indian Department were able to persuade the Government to appropriate enough money to keep the Poncas from starving. In 1859, the Senate got around to ratifying the treaty, but it might as well have saved the time and effort, for ratification brought the Poncas no relief from their terrible plight.

Under the treaty the United States agreed "to protect the Poncas in the possession of this tract of land, and their persons and property thereon, during good behavior on their part; to pay them annuities annually for thirty years—$12,000 for the first five years, then $10,000 for ten years, then $8,000 for fifteen years; to expend $20,000 for their subsistence during the first year, for building houses, etc.; to establish schools, and to build mills, mechanics' shops, etc.; to give $20,000 for the payments of the existing obligations of the tribe."

An agency report told how well the United States carried out its agreements. When funds failed to arrive, and the Agent had no money with which to feed the Poncas, he persuaded them to undertake a hunt on the plains. In less than a month they had returned, begging for provisions for their women and children, whom they had left on the plains half-starved, having been unable to find any game or any food except wild turnips. Some of them went to visit the Omahas, others the Pawnees, where they remained until the little corn they had planted produced roasting ears. In the meantime those who were at the Ponca agency subsisted mainly on wild cherries, plums and wild turnips and traded away most of their blankets and other possessions for provisions.

In 1863, four years after the Senate had ratified the treaty, the annual report of the Indian Bureau contained this letter from a Ponca agent: "They started on their summer hunt toward the last of May, immediately after the first hoeing of their corn. At first they were successful and found buffaloes . . . but they soon consumed what meat they had cured and were compelled to abandon the chase. They commenced to return in the latter part of July. They went away with very high hopes . . . of a large crop, but returned to see it all withered and dried up. In the meantime the plains had been burnt over, so that they could not discover the roots they are in the habit of digging. Even the wild plums . . . are withered and dried on the limbs.

"The building I occupy was constantly surrounded by a hungry crowd begging for food.

"I am warned by the military authority to keep the Poncas within the limits of the reservations; but this is an impossibility. There is nothing within its limits; nor can anything be obtained in sufficient quantity, or brought here soon enough to keep them from starving.

"The Poncas have behaved well—quite as well, if not better than, under like circumstances, the same number of whites would have done."

Some money and some supplies were obtained for the Poncas in small amounts from time to time, as one agent said "more by the Grace of God than by actions in Washington," and somehow the Poncas managed to keep themselves alive. A supplemental treaty enlarging their reservation and taking in additional good farming lands was negotiated with them in 1865, but again the Senate delayed ratification for two years. This treaty would have brought them some funds for education and agricultural purposes over five-year periods, but because of the remissness of the Senate and the red tape of appropriations these periods were all but exhausted before the programs could be started.

In the treaty of 1859, the United States had agreed to "establish and maintain for ten years, at an annual expense not to exceed $5,000, one or more manual labor schools for the education and training of the Ponca youth in letters, agriculture, mechanics and housewifery."

A school eventually was started, but in 1868, this provision of the treaty had only another year of life, and the Governor of Dakota Territory wrote with profound concern to the Indian Department: "A school has been in successful operation at this agency [Ponca] for the past nine months,* with an average attendance of about fifty scholars, and with every evidence of advancement in the primary department of an English education. But just at this interesting period of its existence we are notified by the agent that with this fiscal year all funds for school as well as for agricultural purposes cease,

* This meant that for the first eight years the Government had failed to keep an agreement that had only ten years to run.

agreeably to the terms and conditions of their original treaty. This will be a serious and irreparable calamity. . . ."

If the Government repeatedly failed to heed the time set for the start of an agreement, it rarely overlooked the date on which an agreement was to conclude. Promptly on schedule in 1869, it was announced that the Ponca school was "discontinued for want of funds."

A new governor had taken office in Dakota Territory, and he gave his support to an Indian Department recommendation that Federal funds be made available for reopening the school, adding to his letter that "for the enlightenment of the 35,000 Indians embraced in the Dakota Superintendency, there is not one school in operation."

A year later, in 1870, Congress got around to awarding $5,000 to reestablish the Ponca school. Additional small amounts of money were begrudgingly appropriated during the next several years, but the provisions of the treaties were never fulfilled to the specified extent.

The good use to which the Poncas put the money that was made available to them and their indefatigable efforts to improve their property comprised incontestable evidence of their sincere desire to become a progressive, peaceful and permanent segment of American society. Good houses were built, lands were cultivated, a mission church was constructed. Wild bands of Sioux stole their horses and cattle, drought and locusts destroyed their crops, floods ruined their farms, but they refused to accept defeat, and after each disaster set out to rebuild with undiminished vigor.

Security and prosperity appeared at last to be within their reach. Then disaster struck, and the last vestiges of their hopes and ambitions were destroyed.

White settlers demanded the valuable Ponca lands, and unconscionable officials in Washington decided that they should be moved to the Indian Territory (Oklahoma). It was not necessary to have a treaty under which this evil scheme could be executed, for Indian tribes were no longer foreign nations. All that was necessary was for the Government to obtain the Ponca's "consent," and they could be removed.

How that "consent" was obtained was related in one of the most moving documents to be found in the history of the Indians. It remains an indestructible memorial to the perfidy and brutality of the United States Government. The author was a Ponca leader, Standing Bear.

Feigning a benevolent and paternalistic attitude, the Department of Indian Affairs induced ten Ponca leaders to go with an Indian inspector to the Indian Territory "to see if the land there did not suit them better than their Nebraska reservation." They were solemnly promised that if they did not like the Indian Territory, they would be taken to Washington and given an opportunity to consult on the matter with the President. The first concern of the Great White Father, they were told, was their welfare, and nothing would be done to them that they felt would be injurious to their best interests.

This is Standing Bear's story:[31]

"We lived on our land as long as we can remember. No one knows how long ago we came there. The land was owned by our tribe as far back as memory of men goes.

"We were living quietly on our farms. All of a sudden one white man came. We had no idea what for. This was the inspector. He came to our tribe with Rev. Mr. Hinman. These two, with the agent, James Lawrence, they made our trouble.

"They said the President told us to pack up—that we must move to the Indian Territory.

"The inspector said to us: 'The President says you must sell this land. He will buy it and pay you the money, and give you new land in the Indian Territory.'

"We said to him: 'When two persons wish to make a bargain, they can talk together and find out what each wants, and then make their agreement.'

"We said to him: 'We do not wish to go. When a man owns anything, he does not let it go till he has received payment for it.'

"We said to him: 'We will see the President first.'

"He said to us: 'I will take you to see the new land. If you like it, then you can see the President, and tell him so. If not, then you can see him and tell him so.' And he took all ten of our chiefs down. I went, and Bright Eyes' uncle went. He took us to look at three different pieces of land. He said we must take one of the three pieces, so the President said. After he took us down there he said: 'No pay for the land you left.'

"We said to him: 'You have forgotten what you said before we started. You said we should have pay for our land. Now you say not. You told us then you were speaking truth.' All these three men took us down there. The man got very angry. He tried to compel us to take one of the three pieces of land. He told us to be brave. He said to us: 'If you do not accept these, I will leave you here alone. You are one thousand miles from home. You have no money. You have no interpreter, and you cannot speak the language.' And he went out and slammed the door. The man talked to us from long before sundown till it was nine o'clock at night.

"We said to him: 'We do not like this land. We could not support ourselves. The water is bad. Now send us to Washington, to tell the President, as you promised.'

"He said to us: 'The President did not tell me to take you to Washington; neither did he tell me to take you home.'

"We said to him: 'You have the Indian money you took to

bring us down here. That money belongs to us. We would like to have some of it. People do not give away food for nothing. We must have money to buy food on the road.'

"He said to us: 'I will not give you a cent.'

"We said to him: 'We are in a strange country. We cannot find our way home. Give us a pass, that people may show us our way.'

"He said: 'I will not give you any.'

"We said to him: 'This interpreter is ours. We pay him. Let him go with us.'

"He said: 'You shall not have the interpreter. He is mine, and not yours.'

"We said to him: 'Take us at least to the railroad; show us the way to that.'

"And he would not. He left us right there. It was winter. We started for home on foot. At night we slept in haystacks. We barely lived till morning, it was so cold. We had nothing but our blankets. We took the ears of corn that had dried in the fields. We ate it raw. The soles of our moccasins wore out. We were barefoot in the snow. We were nearly dead when we reached the Otoe Reserve. It had been fifty days. We stayed there ten days to strengthen up, and the Otoes gave each of us a pony. The agent of the Otoes told us he had received a telegram from the inspector, saying that the Indian chiefs had run away; not to give us food or shelter, or help in any way. The agent said: 'I would like to understand. Tell me all that has happened. Tell me the truth.' "

(This Otoe agent afterward said that when the chiefs entered his room they left the prints of their feet in blood on the floor.)

"Then we told our story to the agent and to the Otoe chiefs —how we had been left down there to find our way.

"The agent said: 'I can hardly believe it possible that any

one could have treated you so. That inspector was a poor man to have done this. If I had taken chiefs in this way, I would have brought them home; I could not have left them there.'

"In seven days we reached the Omaha Reservation. Then we sent a telegram to the President: asked him if he had authorized this thing. We waited three days for the answer. No answer came.

"In four days we reached our own home. We found the inspector there. While we were gone, he had come to our people and told them to move.

"Our people said: 'Where are our chiefs? What have you done with them? Why have you not brought them back? We will not move till our chiefs come back.'

"Then the inspector told them: 'Tomorrow you must be ready to move. If you are not ready you will be shot.' Then the soldiers came to the doors with their bayonets, and ten families were frightened. The soldiers brought wagons; they put their things in and were carried away. The rest of the tribe would not move.

"When we got there, we asked the inspector why he had done this thing, and he got very angry.

"Then we said to him: 'We did not think we would see your face again, after what has passed. We thought never to see your face any more. But here you are.'

"We said to him: 'This land is ours. It belongs to us. You have no right to take it from us. The land is crowded with people, and only this is left to us.'

"We said to him: 'Let us alone. Go away from us. If you want money, take all the money which the President is to pay us for twelve years to come. You may have it all, if you will go and leave us our lands.'

"Then, when he found that we would not go, he wrote for more soldiers to come.

"Then the soldiers came, and we locked our doors, and the women and children hid in the woods. Then the soldiers drove all the people the other side of the river, all but my brother Big Snake and I. We did not go; and the soldiers took us and carried us away to a fort and put us in jail. There were eight officers who held council with us after we got there. The commanding officer said: 'I have received four messages telling me to send my soldiers after you. Now, what have you done?'

"Then we told him the whole story. Then the officer said: 'You have done no wrong. The land is yours; they had no right to take it from you. Your title is good. I am here to protect the weak, and I have no right to take you; but I am a soldier and I have to obey orders.'

"He said: 'I will telegraph to the President, and ask him what I shall do. We do not think these three men had any authority to treat you as they have done. When we own a piece of land, it belongs to us till we sell it and pocket the money.'

"Then he brought a telegram, and said he had received answer from the President. The President said he knew nothing about it.

"They kept us in jail ten days. Then they carried us back to our home. The soldiers collected all the women and children together; then they called all the chiefs together in council; and then they took wagons and went round and broke open the houses. When we came back from the council we found the women and children surrounded by a guard of soldiers.

"They took our reapers, mowers, hay-rakes, spades, ploughs, bedsteads, stoves, cupboards, everything we had on our farms, and put them in one large building. Then they put into the wagons such things as they could carry. We told them that we would rather die than leave our lands; but we could not help ourselves. They took us down. Many died on the road. Two of my children died. After we reached the new land, all my horses died. The water was very bad. All our cattle died; not one was left. I stayed till one hundred and fifty-eight of my people had died. Then I ran away with thirty of my people, men and women and children. Some of the children were orphans. We were three months on the road. We were weak and sick and starved. When we reached the Omaha Reserve the Omahas gave us a piece of land, and we were in a hurry to plough it and put in wheat. While we were working the soldiers came and arrested us. Half of us were sick. We would rather have died than have been carried back; but we could not help ourselves."[31]

The incredibly cruel treatment of the Poncas, the destruction of their homes and farms, and their forced removal aroused indignation throughout the Middle West and the East. Newspaper editorials condemned the Government's actions. Many individuals and organizations contributed money to finance a court suit to have them returned to their Nebraska lands and be recompensed for their real losses.

The Poncas who had run away from the Indian Territory were released by an Omaha judge in a celebrated decision. In the trial the Government attorneys contended that an Indian was not "entitled to protection of the writ of habeas corpus, not being a person or citizen under the law." The court ruled against the Government, and the case opened numerous legal channels through which investigations of other crimes committed by Federal authorities against Indians proceeded.

So great became the public clamor for justice in the Ponca case that a Presidential commission was appointed to investigate the matter. The Poncas owned their Nebraska lands in fee simple. The titles were without a cloud. Yet, the Government had forced them at bayonet point to leave as if they had been squatters without a legal claim of any kind to the property.

E. A. Howard, the Indian Agent who had directed the tragic march testified: "It is a matter of astonishment to me that the Government should have ordered the removal of the Ponca Indians from Dakota to the Indian Territory without having first made some provision for their settlement and comfort. Before their removal was carried into effect an appropriation should have been made by Congress sufficient to have located them in their new home, by building a comfortable home for the occupancy of every family of the tribe."[32]

The only money provided by the Government, he said, was "a sum little more than sufficient to remove them." The result was that the Poncas were driven onto an "uncultivated reservation, to live in their tents as best they may. . . ."

The Presidential Commission was able to effect a "satisfactory arrangement of the affairs of the tribe, through which the greater portion, some six hundred, remained in Indian Territory, while some two hundred and twenty-five kept their reservation in Nebraska."

The Government was the victor. It had succeeded in breaking and dividing a small peaceful people whose loyalty to the United States had never wavered. It had killed some two hundred of them . . . men, women and children.

23

The Indians could teach white men nothing about cruelty. No atrocities or tortures of Indians were more depraved or more fiendish than those committed by soldiers and western civilians.

In Denver the bounty on an Indian scalp was $10, and it was paid on several hundred. The bounty in Central City was more attractive, $25, and was paid on more than two hundred. Deadwood, South Dakota, was the best bounty market in the West. There Indian scalps were worth $200.

Inasmuch as payments were not restricted to the scalps of known enemy Indians, settlers, miners and soldiers frequently shot Indians on sight, in the back. A scalp was a scalp. After a fight it was the custom of American troopers to scalp dead Indians. If it was not convenient to obtain bounties for scalps taken in such cases, they could be sent back East as souvenirs or used to decorate barracks. The scalps of squaws were as highly prized as those of warriors.

Emigrants introduced the torture of lashing an Indian to a wagon wheel to die a lingering death as the vehicle bumped over the plain. The Indians retaliated by tying settlers to the wheels of destroyed vehicles and leaving them mutilated and bleeding to die under the burning sun.

Prodding Indian captives with red hot bayonets—sometimes they were held under a prisoner's arms—to make them confess to killing white persons or reveal the whereabouts of companions was a favorite practice of Army officers. One prominent chief who struggled to evade the terrible torture was shot to death for attempting to escape.

At an upper Missouri River military post, Army cooks threw boiling water on starving Indian women and children who attempted to salvage scraps of food from the garbage thrown out of the post kitchen. It was considered great sport to see them run as the burning water struck them and they screamed in pain.

Hunting for Indians to shoot and Indian women to rape was

a Sunday amusement of the gold miners in California, Colorado and the Black Hills.

24

Americans cluck sympathetically at accounts of people in foreign countries being driven from their lands and made homeless wanderers by dictators. One wonders if the same Americans have forgotten that similar tragedies occurred innumerable times in the United States.

A heavy volume might be written about these cruel events, but the disaster suffered by the Potawatomi of northern Indiana serves as a typical case in point. The origin of the word *Indiana* is obvious, but the white persons inhabiting the State spared no effort to rid themselves of the people for whom it was named.

By 1841 most of the Indians of Indiana had been forced to give up their homes and farms, and had been banished to the West beyond the Mississippi. A large group of peaceful Potawatomi farmers, however, stubbornly refused to leave, and for several years stood firm against the pressures of settlers who wanted their lands. At last Indiana politicians succeeded in persuading the State Government to take illegal action against them. A general of the State Militia was ordered to organize a force of a hundred armed citizens and "drive the Potawatomi out of the country." The Indian Bureau cooperated with the Indiana authorities by offering the Potawatomi "new lands" in western Iowa. The offer was rejected, but that fact, of course, had no bearing on the scheme to oust them.

An Indian Bureau agent whom the Potawatomi thought

they could trust sent word to them to meet him at a designated place under the pretext that he wished to have a council with them. The Indians responded, not suspecting that they were being enticed into a trap. When four hundred of them had assembled, the citizen force surrounded them and made them prisoners. The general then led some men to a church where a number of Indians were attending service, surrounded the building, fired guns, and took the worshippers into custody.

"The Indians pled for mercy, and to be let alone, but all to no effect," said one contemporary account.[33] "When evening came and the prisoners did not return home, other Indians were sent out in search of them and they too were made prisoners. All of them were held under guard while troops were scouring the reservation for others and destroying their houses. They also rounded up about four hundred ponies that were to be used in their journey.

"Many tragic scenes were enacted in this roundup. Some fought like demons till they were overpowered and roped; some went in hiding. . . . In one case where they had surrounded the hut and called on the Indian to surrender, he sprang for his tomahawk and rifle. . . . A priest hurried toward him, in the hope of preventing his death, and when the Indian saw the cross, which the priest wore, he threw down his weapons, crossed his arms, and held them out to be tied. This work was kept up until they had gathered near fifteen hundred. . . ."

The priest was permitted to hold a final service. He wrote: "At the moment of my departure I assembled all my children to speak to them for the last time. I wept and they sobbed aloud. It was a sorrowful sight and over this, our dying mission, we prayed for the success of those missions that they would establish in their new home to which they were being driven."

A number of white persons whose "consciences were not at rest" came to bid the Indians good-bye. On the last day the Indians "were permitted, under guard, to visit the graves of their departed friends, and held an impressive service; heart-rending scenes that were indescribable were witnessed." The general had obtained a number of wagons and had hired teams and oxen, and "these were being loaded with their goods such as would be needed, and the old, and the sick of which there were over one hundred, the women and children."

The order to march was given, and the Indians were "lined up, some afoot, some on ponies, followed by the wagons, and all heavily guarded with guards at the rear with bayonets, which were often used to keep the weak ones in the procession.

"Before starting the torch was applied to their village, so that they might see their homes destroyed and they would not want to return.

"When all was in readiness, this gruesome procession, nearly three miles long, like a funeral procession, which in reality it was, started on its final journey."

This was the line of march, as it was described by Father B. M. Petit: First went the "United States flag, carried by a dragoon; then one of the principal officers, next the staff baggage carts, then the carriage, which during the whole trip was kept for the use of the Indian chiefs; then one or two chiefs on horseback led a line of 250 or 300 horses ridden by men, women and children in single file, after the manner of savages.

"On the flanks of the line at equal distance from each other were the dragoons and volunteers, hastening the stragglers, often with severe gestures and bitter words. After this cavalry came a file of forty baggage wagons filled with luggage and Indians. The sick were lying in them, rudely jolted, under a canvas which, far from protecting them from the dust and heat, only deprived them of air, for they were as if buried under this burning canopy—several died thus."

The Indians wanted to take the bodies of those who perished on the march to be interred in their new home, "and when this was denied, they had to leave them at the roadside or camping ground; hence every camping ground became a burial ground.

"In making preparations for this expedition it was thought a picnic for the volunteer guards . . . but at the end of the first day, twenty of the troops, heat-sick, stole twenty of the Indians' ponies and deserted. . . ."

The Indians couldn't desert. Scores fell by the wayside. Mothers carried dead babies they could not bring themselves to abandon. In one town so many persons dropped from heat, exhaustion, lack of water and proper food, if not from utter despondency, that a doctor was called, and he found three hundred "cases of sickness."

"No man can look upon these poor creatures without lamenting the inevitable necessity which drives them from the homes of their fathers," wrote a reporter for an Indiana newspaper who was on the scene.[34] "They are certainly forced away from them at this time, and yet I question if their more judicious and sincere friends will not rejoice at it. If they had lingered much longer, more would have fallen a prey to the hand of violence than can now, by any possibility, die in the attempt to go West at so inauspicious a season of the year. Some affecting scenes have taken place in the camp since and before the Indians were got under way. One chieftain had a mother upwards of a hundred years old, over whom a consultation was held whether or not it would be better to put her to death before she started as no hopes of her long surviving could reasonably be entertained. Fortunately humane counsels prevailed, and the poor creature died and was buried after a journey of four days.

". . . to see eight hundred poor, half-clothed, hatless, breechless creatures in a single file, choked with dust and suffocated with heat, mounted on poor, half-starved Indian ponies, is a sight no man of sensibility can look upon unmoved or with composure."

The compassionate newspaperman was wrong. Such scenes, and worse, were repeatedly viewed by westerners, and if they were moved they made no effort to prevent them. In most cases, they viewed them with satisfaction and fought with each other to take possession of the Indian lands. In one town the guards were prevailed upon to exhibit the suffering Potawatomies on the main street, so the citizens could observe them at close range. With the town band leading the way, the Indians were forced to march around the town square, like animals in a circus. This, too, was America.

The Potawatomies were in their new western Iowa "home" on the Missouri River only a few years when white settlers demanded their lands, and they were again uprooted and driven out on the plains of Kansas. There, after a short time, the same performance was repeated. In less than ten years, some Potawatomies were driven from their homes three times, and their lands opened to white settlement. During this period, the Indian Bureau announced that it had made progress in teaching the Potawatomies to become farmers.

25

The Indian Bureau's annual report for 1868 contains the following dispatch from the Osage agency in Kansas:

"The condition of the Osages upon their reservation the past year has been simply a continuance, in a more aggravated form, of that related by my predecessor. . . . He asks for the assistance of the military to remove the settlers that have intruded on the Osage diminished reserve, and otherwise enforce the laws for the protection of the Indians. . . . Their horses are constantly being driven off by white men. . . . Immigration is still crowding on their lands. They [the white settlers] threaten me with the militia, and say they will hang me if I interfere with them. . . . This should not be allowed by the Government, and I cannot check this settlement without a small armed force.

"The [white] people on and near these lands are made to believe, by speeches delivered by the so-called leading men and newspaper articles, that those Indians have no rights which should be respected by white men.

"Men are taking claims, building houses and mills on the diminished reserve, which disturbs the peace of the Indians very much. If the military is not sent to remove the settlers and enforce the laws . . . there will be much trouble, and the Indians will be driven from their homes. The settlers are preparing to organize a county, entirely on Indian lands, and they have applied to the governor of the State for protection. I can do nothing in the matter without instructions from the Government, which I will await with great anxiety. . . . More than 500 families have settled on the eastern part of the Osage reserve, have built their cabins near the Indian camps, taken possession of their cornfields, and forbidden them cutting fire wood. . . .

"The settlers were generally associated in clubs, pledged to defend each other . . . without regard to the improvements, possession, or rights of the Indians. Many of the latter were turned out of their homes and threatened with death if they persisted in claiming them. Others were made homeless by cunning and fraud. While absent on their winter hunt, cribs of corn, and other provisions so hardly earned by their women's toil, were robbed. Their principal village was pillaged of a large amount of puncheons, and wagon-loads of matting hauled away and used by the settlers in building and finishing houses for themselves. Even new-made graves were plundered, with the view of finding treasure, which the Indians often bury with their dead.

"To my surprise the Indians listened to my advice, and submitted to these wrongs, while the settlers often quarreled among themselves over claims to which they had not a shadow of right, ending their disputes frequently with loss of life.

"The question will suggest itself, which of these people are the savages?"

These were the vaunted pioneers of the West, the heroic men and women so highly praised and revered in song and story, and, regrettably, in so many school histories.

The agent had more to say:

"I encouraged the Indians to plant as usual this spring. They replied that it was useless . . . the herds of cattle and other stock of the settlers would destroy their growing crops, and as their ponies were being stolen in large numbers, they decided that to preserve the balance of their property, and peace with the Government, they would remove to the Indian Territory, permission to do so having been generously given by the Cherokees. . . ."

The Great White Father made no move at all to honor the treaty he had made with the Osages, under which their lands were awarded to them and they had been promised protection. The Federal Government ignored them, and let the white riffraff of Kansas drive them out.

"My efforts," wrote the agent, "thus far have been fruitless to obtain damages for them. The eastern part of the reservation is now mostly surveyed and claimed in 160-acre lots, three counties duly organized. . . . [White people] have been led to believe that the lands are open to settlement. . . . Had the Government at an early stage of these violations of law and of the acknowledged rights of the Indians, which they themselves were not allowed to defend, extended the protection asked for, and that had been solemnly promised, a long list of depredations and outrages that will mantle the face of every true man with shame, would not now be on the record, and a higher standard of morality and justice would obtain. . . .

"The neglect of the Government to assert the supremacy of law over a few border men, professional squatters, was regarded as a tacit approval of criminal acts by men professing to be just and honest; hence this class perpetrated the same crime, claiming the right to do what was allowed by others.

"The attempted purchase of these lands by a railroad company was used as a justification for intruding. Others insisted that they had purchased their claims of Indians, knowing that no Indian could give a title, or even a privilege to settle there; and again, that they were kind and generous to the Indians; that they paid yearly a stipend to some chief, etc. Yet all these do not relieve these men from the reproach of being trespassers, intruders and violators of the nation's law.

"While these efforts were being made to force the Indians from the country, their enemies in Congress were equally zealous to legalize the possession of their lands without reasonable or just compensation."

With the assistance and the approval of the Government, the Osages were driven out of Kansas. This was the year that Congress decided Indian tribes were no longer foreign nations. An act was passed which would permit some Indians to file notices in court of their intention to become citizens, and to remain on their farms with legal title to the land. A few Osages took advantage of the legislation and complied with it, intending to remain on their farms in Kansas.

This is what happened to them, according to an official report of the Indian Bureau in 1871:

"But their claims were soon occupied by white settlers, and the series of outrages and persecutions perpetrated upon them shames humanity. All except eight have abandoned their homes, or taken what they could get from them. Some of their houses were burnt by mobs of white men; one half-breed died from injuries received and exposure on such an occasion. These murderers were arrested, went through the forms of a trial, and were discharged. The eight still remaining will probably lose their land, as they have not the means to engage in a long contest of law; and if the past is an earnest of the future, they can hardly hope that an Indian's rights will be protected in a Kansas court."

Things weren't going any better in the Indian Territory area to which the Osages had been driven, as an agent reported: "Last fall the military removed a number of white settlers who had intruded on the lands bordering on Kansas. Most of them returned promptly when the soldiers had left. Early this spring I asked for the removal of nearly a hundred families from the Osage lands; then applied to the officers in command at Fort Gibson, then at Fort Scott, but the necessary assistance could not be obtained. Immigration has continued to pour in even more rapidly than it would on lands that it was lawful to occupy. My unaided efforts to remove them and prevent immigration have been futile. The Osages feel that their new home is being wrested from them even before they have got possession.

"Last spring a gang of seventeen border men made an unprovoked, murderous assault upon ten unarmed Osages, killing one and severely wounding others, and robbing them of several ponies, blankets and robes."

Three of the attackers were captured and released on $250 bond. End of the case.

A band of twenty-nine Osages, including ten women and children, set out to hunt. "They wandered," reported their Indian Agent, "to the State line of Kansas. Asking some white men who came to their camp if they knew of any buffalo, they were directed forward into the State to a sandy and uninhabited portion of the country, where they at once proceeded and found buffalo, a number of which they killed and dried the meat. They had no thought of doing wrong, as this was their former reservation, where they reserved the privilege of hunting as long as game could be found there, and the country remained unsettled.

"The party was preparing to start home, when they discovered a company of people in the distance. They decided to await their arrival and learn who they were. They proved to be about forty white men, mounted and armed with breech-loading guns and revolvers. They stopped within half a mile of the Osages. The Osages sent two of their men to speak with them; they shook hands friendly, then disarmed the Osages and detained them. Other Osages, two together, continued coming up, until eight were treated as the first and held as prisoners.

"As no more were coming, it was thought best to make sure of these, and the work of death commenced. Four were shot on the spot, and four miraculously escaped the murderous fire. The white men then charged on those who remained in the camp. They [men, women and children] sprang on their ponies, not having time to gather up saddles, clothing, or anything else, and fled for their lives. They were pursued three or four miles under a shower of bullets, but fortunately no more of them were killed.

"At night two of the party returned to look after the dead and their property. Three bodies were found, two of them scalped and otherwise mutilated after death.* Fifty-four ponies, colts, and mules, that they had left behind when escaping, had been driven off by the marauders, and all their other property either carried off or destroyed."[35]

Residents of the Kansas town of Medicine Lodge bragged about these wanton killings as the Medicine Lodge Massacre. It was their very own.

26

The reservation of the Winnebagos was in Minnesota. It had been given to them "in perpetuity." In 1860, the Commissioner of Indian Affairs reported that their progress "in agricultural growths is particularly marked with success. . . . The agent's efforts have been directed to giving to each Indian his own allotment of land. . . . Wigwams are becoming as scarce as houses were two years ago. . . . The school is in a flourishing condition."

The Government continued to fail to honor the treaty it had made with them.

In 1862, after years of waiting for the Government to keep its promises to them, the Sioux went on the warpath in

* Countless white settlers cut ears, fingers, heads, even penes and testes, from Indians they killed, and displayed them in towns.

Minnesota. The Winnebagos refused to join them. Said the annual report of the Interior Department for 1862: "While it may be true that a few of the Winnebagos were engaged in the atrocities of the Sioux, the tribe, as such, is no more justly responsible for their acts than our Government would be for a pirate who happened to have been born on our territory.

"Notwithstanding this, the exasperation of the people of Minnesota appears to be nearly as great toward the Winnebagos as toward the Sioux. They demand that the Winnebagos shall be removed from the limits of the State. The Winnebagos are unwilling to move. Yet the Minnesota people are so excited that not a Winnebago can leave his reservation without risk of being shot; and as they have never received their promised implements of agriculture, and the game on their reservation is exhausted, and their arms have been taken from them, *they are starving.*"

The Winnebagos' agent wrote: "These Indians have been remaining here in a continuous state of suspense, waiting for the Government to cause the stipulations of the treaty of 1859 to be carried into operation.

"I have been notified by the whites that the Indians will be massacred if they go out of their own country; and it is but a few days since an Indian was killed while crossing the Mississippi River, for no other reason than that he was an Indian, and such is the state of public opinion that the murderer goes unpunished."[36]

Congress chose to ignore the treaty with the Winnebagos and to pass an act authorizing the "peaceful and quiet removal" of the tribe from Minnesota. It was ordered that they be located "on the Missouri River somewhere within a hundred miles of Fort Randall, where it is not doubted they will be secure from any danger of intrusion from whites . . . absolutely no time should be lost in emigrating of these Indians."

The people of Minnesota swarmed over the Winnebago lands, snarling and fighting among themselves for possession of them. The Government made no effort to protect the rights of the Winnebagos. What the Government did was to send troops to move them out so their reservation could be stolen, and the greed of the Minnesotans could be satisfied.

The cruelty of the forced removal was augmented by the inconceivably absurd manner in which it was carried out. The Winnebagos, numbering a mere two thousand, were taken from Mankato down the St. Peters to Fort Snelling, loaded on steamboats, thence down the Mississippi to the Missouri, and up the Missouri to the new reservation assigned to them. It was below the Big Bend of the Missouri, 1,363 miles from its mouth, but only about 300 miles by land from their old dwelling place. Men, women and children jammed like animals on the boats were carried more than 2,000 miles, when they might have reached their destination easily and without hardship by wagon caravans on an overland journey of only 300 miles.

The Government added insult to injury by requiring the Winnebagos to pay the cost of the removal from funds due them, a total of $56,042.20.

"They were very much crowded," said a contemporary report, ". . . being without attention or medical supplies. All the Indians were excluded from the cabin of the boat, and confined to the lower and upper decks. It was in May, and to go among them on the lower deck was suffocating. They were fed on hard bread and mess pork, much of it not cooked. . . . They had no sugar, coffee or vegetables. Confinement on the boat in such a mass and want of proper food, created much sickness, such as diarrhea and fevers. For weeks they died at the rate of three to four per day. In a few weeks one hundred and fifty had died, mainly on account of the treatment they had received after leaving Fort Snelling."[37]

The Winnebagos had been promised good homes and good lands. They were unceremoniously herded onto a sandy beach. Around them was only barren prairie burning in summer heat. Not a house had been built.

They had been promised farm implements. None came.

They had been promised food. Very little came in the summer, and much of it was rotten. They were starving, while soldiers patrolled the area to keep them from leaving to obtain supplies. Men who attempted to hunt game were shot down. Women were raped by drunken troopers. They were in a concentration camp.

Some oxen which had been used to pull freight wagons across the plains were killed in January. An official report tells how this beef, which was to feed the Winnebagos until the coming June, was piled in the snow, and it "was black, and very poor—the greater part only skin and bone. . . . In January, the issue of soup to the Indians was begun, issued every other day. It was very unpalatable. On the day the Indians received soup they had no other food issued to them. Some Indians managed to run away. . . .

"There were thrown into the [soup] vat beef, beef heads, entrails of the beeves, some beans, flour and pork. The mass was then cooked by steam. . . . When that was done, all the Indians were ordered to come with their pails and get it. . . . It was about the consistency of very thin gruel. . . . It had a very offensive odor. It had the odor of the entrails of the beeves . . . the settlings in the vat smelled like carrion, like decomposed meat. Some of the Indians refused to eat it, saying it made them sick."[38]

Report of the Commissioner of Indian Affairs for 1863:

"The case of the Winnebagos is one of peculiar hardship. I am still of the opinion that this tribe was in no manner implicated in or responsible for the cruel and wanton outbreak on the part of the [Minnesota] Sioux; but its consequences to the tribe have been as disastrous as unmerited. . . . Contrasting the happy homes, and the abundant supply for all their wants which they have left behind them, and their almost defenceless state, their present condition is truly pitiable.

"*It is not surprising that they have become to some extent discouraged, and are dissatisfied with their new homes.*

"It cannot be disguised that their removal, although nominally peaceable *and with their consent*, was the result of the overwhelming pressure of the public sentiment of the community in which they resided.

"It is to be feared that it will be many years before their confidence in the good faith of our Government, in its professed desire to ameliorate and improve their condition, will be restored. Their misfortunes and good conduct deserve our sympathy."

27

In 1869 President Grant was authorized by Congress to appoint a Presidential Commission "to examine all matters pertaining to Indian affairs."

A few excerpts from the commission's report:

"To assert that the Indian will not work is as true as it would be to say that the white man will not work.

"Why should the Indian be expected to plant corn, fence

lands, build houses, or do anything but get food from day to day, when experience has taught him that the product of his labor will be seized by the white man tomorrow?

"The history of the Government connections with the Indians is a shameful record of broken treaties and unfilled promises.

"The history of the border white man's connection with the Indians is a sickening record of murder, outrage, robbery, and wrongs committed by the former, as the rule, and occasional savage outbreaks and unspeakably barbarous deeds of retaliation by the latter, as the exception.

"Taught by the Government that they had rights entitled to respect, when those rights have been assailed by the rapacity of the white man, the arm which should have been raised to protect them has ever been ready to sustain the aggressor.

"In our Indian wars, almost without exception, the first aggressions have been made by the white man.

"In addition to the class of robbers and outlaws who find impunity in their nefarious pursuits on the frontiers, there is a large class of professedly reputable men who use every means in their power to bring on Indian wars for the sake of the profit to be realized from the presence of troops and the expenditure of Government funds in their midst. They proclaim death to the Indians at all times in words and publications, making no distinction between the innocent and the guilty. They irate [sic] the lowest class of men to the perpetration of the darkest deeds against their victims, and as judges and jurymen shield them from the justice due to their crimes.

"Every crime committed by a white man against an Indian is concealed or palliated.

"Every offence committed by an Indian against a white man is borne on the wings of the post or the telegraph to the remotest corner of the land, clothed with all the horrors which the reality or the imagination can throw around it."

28

In 1849, the Bureau of Indian Affairs was transferred from the War Department to the newly created Department of the Interior.

This legislative action launched an internal conflict in the Federal Government that continued for nearly half a century—the bitter and often vicious fights between the War Department and the Indian Bureau for jurisdiction over Indian affairs.

The War Department was adamant in its contention that, since warfare was involved, control of the Indians was properly its business, and it was openly resentful of what it held to be unwarranted interference by the civilian Indian Bureau.

The Indian Bureau no less stubbornly maintained that it had been created for the express purpose of inaugurating and executing procedures which would civilize and augment the welfare of the backward red people.

Congress, of course, held the power to make all final decisions, but invariably these were shaped more by political considerations than by a desire to see justice prevail.

Often the achievements of one bureau were negated by the counter actions of its rival. And always the mistakes of one bureau were publicly hailed by the other bureau.

While small bureaucrats devoid of human compassion continued senseless wrangling, thousands of Indians hungered and were driven to desperate attempts to survive under the onslaughts of their white persecutors.

29

Organizations campaigning to halt the warfare against Indians, and advocating the establishment of a reservation system that would be impregnable to the schemes of white exploiters, had President Grant's ear. He had not long been in office before he held meetings with leading churchmen, executives of missionary societies and officials of various other groups dedicated to protecting the Indians and improving their welfare. Out of these councils evolved what would come to be known as Grant's Peace Policy, sometimes labeled Grant's Quaker Policy.

Grant had good reasons for endorsing most of the proposals advanced by the conferees. They provided him with the opportunity to shift responsibility for the rapidly increasing troubles with western Indians to other shoulders. He could reason that perhaps they would solve some, if not the bulk, of the problems—at least, he fervently hoped so. If the programs failed, he could not be blamed. In any case, he had nothing to lose and everything to gain.

The announced objective of the peace policy was to civilize and Christianize the degraded, backward, red infidels, instead of exterminating them by the simpler means of starvation and warfare. This humane goal was to be achieved not by civil justice, not by large appropriations of Federal funds, not by the rigid enforcement of existing statutes that prohibited the stealing of Indian resources, but by "the assignment of religious and education work (among the Indians) to the various religious denominations on a regional basis." Persons whose religious faith and integrity had been established would be appointed as Indian agents. Missionaries would be assigned as teachers. Honest mechanics and farmers would be sent to the reservations to instruct the Indians in crafts and agrarian pursuits.

Except in the West the peace policy was hailed as a panacea. Westerners, most of whom were unalterably convinced that annihilation of the Indians was the only means of achieving peace, condemned and blasphemed the whole program as a product of warped minds.

The peace policy was not a failure, however, because of the antipathy of western people. They contributed every effort of which they were capable to make it unworkable, but they might well have spared themselves from the exertion.

The forces which defeated it were four in number:

1. Thieves in the Indian Bureau, and their co-conspirators, dishonest government contractors and merchants throughout the West.

2. Religious fanatics accorded great license and responsibilities they neither deserved nor could fulfill.

3. So-called educators whose qualifications and characteristics made them ineligible for employment as sheepherders.

4. Failure of Congress to approve the enterprises undertaken and to appropriate funds necessary to support the pledges made to the Indians.

The peace policy did not inaugurate corruption in Indian affairs, but it opened the gate to the greatest era of swindling in the annals of relations between white and red people in the West. To the great chagrin and embarrassment of the various religious denominations given jurisdiction "on a regional basis," many of the agents they appointed, all of whom were reputed to be honorable and devout, proved to be totally unscrupulous. Not a few of them quickly established records as the most talented thieves in government service. Cases in which these men appointed by churches and missionary groups stole as much as $50,000 in goods and money appropriated for the relief of Indians were commonplace.

The opening of reservations to missionary organizations was one of the greatest injuries inflicted on Indians. Religious zealots were thereby given sanction by the federal government to force their beliefs on captive audiences by any means, intellectual or physical, they chose to employ, not excluding chicanery, bribery and threats. As a result the Indians suffered an emotional trauma from which they have never recovered, and which still appears to be irremediable.

Once the door had been officially opened to them, many denominations built mission schools, staffed them with fiery-eyed bigots, and hammered their creeds into the heads of the Indian children they lured or forced into their sanctums, under the pretense of giving them an education.

Any secular group or individual desiring to establish a free medical clinic, a trade school or an industrial plant that would contribute to the physical or economic well-being of Indians is subject to searching examination, must obtain numerous licenses and must share profits with the tribe in whose territory the enterprise is undertaken. That is as it should be. But churches are as free as the wind to do as they please, when they please, without any restrictions whatsoever. That is not as it should be.

Indian leaders have not yet found a way to eradicate the turmoil created in the minds of their people by the various creeds being shouted at them and the inane demands being made on them by the apostles of missions. Even if they devised such a means they would not, in all probability, be permitted to use it. Certainly no Congress and no administration has been willing to incur the enmity of church officials—much less the wrath of their blindly devout followers who cast a large number of votes—by restricting the operations of missionaries.

"How are you going to keep them out or even control them?" an Indian Bureau executive said to me. "It's still a free country. If you can keep religious freedom out of reservations, you can keep other freedoms out, can't you?"

The premise is fallacious. A reservation is not a "free country" in the sense that religion can be forced upon the Indians occupying it, nor in the sense that it is open to all groups and all promoters who may wish to enter it. Nor is the contention that doctors and hospitals supported by church funds have greatly aided the Indians sufficient reason for allowing rabid evangelists to wage campaigns within reservations against Indian beliefs. That is analogous to maintaining that any public or private foundation that contributes money to a project to improve the condition of Indians automatically has the right to insist on their acceptance of a particular faith or moral code.

The theory of the educators sent to reservations by the Bureau of Indian Affairs was basically this:

If Indian children were to be fit to enter white society, the first thing to be done was to remove them from their respective environments. They must be prevented from having any contact with their families for at least four, and preferably six or eight years. They must not be allowed to speak their own language. They must wear the clothes of white children. All heathen teachings must be driven from their minds. They must be made to forget the songs taught them by their mothers. They must attend Christian services. They must not play Indian games. They must be made to forget everything they knew. They must be forced to think, act and believe as white children. They must be taught to labor, to assume responsibilities, to behave like civilized persons. They must be severely punished for infractions of rules. They must be given new instincts. Above all, nothing must be permitted to enter their lives that might remind them of their homes, their parents, their brothers and sisters. The world of the Indian must be forever closed to them.

Little children who could not speak a word of English were taken from one world into another. They were whipped and manacled. All phases of the above theory were enforced. For the slightest infraction, such as inadvertently speaking a word of their own tongue, they were deprived of meals or strapped or made to stand in the sun tied to a post for hours or denied time to play, which, anyway, usually amounted to an hour a day at most.

It was a long way from the world of the tepee or hogan or wickiup or sod and clapboard shanty, from the small, tightly knit family group, to the stern and cold military world of the boarding school. Very small was the number of Indian children who made the transition without suffering some permanent psychological or physical injury. They were beaten so cruelly that many of them lost an eye or teeth or were deafened. Most of them were never able to identify in any sense with the strange and conflicting cultural values. Upon release from confinement, all but a very few, actually rare exceptions, returned to their people and attempted to reestablish themselves as members of Indian society. Some had become so emotionally disturbed that they remained hopelessly maladjusted throughout their lives.

The appalling, almost unbelievable, record is available to anyone wishing to read it, in innumerable official government reports and studies made by independent agencies and scholars.

"Oh, that's all in the dim past," people have said to me. "We're more progressive and understanding today."

Is the year 1928 the "dim past?" In that year, at the request of Interior Secretary Hubert Work, Congress authorized an appropriation to finance a study of conditions in Indian schools by the Institute for Government Research, under the direction of Lewis Meriam.

Here are a few excerpts from the Meriam report:

"Malnutrition was evident. The pupils were indolent, and when they had a chance to play, they merely sat about on the ground, showing no exuberance of healthy youth."

The fact was that a heartless and miserly Congress was slowly starving America's Indian children to such a degree that, unless the barbaric practice was halted, they would be deprived of living normal lives. Because of the paltry appropriations the schools were forced to produce much of their own food. The daily food allowance established by Congress was eleven cents per student. The appropriation for boarding schools was set at $225 a year for each pupil. Out of this sum had to be paid the wages of teachers and employees, maintenance costs, and all expenditures for equipment, books, clothing and other supplies.

Under the euphemism "vocational training," the Indian school children were obliged to perform ". . . all the hard, menial labor required to raise food, produce milk and butter, repair shoes, launder clothing and perform other functions necessary to the operation of the institution. Discipline was severe and the use of police remained necessary to enforce the enrollment and continued attendance of the reluctant scholars. Dressed in uniforms, the children 'stood formation,' and marched from place to place."

Stricter regulations could not be found in a prison, as the Indian child ". . . must maintain a pathetic degree of quietness. In fact, several matrons and disciplinarians said that they did not allow the children to talk in the dining rooms. Despite the fact that the children were faced with the problem of learning English, they were denied the privilege of conversation at the table as one informal opportunity to practice, and the use of their mother tongue was prohibited."

The use of child labor in the Indian schools appalled the committee members. "The superintendent of one school said he can get more work out of the children if he keeps large piles of laundry before them. An inspection of the plant verified his statement. A number of small children were literally hidden behind great piles of wet laundry in a greatly overcrowded room filled with steam.

". . . in nearly every boarding school there were children of eleven or twelve spending four hours a day in more or less heavy industrial work—dairying, kitchen work, laundry and shop. The work is bad for children of this age, especially children not physically well-nourished; most of it is in no sense educational.

"Nearly every boarding school visited furnished disquieting illustrations of failure to understand the underlying principles of human behavior. Punishments of the most harmful sort are bestowed in sheer ignorance."

That was in 1928.

If facilities are improved today in these schools, the atmosphere is little better than it was in the past. The Indian children are lonely prisoners. Defiance and spirit, strongly inherent in them, is still countered with reform-school methods. Most of the students dream only of escaping, and few among the many who do seek further education. They have had all they want of Indian Bureau schools, and the same bitter attitude is harbored by boys and girls taken away to mission boarding schools.

The curriculum of Indian schools still is designed to turn out laborers and mechanics. Little thought is given to graduate students qualified to be trained in business or the professions.

"Hell," an Indian lawyer—one of the few who exist—said to me, "we've got fifty thousand Indian welders, and nothing to weld."

30

There were no distinct and self-contained Indian wars in America. No matter how the innumerable violent encounters between red and white men may be described—conflict, battle, engagement, outbreak, campaign, uprising, massacre—no matter when or where they occurred, each stemmed from a common root.

There was only one Indian War, and the conception of its single basic cause coincided with the establishment by Europeans of military garrisons and civilian settlements in the Western Hemisphere.

This progeny, this cause, sired by many bloods and imbued with diverse characteristics, was nurtured on a formula of political corruption, social depravity, economic rapacity and religious humbug. Instilled in it by the human structure on which it suckled were all the bad qualities of mankind and none of the good. On this venomous fare it thrived, becoming lustful, hypocritical, brutal, ugly and, at last, a monstrous uncontrolled force.

From a military standpoint, the War of the Red and the

White in North America began on the eastern seaboard and the islands adjacent to it as the fifteenth century drew to a close. It ended almost exactly four hundred years later in the deserts and mountains of the western United States.

On the part of the whites, it was unqualifiedly a war of aggression, of immoral appropriation and illegal confiscation.

On the part of the Indians, it was from its very beginning a war of defense, a ceaseless struggle to save their homes, their resources, their lives. With legal actions, instead of arrows and guns, they are still fighting it.

31

They were not subjects of fascism who clubbed to death infants in the arms of Indian mothers. They were not Nazis who shot running Indian children to demonstrate their prowess as marksmen.

It was not a dictatorship which condoned the illegal appropriation of territory awarded Indians by solemn treaty for "as long as the waters run and the sun rises."

It was not an "apartheid" that drove thousands of Indians from their ancestral homes, from the farms and hunting grounds upon which they depended for survival, not a *führer* or a *duce* who herded them into prison camps and let them die of malnutrition, cold and disease.

It was not a *komissariat* in the White House which permitted and condoned the ridiculing and deprecation of the Indians' religious beliefs, blasphemed their gods and their rituals and took no steps to halt the destruction of their shrines and the places in which they worshipped.

The bugle calls of American history proclaim not only noble victories and morally justified accomplishments. They proclaim, as well, base deeds and infamous triumphs.

The books cannot be balanced, but it should be noted that there was no end to the efforts of numerous government officials, celebrated persons and people of no prominence but of great conscience, to obtain justice for the victims of American expansion. If they achieved little, it was not because of insincerity, indolence or ineptness but because the social and political barriers with which they were confronted were too great for them to overcome.

Nor may the progress which has taken place in this respect be attributed to improvements in the human makeup. If the potency of the cause of the War of the Red and the White has been decreased, if its power has been dissipated, its condition is far from fatal. Its present dormancy is not the result of a developing weakness, for it has no weakness, not the toll of age, for it is ageless. It is the result of pressures from new ways of life, from new conceptions and standards, which Americans find profitable in the prevailing environment and under the circumstances and conditions of the time.

Behind this pleasant and encouraging façade, the cause of the War of the Red and the White remains a constant of steady pulse in our national behavior. Corporations, groups and individuals continue to covet the assets of the Indians. Government departments, including the Presidential Office, the Congress, even the Indians themselves, have before them at all times well-disguised schemes to gain control of reservation lands, water, hydroelectric power, timber, minerals and other Indian resources.

The fact that the game of defrauding the Indian has become more difficult to play, and more burdened with complex rules, has not by any means driven away all who would engage in it.

The old cause still breathes, and it can endure severe debilitation, but it cannot be interred without the simultaneous destruction of the greed and the corruption which comprise its bones and its meat.

If that ever happens, surely the day of man's salvation will have arrived.

32

Countless monuments have been erected by public subscription to brave soldiers who fought in the campaigns against the Indians, and other carvings in marble stand to the intrepid pioneers who faced the perils of the West.

In all fairness, perhaps at least one piece of sculpture should be created which depicts a trooper in the uniform of the United States Army shooting a child in the arms of its Indian mother. It would be fitting in such a memorial to have a background composed of pioneer settlers holding aloft the scalps and other anatomical parts which they have just torn from the bodies of Indians they shot in the back.

The inscription at the base might be composed of the adage, so long popular with Americans:

"The only good Indian is a dead Indian."

Part Two

THE FUR TRADE IN THE WEST

The acquisition by the United States of the immense Louisiana Territory opened the way for the spread throughout the West of an American industry which for dishonesty, destructiveness, exploitation, cruelty, immorality, criminal negligence, viciousness and avarice has no counterpart in western history. It was the fur trade.

1

From the day on which the English colonies won independence, the American fur trade had been lawless, uncontrolled and a contaminated spring from which poison seeped into the channels of commerce and permeated the highest levels of the Federal Government. When, in 1803, the bars to its expansion west of the Mississippi and Missouri Rivers were removed by the Louisiana Purchase, the noxious qualities which characterized it were freed to infiltrate an untouched and incalculably rich empire larger than western Europe, there to be augmented and compounded until they had reached monstrous proportions.[1]

At the time the Lewis and Clark Expedition, followed closely by the first American Mountain Men, ascended the Missouri River, the fur trade of the North American Continent was more than three hundred years old, but it had been carried on west of the Mississippi only to a very limited extent. British agents and French *voyageurs* had pushed far westward through the forests and lakes of Canada, and the Spanish had long traversed ancient Indian trading trails along the western edge of the Great Plains, as far north as the Platte, and through the southwestern mountains. On the north Pacific Coast the slaughter of sea otters by Yankee, English, Spanish and Russian sailing crews had been so great that hunting them was swiftly becoming unprofitable. Between these three perimeters, however, lay a vast region that was for the most part wreathed in the darkness of geographical ignorance. Except for a few inconsequential penetrations, such as the explorations of the Verendryes to the Powder River area and the journeys of a few itinerant *voyageurs* who left no written accounts and whose names have been forgotten, it was known only by the Indians lost in its immensity.

If the early American fur traders opened paths and supplied practical knowledge, they contributed nothing to the economic improvement or development of the West. The Mountain Men lighted lamps, their intrepidity was incomparable, their feats heroic, their courage unquestionable, but the industry they represented was without a redeeming quality, and wherever they went corruption, disease and ruination were sure to follow.

In four decades the American fur trade had not only exterminated that which had made it possible in the West, but it had left debased, weakened and grievously injured the native peoples whom it had tricked, or forced, into its service. Its legacy to society was the diabolical system it had inaugurated, an inheritance appreciatively received and extensively utilized by the brutish, covetous settlers and a conscienceless corrupt national government in the drive to bring about the final destruction of the Indians.

When the American flag was raised over St. Louis in 1804, it had a population of little more than a thousand, yet it was the trading center of a region larger than the entire eastern and southern United States.* Almost its entire economy was derived from a single source, the fur trade. Money was valued in terms of deer and buffalo hides, beaver, otter, lynx, muskrat, wolf and bear skins. The leading families, almost without exception French, were and had been since the founding of the town in 1764, engaged in trade with the Indians, from whom the great bulk of the furs were obtained.

At the time of the cession, life in St. Louis was easy, pleasant and orderly. Commerce was controlled for the most part by monopolies. It was a pattern which had prevailed for four decades and was rarely contested. Trade rivalries seldom developed, but if one did arise, it was invariably settled without recourse to legal proceedings or violence. Courts and lawyers were almost non-existent. In dealings among themselves, the traders were honest and punctilious. A strong jail was not required, for there was little crime. A log hut in which an obstreperous laborer who had indulged to excess in home brew might be temporarily confined sufficed. Thefts were not a problem of the residents. Great wealth was absent, but so was beggary. Largely, St. Louis was a ragged cluster of board, stone and log buildings, but there were a few spacious and carefully tended residences which denoted the presence of some persons of taste and culture who strove to preserve something of the gracious manner of living they probably would have known had they remained in New Orleans.[2]

If they were scrupulous in transactions among themselves and respectful of the rights of one another, the attitudes and customs of the St. Louis traders were quite different in their relations with the Indians. Here in another way the control of competition, that is, the monopolistic pattern, was an advan-

* Indians and Negroes were not counted.

tage. They could keep the prices of furs low without fear of interference. They could offer inferior merchandise, and their red customers had no recourse but to accept it or go without the articles they were very desirous of possessing, indeed on which many of them had come to depend. Indians who appeared in St. Louis to protest being cheated were unceremoniously driven out of town at gunpoint and not infrequently beaten or otherwise mistreated. In the view of the St. Louis traders the people from whom they derived their living were worthy of no more respect and consideration than the animals from which the furs were torn.

At the end of the few lanes which trickled through the farms on the terraces above the town, the wilderness began. Rolling hills gradually diminished, melting into widening prairies. Woodlands decreased, breaking apart in scattered islands, and at last only a few trees remained to trace the crooked courses of shallow streams across flat earth that touched the sky, the grass seas of the high plains, growing steadily more immense, sweeping onward for a thousand miles until they washed against the towering impregnable wall of the western mountains.

3

The St. Louis traders conducted their regular commerce for only comparatively short distances, in most cases no more than three or four hundred miles, into the vast wilderness region. They dealt with Indians as far south as the Arkansas, as far west as the same river (Central Kansas), and as far north as the Platte. It was business enough, all they could readily handle. Great ambition was not a quality with which they were imbued, but neither did they see anything to be gained in endangering their enterprises, as well as their lives, by attempting to reach out into territory and among tribes virtually unknown to them.

Another practical reason dictated the limit of their northern operations. Competition between the British and Americans for the trade of the tribes inhabiting the upper Mississippi and its tributaries was bitter and bloody, and the British were firmly entrenched among the Indians of the upper Missouri.

4

Almost overnight every condition St. Louis had known was changed. Peace evaporated. Monopolies were shattered. Competition raged. Social life was transformed.

In the years immediately following the acquisition of Louisiana Territory by the United States, Americans swarmed across the Mississippi. The quiet of St. Louis was supplanted by a continuous uproar. Enterprising American shopkeepers opened emporiums, which if they were not directly involved in the fur trade, would live off it. New brick and stone buildings arose, hemming in the old structures, as well as the dignified French houses with their open casements and spacious gardens. Billiard parlors, saloons and brothels appeared, remaining open night and day, and for the first time in its history, the old frontier settlement knew a serious crime rate. There were robberies, muggings, beatings, stabbings and shootings. *La Rue Principale* was crowded with French-Canadian *voyageurs*, British, Scotch and Irish factors in the pay of American traders, hunters with long rifles over their arms from Virginia, Kentucky and Tennessee, river louts, boatmen, woodsmen and plainsmen who looked and acted like Indians, the Indians themselves, both full bloods and breeds of all fractions, prostitutes of varied shades, soldiers and government officials, gamblers, thieves, degenerates and false prophets.

The old St. Louis traders quite naturally resented most the intrusion upon their private trading domains, and the influx of American money. Yet, there were other things to trouble their sleep. They had good reason to worry about how the advent of the unprincipled American Government would affect relations with the Indians. During the French and Spanish regimes, there had not been a major Indian war which had affected either their trade or their safety. Only once, in 1780, had St. Louis been menaced by red invaders, and that had come as an aftermath of troubles on the east bank of the Mississippi. Indians had made an abortive attack on the village of Kaskaskia, and some of them had crossed the river and had killed six persons at Grand Prairie, five miles northwest of St. Louis. Up to this time St. Louis had no defenses. Then some fortifications were constructed, but they were never needed.

The United States could boast of no such record. Since the colonies had attained independence, the United States had fought numerous wars with Indians. Tribes which had lived from time immemorial east of the Mississippi had been driven westward across it, and they all were bitter enemies of their destroyer, the government which had permitted settlers to rob them, take their lands, destroy the game on which they lived and had forced them to migrate in a starving condition hundreds of miles from their ancestral homes.

Not only were American traders known to be unscrupulous in their dealings, but they were not above employing violent tactics in competing with each other, nor were they above starting tribal wars, if by so doing they could gain some commercial advantage.

St. Louis traders began to think in ways they did not enjoy, to act with an alacrity they had never displayed. Yet, resignation and retreat was their only alternative. Whether they liked it or not, they were Americans.

5

If the early administrations of the Federal Government had possessed the courage of their convictions, much of the tragedy and bloodshed of the American fur trade would not have occurred.

Shortly before the beginning of the nineteenth century, Congress gave its first endorsement of a system designed to bring trade with the Indians under governmental control through the establishment of a number of Federal trading posts, called factories, at strategic locations, in the wilderness west of the Appalachians and in the South. It already had become apparent that this trade could not proceed and develop under peaceful conditions because of the dishonesty and recklessness of American traders and the machinations of Canadian and Spanish traders in the northern and southern border territories. Some form of government supervision was mandatory.

President Washington had defined the official policy: peace with the Indians could be attained only by giving them justice. Therefore, "commerce with them should be promoted with regulations tending to secure an equitable deportment toward them." The accepted theory was that next to a "rigorous execution of justice on the violators of peace, the establishment of commerce with the Indian nations on behalf of the United States is most likely to conciliate their attachment. But it ought to be conducted without fraud, without extortion, with constant and plentiful supplies, with a ready market for the commodities of the Indians, and a stated price for what they give in payment, and receive in exchange." The traders would not "pursue such a traffic, unless they be allured by the hope of profit, but it will be enough for the United States to be reimbursed only."[3]

Here was a sensible and practical approach to a problem which was becoming more critical and more menacing with the passage of each day. It could have and should have succeeded. Properly administered and honestly conducted, it would have been of incalculable benefit to the Indians. It would have served greatly to bring them into peaceful pursuits. It would have led them by easy stages to an understanding of the ways and pressures of a settled land. It would have averted much of the bad faith and corruption, which they came to know as the hallmark of every proposal made to them by the national government.

The Federal factory system was a miserable and scandalous failure. The reasons are easily explained.[4]

Monopolies were instruments of European governments, and were forced upon peoples held in bondage by tyrannical sovereigns. The thought alone was enough to make them anathema to the American individualist savoring his first real taste of freedom, but there was another important source from which his hatred of them sprang. They were in conflict with every belief and theory contained in the fundamental concepts upon which the United States had been founded, and not the least of these was the privilege assertedly granted every man to build for himself with all the ability nature had given him, and without interference, restraint or coercion on the part of his government.

The individual's detestation of monopolies was no less pronounced in the members of the Congress. They voted to establish the factory system, but they refused to take over the field. They continued the practice of permitting licenses to be issued to private fur traders.

Under such a situation, the factory system was doomed from its inception. Congress put the government in the fur trading business and then degraded it to the level of a competing trader, forced to fight totally irresponsible and lawless rivals.

There was no fur traders' lobby at this time. If the American traders were opposed to the factory system, they had no funds and no organization to fight it in Washington. They didn't need them, however. Congress itself provided the legislative afflictions that made the system's early demise inevitable. It is improbable that any more stupid provisions and rules ever burdened a Government program. Their inanity makes one suspect that Congress did not, after all, have the best interests of the Indians in mind or sincerely endeavor to attract them into peaceful ways. Whatever the case, curtailment or infringement of individual rights or private enterprise was not to be countenanced.

Under the factory law, trading licenses were not restricted to American citizens. The door was left open to Canadian and British traders to operate in American territory, although Americans were not granted the same privilege north of the international boundary. Not until American fur companies had become affluent and politically strong enough to influence Congress and another war had been fought with England were foreign traders excluded from United States soil.

The clerks and managers, or factors, of the Government stations were forbidden to leave their posts. They were not permitted to go into the wilderness, among the Indians, to solicit business or to trade. All trading had to be conducted in the factories, and the Indian trappers were obliged to bring their pelts to them.

All Government merchandise was to be traded at a markup of 33 ⅓ per cent. There was to be no deviation from this price which was thought to be sufficient to make the factories self-sustaining and not a burden to the general taxpayer. This would have been the result had the business been large enough. Actually, with a monopoly, the Government would have been in a position to have made a tidy profit, which the desperate Federal Treasury would have welcomed. Obviously, that did not happen.

The factories were not permitted to extend any credit.

The factories were not permitted to dispense any liquor.

The factories were permitted to sell, or exchange, only for cash paid over at the time of the transaction.

The factories were permitted to stock only goods made in America.

It was not required that a factory trader speak any Indian language. The jobs were awarded as political rewards, and rarely did a factory trader have a real interest in the work. He took his salary and cared little whether he operated at a gain or a loss. That was a problem of the Congress.

The private trader, often operating without a license, established his post at a strategic location, usually within gunshot of the Government factory. To Indians he knew to be reliable he extended credit, thereby obtaining a mortgage on their season's catch. He was free to protect his investments by going into the wilderness and collecting furs from his debtors as fast as they were taken from the traps.

The private trader could smuggle liquor to the Indians. Generally he could dispense it openly, for there was little likelihood that he would be arrested.

The private trader could offer higher-grade merchandise than that to be found in the Government factories. British manufactured goods were invariably superior to any others. The Indians came to understand that soon after the first American traders pushed their way over the eastern mountains with articles made in the cities of the Atlantic seaboard. American blankets and cloth were shoddy. American manufactures were poorly made of inferior materials. American gunpowder was generally second quality. American whiskey was not only raw but highly diluted. American traps and axe heads were sometimes brittle. The colors and gilt of American ornaments faded.

The Government factories forced prices down, but not enough to make them a major threat to the American traders. Liquor, credit and superior merchandise, the inducements proffered by their private competitors made them unprofitable. Yet, for a quarter of a century the Congress defended and maintained the factory system, while steadfastly refusing to provide it with the medicine that would have cured its ills.

If the Government had taken over the Indian trade the way it had taken over the handling of the mail, the coinage of money and the imposition of customs and federal revenue taxes, many of the crimes committed against the Indians would have been prevented. Instead, it wantonly adhered to the fallacy that private enterprise was a supreme right, not to be abrogated by any policy or program, even though that policy or program be beneficial to the general welfare and conducive to the improvement of the national economy.

No amount of rationalizing can free Congress of its guilt,

for its own actions make it clear that it recognized its own weaknesses and fully understood that the factory system, which it adorned with garlands of lofty phrases, could not succeed. Congress protected the criminal activities of the private traders to the detriment of the whole society. As an early historian of the fur trade so correctly charged, the Government "sinned knowingly—sinned with the consequences patent to its eyes—and from the paltriest and basest of motives that can guide the policy of a nation."[5]

The factory system was slowly enlarged, unquestionably because Congress knew that its defeat and destruction were inevitable. Yet, it recognized the danger to its own public image, the exposure of its own dishonesty, which it had sought to conceal behind artificial wreaths of noble motives, by the sudden cessation of the program. Less than a score of factories were opened altogether, and no more than a dozen ever operated at one time. Only one was established on the Missouri River.

6

The American fur trade knew its greatest prosperity in the decade following the War of 1812. If the traders professed to despise monopolies in control of the Government, they had no such feelings against them in private realms. They fought bitterly to create and maintain them. Strong combines began to emerge.

With every reason to believe that good times would be theirs to enjoy for years to come, the St. Louis traders opposed the extension of the factory system into the virtually unspoiled fur areas of the Upper Missouri and the mountain West. In this stand they found their bitterest enemy, the "Company," by which they meant Astor's American Fur Company, to be their strongest ally. The Company had senators on its payroll, one of them a distinguished statesman from St. Louis and an unqualified champion of private enterprise and individual rights, Thomas Benton, and maintained a lobby, the members of which were easily identifiable on Capitol Hill by the weight of the money bags they carried. The Company had waged its own war on the factories for years, and it readily agreed to unite with the St. Louis traders in a new assault.

By design the attack was launched in 1816 from the West. Congress received a petition asking for the abolishment of the system. The Company's lobbyists added their voices to the appeal, as did the Governor of Michigan, Lewis Cass, a company stooge whose national political influence was rapidly growing. For six years the battering against the factories continued without abatement.

It was the contention of some high Federal officials that inasmuch as a policy of moving the Indian tribes from the East and the South to the West had been launched, it was the Government's responsibility to protect them from exploitation by private individuals and companies. This meritorious stand brought an increase in shelling from the traders and the Company's well-oiled propaganda machine. Criticisms of the system which were inspired and paid for by Company agents appeared in newspapers. Government factors were accused of trading surreptitiously on their own accounts, in violation of the law. Smears were directed against the characters of Government employees. It was charged that the factories, instead of selling furs taken in from Indians at auction, as required by statute, were selling them at low prices to individual traders.

Congress saw the need of a move to stem the rising tide of complaints, if only to protect itself from the abuse, and in 1818, it directed that not only superintendents of the Government system but "all agents and assistant agents of Indian trading houses and the several agents of Indian affairs" were to be "appointed by and with the advice and consent of the Senate." Rigid congressional control, it was hoped, would eliminate the evils which were bringing public condemnation of the Federal program.

The House of Representatives did not propose to be left out of the act, and ordered the War Department to prepare "a system providing for the abolition of the existing trade establishments of the United States and providing the opening of the trade with the Indians with suitable regulations."[6]

Both Houses were doing nothing more than sticking their heads in the legislative sand to keep from facing reality.

The War Department attempted to obey the House's order, but its very vagueness made the task difficult. No one seemed to know exactly what the congressmen had in mind. The best the Secretary of War could do was to point out that it would be extremely hard to plan a trade by individuals. However, if that was what Congress desired, a superintendent should be appointed to issue licenses and enforce regulations. License fees should be raised to $100, or perhaps $500, and provision should be made for a penalty of at least $1,000 for trading without a license. Trade permits should be issued for specific areas, and traders must be prevented from selling or giving away liquor. Also, the Government's superintendent should have the power to control prices.*

* Indian affairs at this time were under the jurisdiction of the War Department.

The War Department further stated:

1. That trade should be concentrated under strict laws in a few sections. This would make it easier for the Indian Bureau to prevent frauds and to maintain peaceful relations.

2. Actually, two programs were necessary, with the Mississippi River the dividing line between them.

3. If a system was to be formulated under which the trade would be carried on by licensed individuals, it should be carried on only in areas east of the river. The tremendous slaughter of wild animals in the old Northwest was swiftly reducing the trade to a point where it would become inconsequential. Indians who continued to live there should be forced to become farmers, or turn to some other means of livelihood.

4. The future of the trade was west of the river, and for that enormous territory an entirely different kind of plan should be established.

5. All foreigners should be excluded from the West. Posts should be built along the Mississippi and up the Missouri to its headwaters. An organization strong enough to compete with the British to the north, and the Spanish to the southwest, should be formed with the sanction of the Government. This would bring the trade completely under American control. Individual private traders would be unable to inaugurate such a program, nor could they make it effective. The western trade, therefore, should be invested "in a company with sufficient capital," and this company should have "a monopoly of the Indian trade for twenty years." Such a company not only would eliminate all foreigners, especially the British, and insure peace on the frontier, but would be able in a few years to push over the Rockies to the Pacific, and "the most profitable fur and peltry trade in the world would be ours."[7]

The most remarkable aspect of the War Department's proposals was the exposure of the ignorance of its authors about the fur trade and the low caliber of the trade's leaders. It was proposing to place in the hands of men without business ethics, morals or integrity not only the economic control of the western United States, but also the welfare of the red people. Moreover, such a scheme could have succeeded only in a nation strong enough to control the actions of its citizens, to enforce laws. The Federal Government's strength in this respect was one of its greatest weaknesses.

The Senate also appointed a committee to work out a plan for abolishing the Government factories. Contrary to expectations, the committee decided that the system wasn't as bad as it had been painted. It expressed a fear of independent traders, regarding them as of bad moral character. It found—certainly not a discovery—that private traders played dirty tricks on each other, stole each other's furs, murdered each other and debauched the Indians with liquor. For these reasons, it recommended that the factories be continued, even though they operated at a loss.

The War Department did not wait for either House of Congress to take final action on its suggestions. It ordered that licenses be refused to French-speaking persons, who had previously considered themselves British subjects, until they became naturalized American citizens. The order applied even to such persons who had been born on American soil. Licenses already issued to traders who came within these categories were to be revoked.

It was a shrewd move to help the factories. If it had been carried out, there would have been so few licensed traders that the factories would have had a clear field for expansion. Many of the leading traders would have been unable to obtain a license.

In Washington, the Company stepped up its drive against the factories, and quickly demonstrated its influence. The Congressional Committee on the Indian Trade, in February, 1820, reported that the Federal posts were "productive of very serious injuries." It advocated that the Government either take over the entire trade, a thing it knew Congress would never do, or grant it to a single company which could be held responsible for all violations of the law and any mistreatment of the Indians.[8]

Officials of the War Department and the Indian Bureau continued their opposition to such proposals, maintaining that the Government houses did much to control the Indians. Ensuing events showed that their opinions still carried considerable weight. Less than two months after advocating the abolishment of the factories, the Indian committee reversed itself and recommended that they be continued. There were some men in the Congress who were sincerely fighting for a just and sensible solution to the problem.

The Company suddenly received unexpected support from a most unlikely source. The War Department had taken the position that the factories had prevented Indian wars and had improved the way of life for the red man. In this contention it was supported by eastern groups interested in bringing cultural advantages to American savages. It was on the recommendation of these naive but well-meaning easterners, among whom were many prominent persons, that the War Department sent a highly respected Congregationalist minister and educator, Reverend Jedidiah Morse, on an extensive tour of the Indian country to report on conditions.

Morse, who was also an author of textbooks on geography, visited factories and talked with a large number of Government employees and private traders. He learned to his astonishment that the Government agents had no authority to prevent independent traders from selling whiskey to the Indians, at exorbitant prices moreover. This prompted him to ask what value the factories had, if they could not prevent the evil debauchery and robbery of the Indians. Probably he did not get a satisfactory answer to that question, but he did gather enough evidence to convince him that the Government's operations left a great deal to be desired.

The private traders poured tales into his ears of how the factories cheated Indians by selling them inferior goods. As proof of their accusations they displayed both British and American goods side-by-side. Even an untrained person could see the difference.

The detective man-of-the-cloth was principally interested, however, in finding out how the Government houses had contributed to the cultural improvement of the Indians. He soon obtained the information.

The Indians on the frontier were as savage as they were at the time the first factory was built. In fact, the Government system had done nothing whatever to aid them in adopting the ways of civilized Christians. On the contrary, the factories had done much toward keeping the Indians on wilderness hunting trails. The whole picture was simply drawn for the War Department's investigator. Factories gave the Indians goods for pelts. If an Indian had turned to farming or some craft, he would not have been able to secure a single pound of flour in exchange for his products at a Government post. They accepted only furs. Obviously, the investigator knew a great deal more about geography and the Bible than he did about wilderness economics.

He could discover no qualities in the political appointees who worked in the factories which might have aided the Indians in improving either their mode of living or their culture. He was surprised to learn that the Indians had never been told what the Government's program was designed to do for them. They didn't understand it at all, therefore, and they had no respect for the men in charge of it. Apparently sociology was a subject which also had been omitted from his education.

He returned to Washington disillusioned and much wiser, and his report advised that the factories be abandoned.[9]

A letter from John Jacob Astor, president of the American Fur Company, to James Monroe, President of the United States, whom he knew intimately, was notable for its implications. It expressed the hope that if the Chief Executive was contemplating any change in the Government's fur trade policies "it will not be to operate against Citizens who are at present engaged in that trade under the System which government adopted Some years ago." This was a reference to the "System" under which the Company had obtained licenses and which permitted the employment of foreigners. The order of the War Department would have halted this practice.

"Relying," the letter said, "on that we shall be permitted to trade under that System we have made many and extensive engagements, Some of which will not expire for Some years to come. In fact our men for the conducting of that trade are generally engaged for 4 to 5 years & whether the trade is good or bad they must be paid & must be fed at a great expense. Our property too becomes So engaged that it takes years to retire. . . . No favor is asked, but I trust that no new measure will be adopted by government to the Injury of us or other Private traders & that if congress who perhaps may not bee fully informed as to the nature of the trade pass any act that will Leave it to the Discression of the executive to Carry the Same into effect as the good of our Country may Require . . . Your friends here all Speeck of you with muish cordiality . . ."[10]

This was an attack on the factories from a side door, but it was effective. The great majority of experienced wilderness fur traders had been born British or French subjects, and to have excluded them would have eliminated the greater part of the competition of the factories. Incidentally, the President to whom the letter went had for several years owed some $5,000 to its writer, which he had been unable to pay. It was at the time a considerable sum. The President had at last obtained "a release in that amount" from the loan, which he acknowledged had been made when "I was pressed for money," by selling his slaves.[11]

Early in 1822, the forces of the traders gathered in Washington for a final push against the factory system. The Company's leading lobbyist, Senator Benton of Missouri, had got himself appointed chairman of the Senate Committee on Indian Affairs. He introduced a bill calling for the complete abolition of the Government program and then presided at hearings on it. With knowing dishonesty, he argued that the factories had been established because Jay's Treaty allowed British traders to operate in the United States at a time when American traders were not numerous enough nor strong enough to hold their own ground. Since then, he declared, independent American traders had acquired the resources and the ability to serve all the needs of the Indians. He charged that the Government houses had been badly managed, and had failed to furnish the goods which the Indians most needed. He was violently sarcastic when he shouted that the factories carried stocks of such things as jew's harps.

The Government was accused of selling goods bought for the Indian trade to soldiers and private white citizens, even to competing traders, in flagrant violation of the law. It was maintained that "Nothing but individual enterprise, individual industry and attention, is equal to such a business. In every competition, individual interest is always too sharp-sighted where the government is a party."

The bill passed the Senate on May 2, 1822, and went through the House two days later.

Ramsay Crooks, a high official of Astor's Company, wrote to Benton: "The result is the best possible proof of the value to the country of your talents, intelligence, and perseverance, and you deserve the unqualified thanks of the community for destroying the pious monster, since to your unwearied exertions and sound practical knowledge of the whole subject is indebted for its deliverance from so gross and unholy an imposition."

Inasmuch as Benton had been paid by the Company to accomplish the destruction of the factories, the letter was not only maudlin and flowery, but hypocritical.

The Government factory system was dead. It would be supplanted by a licensing plan which did not exclude persons of foreign birth or those who had not taken the trouble to become American citizens. The Company could obtain a license for any man it wished to employ. Actually, even that was not necessary. A trader needed only to obtain a license for himself, and any number of factors or *bourgeois* could operate for him under it.

The American fur trade stood on the threshold of its greatest days, an era of prosperity that would never be surpassed. Indeed, once that period had ended there was no possibility of its ever being repeated.

The fur trade consumed its own life blood, destroyed that which it required to survive, as it advanced westward.

The abolishment of the factory system not only took the Government out of the fur trade but removed all possible Government restraints upon it. The traders' only competition came from within their own ranks. Laws were not a burden in the Indian country, for the Government did not have the means to enforce laws, and, as events demonstrated, corruption and criminal negligence in both high and low Federal offices negated most measures designed to bring about enforcement.

The Government turned the West over to organized brigands and plunderers. It abandoned the Indians to unscrupulous exploiters who were devoid of conscience and any sense of responsibility, who were motivated only by greed, who possessed neither honor nor compassion.

7

"The neighborhood of the trading houses where whiskey is sold," an Army officer wrote to the War Department in 1825, "presents a disgusting scene of drunkenness, debauchery and misery; it is the fruitful source of all our difficulties, and of nearly all the murders committed in the Indian country . . . I have daily opportunities of seeing the road strewed with the bodies of men, women and children, in the last stages of brutal intoxication. It is true there are laws in this territory to restrain the sale of whiskey, but they are not regarded . . . He who has the most whiskey, generally carries off the most furs . . . I will venture to add that an inquiry into the manner in which the Indian trade is conducted is a matter of no small importance to the tranquility of the borders."[12]

Neither the Federal Government nor the American fur traders inaugurated the system of debauching the Indians with liquor. Far from it, but the Federal Government failed to halt it, and the American traders used it to a far greater extent than their predecessors. Powerful voices and pens continually railed against the diabolical practice in Congress, in pulpits and the press, but they spoke no words which had not been heard in colonial times.

From the beginning of the sixteenth century, when the first fishermen from northern Europe began to trade for furs among the Indians of eastern Canada, the red man had suffered the curse of the white man's liquor. Neither kings, parliaments, presidents nor honorable individuals had been able to stem its flow into the wilderness.

Samuel de Champlain had been one of the first officials to attempt to halt the sale of alcohol to the Indians. Recognizing it for the evil it was in the fur trade, and having seen the deleterious effect it had on commerce with the Indians, which he was struggling fiercely to maintain and expand, he issued orders forbidding the importation of all spirits, and he joined with the Jesuits in their efforts to convince the Indians that only harm could come to them from strong drink. Champlain and the Jesuits for a time achieved a moderate success, but they were in no position to prevent the English traders from supplying the Indians with unlimited quantities of rum, and neither their police power nor their political influence was great enough to stop the *coureurs de bois* from using liquor in the wilderness trade.

Contrary to popular belief, it had not been easy to induce the Indians to drink. In the beginning they had been unwilling to exchange their furs for the unfamiliar fiery liquid. They wanted mostly the marvelous ironware which the white man possessed, and bright ornaments and utensils appealed to them much more than a sour stomach and a headache. Both the British and French traders had persisted in offering liquor, and at last succeeded in making it a requisite of the trade. The

French and the British knew what they were doing. An Indian who could be persuaded to take a few drinks became wild for more. Those who developed a craving would give anything they had for it. Returning from a successful hunt, an Indian who had known the delights of intoxication would trade his season's catch for a few bottles of raw, impure liquor.

"It is useless," wrote a Jesuit, "to forbid the trade in wine and brandy with the Savages. There is always found some base person who, to gain a little beaver fur, introduces by moonlight some bottle into their Cabins."[13]

When the Indians with whom they were conducting a trade became impoverished and began to degenerate, with the result that they were unable to hunt, the *coureurs de bois* simply pushed farther out into the wilderness until they found unspoiled tribes to debauch. That was the pattern, and it was not to change as long as there were new territories to be conquered.

On many occasions the Indians themselves sought to stop the bottled fire that was consuming their people. As early as the middle of the seventeenth century, many Algonquins and Hurons avoided traders who offered alcohol, and they petitioned the French Government to forbid its gift or sale to them. One governor granted such a petition, but it had no effect.

The problem became so acute and disruptive that the French Crown at last ordered the leading traders of New France to meet and settle upon a definite policy. The Governor and the members of the provincial Council met with twenty of the largest traders in what was dubbed the "Brandy Parliament."

One trader argued that it was impossible to keep liquor from the Indians, that if the *coureurs de bois* were not allowed to sell it, unscrupulous individuals would smuggle it into the Indian Country, and he insisted that Indians would not trade with those who did not furnish them drinks. He cited a case in point: three hundred Iroquois were en route to Montreal with furs, but when told they could not obtain liquor there, they turned about and went to Albany, where the Dutch willingly supplied them with all the drink they desired. If the French forbade the use of liquor in the trade, the English and Dutch would continue to hold the alliance of tribes and would secure the loyalty of western Indian nations. As it was, the French drinks were more delicious, the Indians liked them better than the English drinks, and this advantage should be maintained.

Others attending the "Brandy Parliament" took the stand that brandy was helpful in saving the Indians' souls. If the British and Dutch held the Indians through drink, they would also convert them to heresies which would send their souls to perdition. It was also asserted that Indians could not afford to purchase enough alcohol to hurt them.

Taking another position, one trader pointed out the violence of Indians when intoxicated. They would run deeply into debt to get brandy, he declared, and their deterioration made them poor hunters. Thus, the fur trade suffered. So extreme were this man's views on the subject that he urged the death penalty for those who used liquor in the fur trade.

The "Brandy Parliament" voted to continue the liquor traffic. Accepting the will of the majority, the Crown amended it by limiting the sale to the French settlements and allowing only a small number of permits for transporting liquor into the wilderness. The edict meant less than nothing. It was ignored, and the Indian Country was in reality thrown wide open to unlimited traffic in alcohol.

Conditions to be met in a given area, however, often affected policy when it came to selling liquor. In northern Canada, the Hudson's Bay Company, before learning better from bitter experience, sold spirits to the Indians. Widespread impoverishment was the result. French traders, in deadly competition with the gargantuan British monopoly, well understood the error the British were making, and took advantage of it. The Indians of the Far West had not yet been corrupted by liquor, and the French, wise in the ways of the trade through decades of experience, realized the advantage to be gained by refraining from its use.

The French traders moved out to the Moose and Albany Rivers, to Lake Winnipeg, and pushed southward around Lake Superior, out to the Minnesota and the St. Peters, the Rivière au Jacques, and the upper Missouri, an enormous virtually untouched empire, and cut off much of the trade that otherwise would have gone north to the British posts.

The French were always more adroit than the English. They lived with the Indians, won their affection, supplied them with guns, traps, axes, brilliantly colored warm clothing and fascinating trifles, but they offered no liquor. The western Indians with whom they traded were sober and vigorous and brought in great quantities of fine furs. However, greedy *coureurs de bois* in time began to undermine this advantageous condition, and it did not long prevail.

The British, victorious in the great colonial war with the French, tried but failed to halt the destructive traffic. England's Imperial Plan for the fur trade in its American colonies contained provisos against the use of liquor in transactions with Indians. They were seldom obeyed. Canadian merchants complained that large quantities of spirits were smuggled into the Indian Country, and the Indians themselves complained that traders were offering them quantities of brandy and other spirituous liquors in exchange for their peltries. The Lords of Trade ordered that justices of the peace cancel licenses of all traders who retailed spirits to the Indians. Troops were sent on occasion to stop the sale of rum, but they had no success.

A British general reported that quarrels between "drunken Indians and licentious whites" were common. "The most general complaint at present about the Trade is of the vast Quantitys of Rum carried amongst the Indians," he said. It was so "easy to smuggle it past posts and profits so great that it will likely continue." He termed the Indian trader as being "generally a pretty Lawless person," and he suggested that Indians be allowed to police themselves and take on the responsibility of preventing "Spirits being carried into their villages and hunting Grounds." The colonial government decided that such an experiment might prove "too dangerous, and it would give Pretence for plundering, and if they began to seize one article, it's uncertain where they would stop."[14]

The British general was right: the liquor trade would continue. When the Americans were at last victorious over the powers of Europe, and had more than doubled the size of the United States by acquisition of Louisiana Territory, it would remain as the most complicated, controversial problem having to do with the Indians. Every argument for and against the liquor trade in the Indian Country would be repeated over and over again. The American Government, looking toward westward expansion, would be faced with the same troubles the earlier continental rulers had known. It would fail to solve them. It would take cognizance not at all of history, of the experiences of the British and French, from which it might have greatly benefitted. Each succeeding administration in Washington would talk loud and long about preventing whiskey from reaching the Indians, and each administration would fail to practice what it preached, each would close its eyes and do little more than make meaningless gestures in the air.

The Congress had no more than assembled in its new Washington home when it passed an act which authorized the President to "take such measures, from time to time, as to him appear expedient to prevent or restrain the vending or distributing of spirituous liquors among all or any . . . of the Indian tribes."

It was a weak, vacillating measure. If it put Congress on the side of righteousness and good sense, it did nothing more. All action was left to the discretion of the President, and every President had a great many other pressing problems, involving voters and Americans living closer to home, about which to worry.

For the next twelve years, no President used his powers to halt the trade in alcohol. It was a fact, of course, that the sale of corn whiskey to traders brought welcome revenue to western farmers, and only a careless politician would have ignored the growing strength of the western electorate. It was also a fact that British traders trafficked in alcohol, and it was deemed unfair to deny the same privileges to Americans who must compete with them. Business and politics first, humaneness and decency second.

The horrors, the crimes, the terrible butchery and suffering that took place on the frontier in ensuing years, however, moved Congress to give brief attention to the problem once more, and in 1815, it forbade the setting up of a still in the Indian Country under pain of a fine of $5,000. The penalty was more than even a highly successful country moonshiner could have paid, but it might as well have been ten times as large. If

Congress had deliberately set out to pass a law which would have little or no effect on the situation it could not have done better. Few persons wanted to distill whiskey in the Indian Country. It was too easy to take it in.

There the matter stood, with liquor pouring into the West, transported up the Missouri River by the boatload. Congress at last got around to saying that use of the whiskey in the Indian trade was illegal, but even this sterner language did little good. The War Department and the Indian Bureau, infiltrated with grafting bureaucrats, failed to enforce the new statute.

The protests and denunciations of a famous Black Robe, Father Pierre Jean De Smet, were censored by his superiors, who feared that they "savored too much of hostile criticism of the government." Scathing letters he wrote directly to the Indian Department became "lost in official files." Some papers he prepared on the subject were not "discovered" until years after he had written them.[15]

In one of his earliest reports from the wilderness this distinguished missionary warned that liquor, "which brings in its train war, famine and pestilence, all together," would be the ruination of all tribes along the Missouri River and in the western mountains, unless it could be halted by force of law and, if necessary, by arms.

"The [Indian] country is overrun with vagabond Americans," he said, "and the government, which alone could put a stop to this abominable traffic, in spite of the severity of its laws, pays no attention to the matter."

He spoke of a tribe which had been guaranteed $50,000 per annum, and "such a sum, well placed, would procure for the savages victuals and goods in abundance, and would render them happy in regard to temporal things. But alas! all this money goes for liquor. As long as it lasts they neither work nor hunt. . . .

"They quarrel and fight from morning to night; their bodies become veritable furnaces, full of foul humors, which cause them all sorts of maladies. Their love for liquor is really inconceivable. . . . It is a regular tarantula to them; as soon as they are bitten by it, all their blood flames in their veins, and they are crazy for more. . . . More! More! is their war cry, until, as the flames consume them, they fall over . . . and when the fumes of drink evaporate from their brains their first and only cry is 'Whiskey! Whiskey! Whiskey!' as if it was a matter of life and death.

"The other day I counted nine bitten-off noses in a single group of Indians. In their rage, this little member is the principal object of their attack, and a drunken Indian who deprives a comrade of his nose, boasts of it as much as a brave soldier of having carried off a flag from the enemy.

"When they are sober, no one would recognize them; they are mild, civil, quiet and attentive; but there is no safety in the presence of a drunken savage. Several times our lives have been in the greatest danger; but fortunately by gentle and moderate words we have managed to appease the rage of these barbarous drunkards, who were breathing only blood."

Following the arrival of a fur trade steamboat that brought liquor to an upper Missouri tribe, Father De Smet wrote a friend in Europe: "Already fourteen among them are cut to pieces in the most barbarous manner, and are dead. A father seized his own child by the legs and crushed it, in the presence of its mother, by dashing it against the post of his lodge. Two others most cruelly murdered an Indian woman, a mother of four children. . . . I wrote an energetic letter to the government against these abominable traffickers."

During one period of twenty days, the Black Robe wrote in his diary of twenty murders, one poisoning, four drownings, several stabbings and a number of fights during which half a dozen noses were bitten off, all attributable to liquor obtained from fur traders.[16]

There was no such thing as a moderate drinker among the wilderness Indians. They were either teetotalers or sots. Wrote a state governor: "Their attachment to ardent spirits is a moral phenomenon, and to it they sacrifice every consideration public or private."[17] In professed horror he told the War Department of the revolting conditions resulting from the distribution of intoxicating drinks among the Indians. This statement was for the public record, to benefit his political image. At the same time, he was taking bribes from traders who were openly transporting liquor, in violation of the law, to the Indians in territory under his jurisdiction.

Thinking of their own interests first, and the welfare of the Indians second, if at all, some traders made a sincere effort to halt the liquor traffic and appealed to the Government to enforce laws prohibiting it. One prominent trader, undoubtedly with the assistance of money, induced an Indian Agent to grant his men the authority to destroy all liquor found in the area in which they wished to hold exclusive trade. This extralegal power was withdrawn by higher officials as soon as they were apprised of it.

"Liquor secretly introduced has hurt our trade," a leading western trader complained, although he was not without secrets of his own of this kind. "If government agents will not stop it, although the proof of guilt is easy, I sincerely hope the opportunity will not be lost of punishing such miscreants. If the government permits the sale of this pernicious liquid we can have no hesitation of availing ourselves of the privilege although we are convinced its total prohibition would benefit both the country at large and the natives who are its victims. But to succeed in the trade when our opponents set the law at defiance and we implicitly follow its dictates is wholly impossible."[18]

Between the years 1822 and 1840, although he would have liked to see the liquor traffic halted, this trader sent far more alcohol up the Missouri River than all his competitors combined.

The Canadians, making a last desperate stand against advancing American traders, sent a flood of whiskey over the border. Washington protested that it was impossible to guard such a remote and lengthy frontier. That was true, but it wasn't the only reason for the condition. Also responsible were the vagueness and ambiguity of regulations. No official was certain of exactly what he could do, what police powers he possessed or how far he might go to curtail the smuggling.

One honest Indian Agent quickly found the answers to these questions. Stationed in a western town, he issued an order prohibiting "the landing of every description of spirits in this agency, for the purpose of trade or Barter." Official reaction came quickly, and he was advised that while "there is no treaty or law which extinguish the Indian title in the vicinity," his town "could not be classed as Indian country," and, therefore, "the sale of liquors to the inhabitants of the country ought not to be wholly prohibited, but only limited or guarded in such a manner as to prevent their subsequent transfer to the Indians." The agent threw up his hands in disgust.[19]

Once again the Congress, disturbed by stories reaching Washington in newspapers and official reports of murder, arson, rape, stabbings and plunderings in the fur trade, took action. In 1822, it passed a law forbidding traders to take ardent spirits into Indian territories under penalty of forfeiting all their goods. It was a good law as far as it went, but it failed to bring the desired result, for the simple reason that it failed to define what was not Indian territory.

A major in command of a frontier post wrote the War Department in an effort to determine whether his station and the area under his jurisdiction, which was "resorted to by some powerful tribes," was actually "Indian territory" in the official interpretation of the new liquor statute. He also asked whether American citizens who were not fur traders could pass through Indian Country with liquor.

He went on to say that if the answer to his first inquiry was No, and the answer to the second was Yes, then the new law was inoperative in his post and in all the Indian Country supplied from it. He also dared to volunteer the opinion that only by prohibiting all persons from transporting alcohol for any purpose whatsoever could the traffic be controlled.[20]

No one in the War Department seemed interested in enlightening the major, or in his personal views, but he was soon transferred to another command.

Hudson's Bay Company agents brought whiskey across the Canadian border in large quantities. American traders, after considerable efforts by their Washington lobbyists, obtained an order from the Secretary of War suspending liquor regulations at all points of the boundary west of Lake Superior where Hudson's Bay Company posts were located. Their plea had been that this move would allow them to compete with the foreign invader.

Of course, they took advantage of this breech in the legal dike, and poured liquor into all the northern Indian Country, hundreds of miles below the border where no Canadian agents were working. This liquor was distributed from American posts at Chicago, Milwaukee, Green Bay, Mackinac, Fond du Lac and points on the Mississippi. Traders at Chicago, said an Indian Bureau report, were "selling quantities of whiskey to the Indians . . . of Lake Michigan."[21] The Superintendent of Indian Affairs disclosed that the Indian Agent at Fort Wayne, in Indiana, had seized a large supply of liquor en route to Indians of his area. Clicking his tongue in disparagement of the situation, the Superintendent remarked that the "forbidden and destructive article, whiskey, is considered so essential to a lucrative commerce, as not only to still those feelings . . . of repugnance . . . but lead the traders to brave the most imminent hazards, and evade by various methods the threatened penalties of law."[22]

Fur trade representatives in Washington were able to get the Indiana liquor released on the ground that it had not been seized in Indian Country.

The whiskey traffic continued. In 1829, an Indian Bureau official at St. Louis informed the Secretary of War: ". . . there is but little doubt but a clear gain of more than fifty thousand dollars has been made this year on the sale of whiskey to the Indians on the river Missouri; the prices are from $25 to $50 a gallon." The commander at Cantonment Leavenworth "says that thousands of gallons of alcohol have passed that post during the present year, destined for the Indian country."[23]

Cargoes of liquor were being transported on steamboats up the Missouri, passing without difficulty the largest military establishment on the western frontier. The hands of commanders were tied by grafters in Washington.

Continued the St. Louis agent: "The capital employed in the Indian trade must be very large, especially that portion which is employed in the annual purchase of whiskey and alcohol . . . for the purpose of trade with the Indians. It is not believed that the superintendent is ever applied to for a permit for the one hundredth gallon that is taken into the Indian country. The whiskey is sold to the Indians in the face of the agents. Indians are made drunk, and, of course, behave badly. . . . The traders entertain, as I know to be a fact, no sort of respect for our citizens, agents, officers of the Government, or its laws or general policy."

The evidence was in the reports, all the evidence Congress needed to bring government, law and at least a semblance of justice to the Indian country beyond the Missouri, but Congress still chose to move cautiously. Beset by pressures, it defended itself by pointing out that a law forbidding the use of liquor in the Indian trade was on the books, and it argued that finding the means of halting violations was not a simple matter. Enforcement involved great expense, which the taxpayers must underwrite, and presented other difficult problems, such as international relations, severe headaches that did not come out of a bottle.

However, demands that a strong new liquor statute be passed continued to increase. The agitation was carried on not only by "drys" but by politicians in high offices. Congress was flooded with reports of tragic conditions on the frontier, and the politically sensitive members began to take cognizance of the growing public resentment of them.

The fur trade lobby waged a vigorous fight against all proposals to change or strengthen the law. Their opposition purportedly was based on the old ground: they could not compete in the West with Canadian traders as long as liquor was allowed to cross the international border.

The Astor Company accepted the task of proving that all

hope of inducing foreigners to stop the destructive traffic was futile. A letter was sent to the Hudson's Bay Company stating that American traders would "not in the future, either directly or indirectly, carry in, or in any way give ardent spirits to the Indians . . . provided the Hudson Bay Co., pledge themselves to the same effect."[24]

A reply from the Hudson's Bay Company office in London said: "The Governor and the Committee have this season confirmed and repeated the orders given last year . . . that in the event the American Traders discontinue the practice, those in the Service of the Company should do the same; But the Governor and Committee do not feel justified in leaving their trading Posts on the Frontier totally deprived of Spirits, at the same time I am directed to assure you, that the Governor and Committee have the means of strictly enforcing the instruction given to their Traders; the discontinuance of the practice will therefore entirely depend on the conduct of the American traders, to which I am to call your attention."[25]

The Governor and the Committee were well aware of the inability of the United States Government to control American traders or to enforce laws in the wilderness, and they were not going to be hoodwinked into an agreement that would leave them holding the short end of the trading stick. The lobby of the American traders stood firm in its position that "if the Hudson's Bay Company did not employ ardent spirits against us, we would not ask for a single drop."

Politics, goaded by the rising voice of the American people, won the fight, however, and in 1832, Congress passed a new and stringent liquor law. It provided simply that "no ardent spirits shall be hereafter introduced, under any pretense, into the Indian country." Customs, military and Indian Bureau officials were given the power to examine all cargoes destined for the fur trade, and to confiscate all liquor they found.

The statute imposed the greatest hardships on the big traders who shipped large cargoes by steamboat up the Missouri River. Avoiding inspection was virtually impossible, unless inspectors could be bribed to keep their eyes closed. That was, of course, done, but it was extremely costly. The small trader who went overland with a few packhorses or made his way stealthily up the river in a small craft could easily escape detection.

"I have no alternative," declared Astor to his chief lieutenant in St. Louis, "if I want to stay in business but to violate the law. In self-defence I am forced to become a smuggler, placing myself on the same level with lawless adventurers who have little investment to lose in the event of arrest."[26]

This would be a familiar role for him. He had been a liquor smuggler for years, the largest in the West. Now he went a step farther. He became an illegal distiller. The manager of the Company's main post on the upper Missouri River was permitted to install a still, and he was soon able to report to St. Louis headquarters: "Our manufactory flourishes admirably. We only want corn to keep us going. The Mandan corn yields badly but makes a fine, sweet liquor. . . . I have a good corn mill, a respectable distillery, and can produce as fine a liquor as need be drunk. . . . Do not load the boat too heavily at St. Louis, that a few hundred bushels of corn may be placed on board at the [Council] Bluffs. . . . Surely you will contrive some means of passing alcohol to the Bluffs for the Sioux trade."[27]

Western traders were delighted to find that the new liquor law contained a major loophole. It was the provision which permitted them to carry a certain amount of alcoholic beverages with them into Indian Country for their boatmen. Congress had made sure that it did not deny a white boatman, who might have a vote, a relaxing nip at the end of a hard day.

Quickly the traders took advantage of the opening. In the year after passage of the law one large post alone received more than 5,500 gallons of whiskey for its *voyageurs* and *engagés*. Diluted in the customary way, it made no less than 20,000 gallons for use in the Indian trade. The boatmen got precious little of it.

Suddenly the high dry West seemed to be filled with boatmen.

A St. Louis trader wrote one of his factors: ". . . it is permitted to take one gill per day for each boatman during the period of their absence—that is, for twelve months. It is on this ground that I have obtained permission to take an amount corresponding to fifty men . . . [including] the names of those . . . previously sent to you . . . and without knowing whether you will keep them or send them back. That makes no difference, however, for I explained the matter to the Indian Agent."[28]

The men previously sent out by this trader numbered twenty-three. By using their names, he was able to add more than three hundred gallons of whiskey to the amount allotted to the twenty-seven men going out—a total of fifty men.

In the spring of 1833, one of the prominent mountain traders was preparing to send a large supply packtrain to the annual fur rendezvous in the far-off Snake River country. He was given permission to carry 450 gallons of whiskey "for his boatmen." Obviously the packtrain was going across the plains. Its announced destination was Pierre's Hole, just west of the Teton Range.

Despite widespread usage of the boatman's loophole and outright smuggling—the highly successful still at the upper Missouri post was only put out of business when rival traders squealed about it to the authorities—the importation of liquor into the Indian Country was curtailed under the new law.

Officers, although handicapped by insufficient manpower, strenuously sought to search all cargoes, whether going by land or water, and their efforts had an effect.

Enforcement, however, was not equal to the task, and graft and corruption in both high and low places continued to eat holes in the dikes.

8

In the code of the fur trader, cheating was a virtue. The greater his accomplishment in the practice, the more a trader was to be congratulated and envied.

Whatever else they might be, Indians, especially those of the northern forests and plains, were not stupid. "The Indians, it is admitted," said a Government report in 1822, "are good judges of the articles in which they deal, and, generally, when they are permitted to be sober, they can detect attempts to practice fraud upon them . . . however, few of the Indians are permitted to trade without a previous preparation in the way of liquor." The report cited cases in which "as much as one dollar and fifty cents had been demanded by the trader of the Indians, and received, for a brass thimble, and eighteen dollars for one pound of tobacco!"[29]

Nine years later, the Indian Bureau informed the Senate about prices then current in the fur trade: "For a white 3 point blanket which cost $4.00 Indians were charged $10; for a beaver tray costing $2.50, the charge was $8; for a rifle costing $11 they had to pay $30; a brass kettle which a trader could buy for 48 cents a pound, he charged the Indians $30; powder cost him 20 cents a pound; he sold it for $4 a pound;

he bought tobacco for 10 cents a pound and sold it at the rate of five small twists for $6 . . ."[30]

A craving to possess the weapons and manufactured articles of the white man helped to decrease the sales resistance of the Indians, and whiskey was certain further to do that, but these were forces that created conditions that could not be depended upon to endure. The American fur traders of the upper Missouri and the mountain West had no illusions in this respect. The eagerness of the Indians to buy and the use of liquor would not alone assure a successful and profitable trade. To meet fully the Canadian competition they had to offer British goods.

A tin tea kettle, then, purchased in England, had to be shipped to New Orleans, and brought up the Mississippi by keelboat.* There it had to be placed in a pack on another keelboat and taken by more brute strength to the upper Missouri, perhaps on up the Yellowstone and the Big Horn. It might have to be carried far beyond these points, hundreds of miles by packhorse, into the mountains, before it passed across a trading robe in exchange for beaver pelts.

It is approximately eight thousand miles from Liverpool to the confluence of the Yellowstone and Big Horn Rivers. Orders for goods might reach England from St. Louis, going overland by express to New York, thence by fast mail ship across the Atlantic, in nine or ten weeks. It could, and often did, because of blizzards and gales, take twice as long. Shipments of British goods, even though they moved directly to New Orleans, took from six to eight months to reach St. Louis.

* The first steamboat reached St. Louis in 1817, but it was not until a decade later that it was regularly in use on the upper Missouri, eliminating the keelboat.

Buying from the manufacturers in England was the cheapest way to obtain trade goods, in spite of the great distance they had to travel. To be safe, a St. Louis trader had to order goods at least a year before he would need them. This was normal procedure and did not increase the cost of his inventory.

The fastest method open to a western trader was to buy the British goods in New York or Philadelphia, but this added a middleman's or wholesaler's profit to the cost, and it often was high. From New York or Philadelphia, the goods might be sent overland to the Ohio, then travel by that river and the Mississippi to St. Louis, or they might be sent by ship to New Orleans. Enormous profits permitted western traders to absorb the wholesaler's markup with ease, and when the War of 1812 ended, New York quickly became dominant in merchandise sales to all the American fur trade west of the Alleghenies.

For example, suppose a tin tea kettle cost a New York dealer 20 cents in England. Transportation, insurance handling, import tax, license, etc., would add another 20 cents. Total: 40 cents. To this he would add a markup of two hundred per cent, or 80 cents. Total: $1.20.

The St. Louis trader purchasing the tea kettle would add to the cost of $1.20, about fifty per cent, or 60 cents, for wages, transportation up the Missouri, etc. Total: $1.80. To this the St. Louis trader would add another two hundred per cent, or $3.60. Total: $5.40.

The Indian purchaser would not pay the $5.40 with coin. He would pay with beaver skins, possibly four prime pelts, with a total weight of six or seven pounds.

The St. Louis trader would charge off 25 cents for transporting the four skins down the river to St. Louis. They would bring $4.00 a pound from the New York dealer. Total: $28.00. Less the 25 cents downriver freight cost, $27.75.

Allowing for normal losses and all other incidental expenses, the St. Louis trader would make more than $25.00 on the tea kettle transaction.

Cost to the New York dealer-trader for the four skins (purchase price plus shipping to London) was $30.00. He would sell the skins in London for $8.00 a pound, or $56.00. Profit to him on the skins alone would be $26.00. He also had made two hundred per cent profit on the tea kettle.

How a large international fur trader, who was also a New York merchandise wholesaler and shipper, operated may be seen from the following transaction.

A ten-pound keg of gunpowder cost him $2.00 in London. It traveled in one of his own vessels to New Orleans. There it was placed on a steamboat which carried it up the Mississippi to St. Louis.

Transferred to a keelboat–in later years to a small Missouri River steamboat, which he also owned–it was taken to his trading post at the mouth of the Yellowstone. The price to Indians was $4.00 a pound, or $40 for the contents of the keg. For each pound, the Indians gave a prime two-pound beaver skin (or the equivalent in lighter skins), ten skins with a combined weight of twenty pounds for the keg.

The beaver skins traveled to London over the same route. Presuming they were sold at the moderate price of $7 a pound, they brought the trader $140.

On the original investment of $2.00, there was a gross return of $140.

The trader deducted two per cent commission for buying the gun powder, or four cents, leaving a gross of $139.96.

He deducted five per cent commission for handling the sale of the furs, or $7 of $140.00, leaving a gross of $132.96.

Next, twenty-five per cent was deducted for transportation, wages and other expenses. This amounted to $35.00.

The remainder, $97.96, was considered net profit.

Fifty per cent of the net was given to the partners who managed the trade for him in the St. Louis office. Therefore, his net on his original investment of $2 in the keg of powder was:

Commission on purchase	$ .04
Commission on sale of furs	7.00
Fifty per cent of net	48.98
Total	$50.02

Actually, the New Yorker's profit was greater. He charged interest on the money he advanced to make the purchase, and in using his own vessel between London and New Orleans, round trip, he made money on freight charges. But these figures were concealed by the haze of his bookkeeping.

9

Indian leaders and some honest Indian Bureau officials continually protested to Washington about the dishonest practices and brutality of the traders, but neither the Congress nor the War Department (much less the White House) made an effort to halt the evils. To the contrary, as one Senator charged, the Government was "quick and generous in affording the greatest protection and the widest latitude" to the traders.

The fur trade lobbyists cried out dramatically that in fifteen years more than a hundred and fifty traders had been killed by

Indians. No count of the number of Indians killed by traders seemed to be available, but it was obvious that if a hundred and fifty traders, "hardworking men simply trying to conduct a legitimate business and help the Indians," had lost their lives defending themselves, their attackers had suffered a much greater loss, probably ten or twenty times as great. Traders could not be expected to go about letting Indians kill them. Certainly not, said official Washington.

The traders, through their political sycophants, presented evidence purporting to illustrate the hardships and problems—the losses in goods, horses and men—which they faced in trying to keep the British out of the fur trade on American soil. It was, they soberly informed the Government, very difficult to make any profit under such unfavorable conditions.

In some years, traders informed the War Department, they made no profit at all, merely broke even, and there were years when they suffered heavy losses. To these sad tales they did not fail to add the opinion that they thought they were performing a great service for their country by their efforts to develop the economy of the West, always their greatest desire.

If the Government had wished to look even slightly beneath the surface of the matter, and to take steps to halt the bloodshed, slaughter and cheating, it had the material before it. War Department files stated in plain language that numerous tribes not only were forced to trade their entire catch of furs to a certain trader, and at prices set by him, under threat of being punished by force, but that some tribes were so deeply in debt to certain traders that they could never hope to escape. In 1829, for example, the Winnebagos, Sacs and Foxes owed one trader $40,000, and two years later the debt had risen to $50,000. The Cherokees, Chickasaws and Sioux owed similar amounts to this same trader.[31]

The debts did not mean that the trader was in danger of losing money to these tribes. Not at all. His profits were so great that he could well afford to extend that much credit. If the debts were never paid, he would still net three or four hundred per cent gain on transactions with them. Also—and here he could obtain ample protection from the courts, if necessary—the debts obligated these tribes to trade with him and no one else.

The law, moreover, made it possible for him to apply the debts as mortgages to lands occupied by the tribes owing him the money. If the Government saw fit to move one of these tribes to another reservation, or the tribe was wiped out by invading settlers, the trader got land in the property to be abandoned commensurate with the amount of his debt. In this way a number of traders got title to immense areas of valuable timber, mineral and agricultural lands. Indians were helpless, for they had no standing in American courts.

Some laws came in handy at times, but for the most part the traders wanted no Government interference in their private affairs.

In 1831, an Indian Bureau officer who had spent more than forty years on the western frontier made an impassioned appeal, the last of many he had made in his long career, to the Secretary of War for measures which would improve relations between Americans and western Indians.[32] He had watched conditions deteriorate until the Indians, debauched, robbed, cheated and brutally treated, had lost all respect for Americans.

More than ten years previously, he had gone to Washington and had laid the same "lamentable" problem before the War Department. He had several long conversations on Indian affairs with the then Secretary of War, and he had told him "that it must appear strange to many people to perceive that we, as Americans, speaking the same language with the British, whose manners and customs were the same, exceeding them perhaps in our Indian expenditures, and having all the Indians residing in our own territories, still had not the same influence over them that the British had. To which the Secretary replied, that I ought not to point out an evil without showing a remedy for it."

The Indian Agent submitted the only remedy he knew. It was "to follow the same policy . . . towards the Indians that the British pursued with success." The Secretary had not thought very highly of the idea.

In his 1831 appeal, the Indian Agent spoke with some bluntness, saying: "The British government have a well-regulated Indian Department. No person is eligible for an Indian agency under that department unless he can speak some one of the Indian languages; for it is natural to suppose that a man understands at least the general manners and customs of all Indians if he had been among them long enough to learn any one of their languages. . . ."

The Indian Agent deplored the intelligence of American agents and their lack of training, declaring indignantly that "our government appoints young men to Indian agencies . . . who, in all probability, have never seen more than three or four together in the course of their lives, and those Indians perhaps civilized."

He continued:

"When the old chiefs and warriors hear of the arrival of their new father (as they term the new agent) they call at the agency to see him, but the agent does not know what to say or do to them and perhaps does not give them a pipe of tobacco, or even a good or bad word. The Indians then go away dissatisfied, and consequently in cases of this kind, everything depends on the interpreter. If the interpreter is an honest man he may teach the agent something in the course of years; but on the contrary, if he is a designing man, and wishes that no one should share his influence, he will keep the agent and the Indians in continual broils and quarrels, and nothing being rightly done, the public must suffer. Instead of trying to heal the old sores that have existed for the last fifty or sixty years between the American people and the Indians, the breach is made wider and fuel is added to the flame. . . .

"A young man who was appointed an Indian Agent on the Missouri River cut off the ears of a halfbreed who resided among the Sioux Indians because, being in a state of intoxication, he made use of some extravagant language disrespectful to the American people.

"Another agent . . . turned out of the guardhouse an innocent Indian to other Indians, his enemies, who shot him down and butchered him in a horrid manner, in the presence of an American garrison of soldiers.

"Another Indian agent also invited some chiefs to a council, when a number of their enemies organized themselves, attacked the chiefs and others who were invited, and killed nine and wounded three of sixteen persons."

Astor and other traders scoffed at such appeals in Washington, terming them overly sentimental, inaccurate and inconsequential. The last thing they wanted were efficient, honest and intelligent Indian Agents assigned to the western tribes. Agents of this type invariably had a habit of writing long and truthful reports, and some of these found their way into public print. If there was anything the traders despised, it was a Government man who was sincerely concerned with the welfare of the Indians. Who could make money by raising the living standards of the impecunious and ignorant, be they red or white? No interest was paid on investments in social improvements. A man had a right to get all he could in business, no matter how he got it, and the Government had no right to interfere with him. That was the American way, by God.

Let the stupid Government officials propound laws that theoretically gave the Indians some protection, if that amused them. When at last there were no more good profits to be made in trading with savages, the naive and impractical public hacks could have the West, and then they could pursue their ridiculous schemes to develop and improve it.

"Suffer the Indians, in particular cases as in Robbery or Murder, to give testimony in our courts, and it will go far to do away with many of the Evils they at present suffer from our violence and our avarice," wrote another Indian Agent to his superiors in Washington.[33] Speaking of the fur traders, he pleaded with the Government to "call this great monied Aristocracy to account, not only for aggressions practiced on the red man, but for any maltreatment . . . and you will at once divest them of a great portion of that power, which is but too often used to grind down and oppress all within the Circle of their influence." He advocated that "a Board of Comptrol, or of accounts, be established" to accomplish this desirable end.

Some Indian Agents, men of the highest character and integrity, spent their lives fighting to protect and improve the lot of their helpless charges.

The Government did no more to keep the Indians from being robbed, debauched and murdered by traders than it did to halt the use of liquor in the fur trade.

Yet, a "board of control" was established. It was created by economic forces. Beaver hats went out of fashion. Farmers pushed up the Missouri River. Trading posts became villages and towns. The frontier moved steadily westward. The Indians began their final struggle for survival, and their enemy then was not the fur trader with dishonest scales, but a society and a Government with dishonest hearts.

10

The agreements that common laborers, boatmen and trappers signed with fur trading companies said they had to go out to the wilderness. There was no provision stipulating that they had to come back.

The brutality with which the humble *engagés* were treated was often incredible. Many Government officials and Indian Department Agents protested to Congress about the fraud and mistreatment inflicted on the "human mules." The *engagés*, wrote one agent, "perform all the menial services . . . their labor is very hard for in a few years they are completely broken down in constitution, they have to work more like beasts of burden than men, and when they can produce the means they will go into all kinds of excesses; exposed constantly to change of heat and cold; which soon brings them to an untimely grave."

Very few Americans would accept employment for such work. Although physically as strong as any men, they refused to suffer the indignities and cruelty imposed upon the more docile French-Canadians. This was one of the chief reasons why American fur traders fought legislation to exclude foreigners from the trade within the United States.

The *engagés* usually were employed for three to five years.

There was no limit to the hours of their working day . . . they simply worked as long as there were tasks to be performed. Shortly after the War of 1812, the standard wage for *engagés* was about $100 a year. A small advance was given an *engagé* when he was hired, but his employer was not obliged to pay the balance until after expiration of his term of service. Small perquisites normally were allowed *engagés*. As Americans became dominant in the fur trade, an Indian Agent reported: ". . . at present they are seldom allowed perquisites, formerly it was an indispensible rule; but it is gradually losing ground. Some now get a few triffling articles of clothing; tobacco, soap, salt, etc."

Astor's American Fur Company, the largest, managed to dispense completely with the "indispensible rule." The only perquisite it allowed was a ration of "*blé d'Indi*" . . . Indian corn. Under its contracts, this was the only food the company was required to furnish. At permanent posts supplying *engagés* with staples was the problem of the manager. On the trail, they often were forced to sustain themselves on wild game.

This company also succeeded in reducing the wages of *engagés* from $100 a year to $250 for three years, but as if that did not satisfy its inordinate greed, it condoned the practice of cheating them out of all due wages. If one of this company's factors, or *bourgeois*, could by any scheme avoid paying an *engagé*, praise, not criticism, came from the company president.

Any articles an *engagé* might require to protect himself or anything he might desire to alleviate the hardship and monotony of his life with a few moments of pleasure, such as tobacco or spirits or some bright ornament, was sold to him at a high markup. In the season of 1823–1824, on goods sold at retail to *engagés*, one large trading post made a net gain of $7,200 on merchandise invoiced at $8,300, almost one hundred per cent profit. In the view of the owner, this was not enough, and the post manager was severely reprimanded. It was not unusual for an *engagé* to end three years of back-breaking labor heavily in debt, and be forced to sign a contract to work another three years.

"It is difficult to exaggerate the state of affairs which at times prevailed," wrote an authority on the fur trade. "Many an employe . . . who had finished his term of service with a letter of credit for his pay fell by the way and was reported as killed by Indians."[34]

Traders were not above murdering an *engagé* to save two or three hundred dollars. Although the evidence against the murderer might be ample and indisputable, he suffered no punishment. There is not a case on record of any legal action brought against a trader who killed an *engagé* to avoid paying money he had earned.

The French-Canadian laborer had no more standing in an American court than an Indian. He was looked upon as a "dirty, ignorant foreigner." Any effort he might make to collect his wages or to be compensated for injury to his person at the hands of a brutal trader could well result in his death. Traders took the law into their own hands.

Neither the Congress nor the War Department gave heed to appeals from Indian Agents and other officials on the frontier to "give the poor Canadians, hirelings for a term of years to hard taskmasters, an assurance that there is a power vested somewhere in the Government . . . to see that justice is rendered to all & Every Canadian employed [by fur traders] and receiving his discharge. . . ."[35]

Wages ranged slightly higher in the mountain and far

western trades during the prosperous years . . . from $130 a year for *engagés* to $400 for trappers . . . but the credit system under which they were bilked remained the same.

Two thousand miles of wild muddy current would lie ahead of a keelboat after it turned into the mouth of the Missouri. There would be weeks of terrible labor through storms, fierce heat, numbing cold, rain, snow and hail, weeks during which every hour would bring its perils, the treachery of the river, its boils and eddies, crumbling banks, snags and bars, wild animals and Indians who were even more unpredictable than either the weather or the Missouri.

The *engagés*, hunters, trappers and *voyageurs* would always be within the United States, but there would be no law, no civil or military authorities. If the Government was there in theory, it would not be there in reality. If laws were written, they would be meaningless, for there would be no way of enforcing them.

On some far upper waterway, they would occupy a post, and the only law, either there or in the surrounding wilderness, would be the *bourgeois*, the partner or trader. Yet, the *bourgeois* would provide little protection for the individual trapper, *voyageur* or *engagé*. The *bourgeois*, holding supreme power, could act as he pleased, as he thought best. He could cast a man out, rob him of his wages with dishonest bookkeeping, shoot him. Or he could, if he so desired, be kind, considerate, fair. The *bourgeois*' first duty was to guard his company's investment. Furs were more important than men. Even horses ranked above them.

Up there on the northern rivers, two or three thousand miles from the nearest church steeple and altar, a man could not place all his trust in God. There were too many manitous to be reckoned with. It was better that a man looked to his own powers, his own resources, for no matter how great a man's faith he must recognize the cold facts of his situation. All that stood between him and an unmarked grave were his own private superstitions, his own knowledge of ghosts, his own ability to sense danger in time, to smell it in the wind, see it in the markings of the dust, hear it in the whispers of the grass.

It is not enough to say that no man was forced to work in the fur trade. Following the same line of thought, it might be contended that no man was forced to serve as a gunman-cowboy for a cattleman illegally holding the public domain, or no man was forced to murder Indians, *engagés* or homesteaders. Cattle raising was the foundation of the plains economy, and the fur traders controlled the economy of the West in an earlier period.

For more than three decades after the Louisiana Purchase the fur trade proffered virtually the only means of livelihood west of the Mississippi River, especially for the man of little or no education, or no training in another field, and by far the greater number of men on the frontier were in this category. Declared one historian at the end of the nineteenth century: "It remains a terrifying commentary on the lengths to which men are forced to go in quest of a livelihood, and the benumbing effects on their sensibilities, that the fur traders should find a host of men ready to seduce the Indians into a state of drunkenness, cheat and rob them, and all this only to get robbed and perhaps murdered in turn."[36] To which should be added the comment that it remains a terrifying commentary on the weakness and criminal negligence of the American Government of the period.

For ten or eleven months of each year, the *engagés*, *voyageurs*, trappers and subaltern traders faced the dangers of the wilderness. They did not rob because it benefitted them. It was what they were paid to do, what they had to do to hold their jobs. To refuse meant ostracism, unemployment, hunger, even death.

It is little wonder that habits of thrift among them were almost unknown. They were improvident by choice, spurning as futile the idea of frugality. "Scarcely one man in ten," wrote a noted trapper of his comrades, "ever thinks of saving a single dollar of his earnings, but all spend it as fast as they can find an object to spend it for. They care not what may come to pass tomorrow, but think only of enjoying the present moment."[37] Said a celebrated mountain trader: "Almost all the men take up their wages as fast as they earn . . . and would faster, if I would let them . . . in goods at about five hundred per cent on original cost."[38]

A fur trade historian expressed the thought that it "was a sort of mountain pride, a convention of the business, to squander wages as fast as earned."[39]

It was something else, too. It was the realization that death lurked in the tall grass nearby, that the next moment might not come for them. There was no justification for the hope or the supposition that they would live to spend their money in civilization.

11

The traders were as unscrupulous and dishonest in their dealings with each other as they were in their treatment of their employees and the Indians. They robbed each other at every opportunity, broke into each other's caches and confiscated each other's furs on grounds asserted to be legal but which had no basis in law.

They fought to prevent Government interference in their businesss, but on the occasions when Indians who had been cheated attempted to retaliate, they cried out for help, protesting that lawless actions were preventing them from carrying on peaceful commerce. They demanded that their right to steal be defended by military force, and the Government obliged them.

In one notable encounter, the Arikaras struck back at traders by attacking an expedition en route to the upper Missouri in the early summer of 1823. The trader in command found himself in a perilous situation.[40] He had lost more than half the strength of his company of ninety men, at least a dozen dead, six dangerously wounded and more than thirty deserted. He had retreated down the river some twenty-five or thirty miles and had established a camp in a thick wood, which would provide protection in event of another attack. One of his boats, carrying the wounded and the deserters, had been sent down the river to Fort Atkinson, near the Council Bluffs.

The trader also had dispatched an urgent express to the fort for troops to suppress the Indians and open the way for him to continue his trading expedition. It was illegal, he cried, for Indians to interfere with the operations of legitimate traders. In other words, Indians who had been victimized for years should be condemned and punished for attempting to protect themselves in their own land.

While he waited for troops, the trader, who, incidentally, would soon afterward be elected to Congress, penned a long letter to a newspaper in St. Louis.[41] It said in part: "On the morning of 2nd inst. (June) I was attacked by the Ricaree

Indians, which terminated seriously on my part. . . . Not one of the Ricaree Indians did I see until I arrived at their towns, on the 30th of May; my boats were anchored about the middle of the river, and I went on shore with two men where I met with some of the principal chiefs who pretended to be very friendly disposed toward us, and expressed a wish that I should trade with them.

"Wishing to send a party through by land from that point to the Yellow Stone River, for which purpose forty or fifty horses were necessary . . . I consented to send some goods on shore to exchange for horses, but proposed that the chiefs of the two towns would meet me on the sand beach, where a perfect understanding should take place before the barter commenced. After a long consultation among them, they appeared at the place to hold the talk. I made them a small present, which appeared to please them very much. . . ."

By the end of the day, the desired number of horses had been obtained, and the trader planned to leave with them for the Yellowstone the following morning. Several of his men, seeking female companionship, remained in the Indian village without his permission. Shortly before dawn he was awakened and informed that one of the straying men had been killed and that an attack on the boats was imminent.

". . . my party consisted of ninety men, forty of whom were selected to accompany me to the Yellow Stone River by land, and were encamped on the sand beach in charge of the horses.

"About sun rise the Indians commenced a heavy and well-directed fire from a line extending along the picketing of one of their towns and some broken ground adjoining, a distance of about six hundred yards. Seeing that some of the horses were killed and others wounded, as well as two or three men, I attempted to have the horses crossed to a sand bar about the middle of the river . . . but before anything to effect that object could be done, the fire became very destructive, aimed principally at the men on the shore. I ordered the anchors weighed and the boats put to shore but the boatmen, with very few exceptions were so panic struck that they could not be got to execute the order. Two skiffs, which would carry thirty men, were taken ashore for the embarcation of the men but (I suppose) from a predetermination of the men on the beach not to give way to the Indians as long as there appeared the least possibility of keeping their ground, not more than five of them made use of the large skiff two of whom were wounded, the other skiff was taken to the other side of the river by two men, one of them mortally wounded.

". . . by this time the most of the horses were killed or wounded and about half of the men, I continued to make every effort to get the boats to shore but all in vain, although anchored not more than ninety feet out in the stream the most of the men swam to the boats, some of them when shot immediately sprang into the river and sunk. It was about fifteen minutes from the time the firing commenced until the surviving part of the men had embarked . . . and the boats dropped down the stream."

Four days after receiving the call for help from the trader, Colonel Henry Leavenworth was ascending the Missouri River from Fort Atkinson at the head of some two hundred infantrymen. They had with them six pounders and several small swivel guns. This force was augmented by a heavily armed contingent of traders picked up at various trading posts, and by more than three hundred Indian recruits, most of them Sioux eager to take part in any campaign against their traditional enemy, the Arikara.

On August 9th, an attack on the Arikara villages was made.

Details of the brief engagement have no important bearing on the subject being treated here. The results of it do.

Colonel Leavenworth agreed to a parley with the enemy. This was looked upon as a show of weakness by the Sioux, and after stealing the Arikara's corn they departed from the field of battle in disgust.

Following a meeting with some Arikara leaders, in which he received their promise to behave, Leavenworth asked a trader to prepare a treaty of peace. Furious at the turn of affairs, the trader refused; it being his contention that only by severely chastising the Arikaras could peace be secured. At last, the colonel wrote the treaty himself, and a peace pipe was smoked.

The traders understood that in the Indian way of thinking peace without victory was not peace at all. The United States Army had conducted a comic opera campaign. It had been fooled and humbled. It had asked for peace, and the warriors were laughing. More blood would have to spill before the issue could be resolved.

A provision of the colonel's treaty required the Arikaras to restore all property taken from the trader. They restored one horse, three rifles and sixteen buffalo robes. Then, during the night, they vanished. The colonel sent messengers to find them and ask them to return, but they had disappeared into the Great Plains.

The colonel then decided that the Arikaras had been sufficiently frightened and would not commit further depredations against traders. He turned back downstream with his force.

Almost before the soldiers had got out of sight, the traders fired the villages and destroyed them.

"It is my sincere and candid opinion," one trader wrote the

Indian Department, "that the expedition against the Aricaras, *from which so much service might have been rendered to this dwindling and bleeding commerce*, will rather tend to increase, than diminish, the evil; that the situation of affairs in this country is worsted materially; that instead of raising the American character in the estimation of its inhabitants and impressing them with the power and spirit of our government, the contrary effect has been produced; and that the outrages of the Indians will increase in consequence."[42]

He said nothing about the outrages of the traders.

12

The steamboat not only brought drastic changes in the methods of the fur trade, but it brought new kinds of men into the Indian Country, kinds of men never before seen there, who had no rightful place in the scheme of things. Gamblers, petty thieves, confidence men, escaped convicts could ride the river boats, take their prey and retreat to their hideouts before winter imprisoned them beyond the frontier.

"The country is overrun with vagabond Americans, with riffraff," wrote Father De Smet from the upper Missouri, "and the Government, which alone could put a stop to this abominable traffic . . . pays no attention."[43]

The steamboat brought other scourges—venereal diseases, fevers, maladies never before known there and which the Indians had no means of combating.

A boat owned by the American Fur Company, the *St. Peters*, brought smallpox. It was a tragedy that might easily have been averted. Officers of the company were on the boat when several cases of the disease were discovered. They had ample time to turn it back before reaching the upper Missouri, but to have done that would have meant the loss of the summer's trade. They might have unloaded the cargo, fumigated it and sent it on up the river in keelboats, but to have done that would have meant an increase in the cost of operations.

They did neither. The *St. Peters*, carrying a cargo of death, went on. The company officers stupidly attempted to keep Indians from coming near it. If they had commanded the sun not to rise, they would have had as much success. The Indians knew the boat carried supplies they badly needed, and they suspected that the efforts to keep them away from it were part of some scheme to cheat them. They swarmed about the boat, and virtually everything they touched sealed their doom.

On the *St. Peters* went, spreading the deadly bane. Hundreds of Indians died each day. So many bodies were there that it was impossible for those not stricken to bury them, and they were thrown over cliffs, into gullies and into the river. About most villages a terrible stench filled the air.

Of the twelve hundred members of the Mandans, only thirty persons escaped the contagion.

On each side of the river for five hundred miles, between Fort Pierre and the Yellowstone, Indian lodges stood but no smoke rose from them, no sounds of human life, except the wails and screams of the dying, broke the fearful silence. Brave warriors killed themselves, unable to stand the sight of flesh rotting on their women and children.

More than fifteen thousand Indians were victims of the greed, the coldness, the criminal negligence of the officers of the company which owned the *St. Peters*.

Astor, president of the company, who lived in New York and spent a part of each year in his luxurious European villa, criticised them not at all. Had they lost a season's trade as the result of a humane act, they would have heard his thunder and have suffered his wrath. No money could be made being humane.

Nor did the Government take any steps whatsoever to prevent the repetition of such a horror.

13

The western fur trade infected its own body, not with communicable diseases but with the poison of its own avarice and viciousness. In the late 1830s and the early 1840s, it staggered with the sickness it had brought upon itself.

The great arena of the Rocky Mountains then was no longer the scene of bitter rivalry between only a few powerful companies. It had been invaded by numerous small groups, all bent on outdoing each other and picking up the leavings of the larger expeditions. These disorganized, poorly financed little bands were not only annoying the strong traders, but were fighting among themselves like a lot of mongrels after a bitch.

Robberies and murders were almost daily occurrences. The fur trade degenerated into a continual running fight between gangs, both big and little. As a result, the Indians were utterly demoralized by the vicious conduct of the white men toward each other. Taking a leaf from the traders' book, the Indians resorted to all manner of lawlessness, trusting no one and putting the life of every white man in peril at all times.

Traders broke contracts made with each other without hesitation. There was no legal recourse open to victims. Traders, at last, found themselves as helpless as their employees had been since the beginning of the trade.

The American fur traders contributed nothing to the development of the western economy. The Mountain Men were the great explorers of the West, but they brought no improvements.

The fur traders left to history only a bloodstained record of disgrace, dishonesty, unparalleled greed, violence and destruction, destruction of both the resources of the West and the red peoples who depended for their existence on those resources.

Part Three

THE CATTLE BARONS

The annals of the American economy contain no record of an enterprise that was labeled and defended as legitimate business but which was more illegitimate than the raising of cattle on the immense ranges of the western public domain between 1866 and the beginning of the twentieth century.

1

The reigns of the western drovers and ranchers, whom romanticists like to call Cattle Barons, were of short duration, all beginning and ending within the four decades immediately following the Civil War. Their historical significance is not to be found in beneficial contributions to the national welfare, for they made none. Quite to the contrary, they are worthy of note for the political corruption they engendered, for the illegal conquests they executed and for the cold-blooded murders committed in the brief period of their existence.

The Cattle Barons were despots and tyrants who held their domains not by legal right but by force of arms and criminal violence.

The enormous region of the so-called Cattle Kingdom did not produce many cows.

The cowboy as he is pictured and characterized in the novel, the motion picture and in the TV drama never existed.

More money, far more, has been made out of the legend of the man in a wide hat, bright shirt and leather chaps, than was earned by all the cowboys who rode in roundups held during the day of the vaunted Cattle Kingdom.

The great trail drives from Texas to the buffalo plains of

the north were economically inconsequential and for the most part unprofitable.

The cattlemen ruling the western grass seas paid few if any taxes, owned little or no real property, gave no thought to civic responsibility, were dedicated only to their personal aggrandizement and loyal only to themselves.

The cowboys of the open range days were the common laborers of the time and the place, the serfs and mercenaries who carried out the commands, legal or illegal, of the suzerains employing them.

The lords of the Cattle Kingdom—there were a few genuine nobles among them—fought every proposal for development and improvement of the West, every attempt to bolster its economy, introduced in both the State and National Legislatures, and if they lacked strength in numbers they made up for this weakness with coercion, assault and bribery.

Perhaps nothing will ever penetrate the haze of puerile romance with which writers unfaithful to their profession and to themselves have surrounded the westerner who made a living in the saddle. Perhaps nothing will ever generate open public resentment against the maudlin, inane, spurious horse operas pouring from the film factories of Hollywood. Fantasy and folklore survive where reality and history are interred, and there is no preventive, no cure, for inherent stupidity.

The Preemption Act had been long in the Federal law books before Texas cattle were driven to northern markets in appreciable numbers. Enacted in 1841, in response to demands from western States, it provided that squatters could preempt lands and permitted settlers to locate a claim of 160 acres. After six months of residence on a registered claim, a settler was entitled to purchase it from the Government for $1.25 an acre.

This was a means by which a squatter or settler could *buy* land. The 1860 platform of the Republican Party promised *free* land. In keeping with this pledge, the Homestead Act was passed in 1862. It provided that a man or woman twenty-one years of age, either the head of a family or single, could file claim to 160 acres of Federal land in the western States and Territories. To obtain title the claimant was required to reside on the homestead for five years, make certain small improvements on it and pay a nominal fee. Not only Americans were entitled to apply for the free land; the privilege was extended to an alien who had declared his intention to become a citizen of the United States.

The statute was hailed in press, pulpit and political hall as a boon to the poor man, as an instrument devised by a benevolent and conscientious government to give security and homes to the homeless. It was nothing of the kind.

If every recipient of a homestead patent issued in this period had been a bona fide farmer, only one in every six homesteads removed from Federal ownership could be included in the "given away" category. Actually, the record was not even that good. An enormous number of homesteaders were dummies for cattlemen and for mining and lumber companies. Probably no more than one acre in every ten went to the needy settlers whom the Homestead Act was intended to assist.

The Homestead Act was one of the keys which unlocked the western gate, not to the masses, but to the affluent few, the persons with influence and power and a great deal more money than integrity. If its authors were sincere, they were not astute, and they suffered from extreme ignorance of the geography, climate and resources of the region with which they were dealing.

In the 1860s, when the trail herds from Texas began to reach railroad shipping points in Kansas, only seven States had been carved out of the vast western plains and mountains between the Mississippi River and the Pacific Coast, which, incidentally, some members of Congress still called the Great American Desert. Federal laws were still written in the majority of cases by easterners.

Quite naturally, in considering such a proposal as the Homestead Act, representatives and senators from both the East and the Middle West thought in terms of forty-acre farms, adequate rainfall and rich black loam. Only in a relatively narrow strip on the eastern perimeter of the immense region to which the Homestead Act would apply were such conditions to be found.

The ninety-eighth meridian was the dividing line between possible success and probable failure.

East of it, grasslands might be converted with comparative ease into farms, and the normal precipitation was sufficient for most crops. The land was generally level enough to be cultivated without difficulty, livestock could be grazed in lush pastures, and corn could be raised to supplement their feed and speed their fattening. Islands of trees provided shade from excessive heat and protection from blizzards and extreme cold. In eastern Dakota (after the Indians were driven far enough to the west), in Iowa, in the eastern half of Nebraska and Kansas, in Missouri, a farmer had a chance to support himself and his family on 160 acres.

West of ninety-eight, his chances for success diminished with every mile he advanced. The meridian marked the approximate end of the area in which twenty to thirty inches of rain might be expected to fall. It marked the beginning of the shortgrass plains, which became ever higher as they rolled on in giant combers and immense tilted sweeps until they broke against the impregnable bastions of the Rocky Mountains.

The precipitation of these vast, seemingly endless high plains was sufficient to grow the various sparse but highly nutritious grasses that supported immense game herds. Treeless and barren, swept by searing winds in summer and terrible blizzards in winter, plagued by drought and fires and dust storms, they offered no hope to a man with a plow. An area of 160 acres might support a family of jack rabbits, but such a small amount of land was virtually worthless for farming with the methods and facilities of the nineteenth century.*

As it was to unscrupulous persons in other fields, to the cattleman, the Homestead Act was a gilt-edged invitation to commit fraud, and as the herds were pushed steadily farther into the north and northwest, they took good advantage of the opportunity.

3

The story is told in a Government document of how a wagon train of supplies for a military post was trapped in a blizzard

* Water conservation, storage and irrigation would change all this, but that is another story and belongs to another age.

on the Laramie Plains in the winter of 1864–1865. The leader, convinced that any hope of escape was futile, constructed a camp, and turned his oxen and horses out to fend for themselves, fully expecting them to perish. In the spring he was astonished to find that the animals not only had survived, but were in better condition than when he had freed them.

The account is proffered as the first practical demonstration of the nutritiousness of the high plains grasses and proof that grazing stock could fatten on them even under adverse weather conditions. Allegedly, the accidental discovery prompted men of the Wyoming frontier to purchase cattle and marked the beginning of ranching in the area under the shadows of the high mountains.

Undoubtedly the incident occurred, but it seems illogical to assume that it was the first of its kind. Moreover, it is a reflection on the powers of observation of the many freighters, scouts and frontiersmen to suggest they were not aware that domestic animals–horses, oxen or cows–could sustain themselves on native grasses the year round, except under extremely abnormal conditions. The high plains were the natural habitat of enormous numbers of buffalo, deer, elk and antelope. The year of the Laramie Plains event was 1865. In the previous fourteen years thousands of head of livestock had crossed the plains with emigrants, gold seekers and military contingents. The immense horse herds of the Indians, not to mention the great herds of wild horses were not kept alive on cultivated timothy hay, but on grama grass, obtained by pawing through snow.

4

For nearly two decades before the spring of 1865, beef animals and draft oxen had been reaching eastern markets after being driven north to Missouri and Kansas from the great cow incubator of Texas. They also had been used to stock farms and ranches and were held for fattening on the northern prairies. From the year 1848 until the outbreak of the Civil War, Texas drovers carried on a regular cattle trade with northern buyers. A Dallas newspaper noted in 1850, "Several large droves of cattle have passed through this place during the present season en route to Missouri. They are . . . to be sold for beef, or to furnish teams for California emigrants." Four years later, another newspaper reported that fifty thousand cattle had crossed the Red River on their way "to northern states and territories."

Between 1849 and 1861, Westport, Independence and Kansas City, where the long western overland trails started, were the main northern markets for Texas cattle.* Work oxen were sold to persons setting out for the Far West, to fur traders, freighters and the Army Quartermaster Department. Stock cows went not only to adjacent farmers but to hopeful settlers planning on establishing ranches in California and Oregon, two thousand miles across the plains, mountains and deserts. Beeves were bought not only by dealers for Chicago, St. Louis and Atlantic Coast cities, but by Army buyers for Fort Leavenworth, Fort Riley, Fort Kearney, Fort Laramie and to supply military expeditions against the Indians.

* Some longhorns had reached these frontier towns several years earlier, both before and during the Mexican War, although the number was small.

They were for the most part not beef cattle of good quality. The adjective *tough* could be applied with several shades of meaning to describe them. "They were driven nearly or quite 500 miles . . ." a Missouri editor wrote of one herd, "subsisted all the way on grass, and kept in tolerable order, and what is more, they never eat a ear [sic] of corn in their lives. An attempt was made to feed them with corn and provender at the stock yards, but they ran away from it. Texas cattle are about the nearest to 'wild animals' of any now driven to market. We have seen some Buffaloes that were more civilized."

They were also carriers of a deadly pestilence. It was not known at the time that the mysterious disease which periodically appeared in cattle with devastating results was communicated from animal to animal by a tick.* The Texas longhorn was immune to it, but native northern cattle were not. The trails of the Texas herds were not only marked by trampled earth but by waves of fever that destroyed local livestock.

The first great epidemic swept through Missouri in 1855, killing thousands of otherwise healthy cattle in farm pastures. Without laws to halt the Texans, the farmers organized to stop them with guns and barricades at stream crossings, and the trails to the north were marked in another way . . . with the stains of human blood and the graves of determined drovers.

A law forbidding the driving of noxious animals into Missouri was enacted late in 1855 but was inadequately enforced and, indeed, for several reasons was unenforceable. Neither the Texas cattleman nor his heavily armed cowboys

* This great discovery, which opened the way for control of the disease, was made in 1890 by scientists of the U.S. Department of Agriculture.

were easily intimidated, and they continued to move cattle into the State in increasing numbers. The most irritating and mysterious aspect of the Missouri farmer's dilemma, however, was that even when a Texas herd was stopped and the longhorns impounded, spread of the disease was not halted.

The difficulties of enforcement stemmed from a number of sources. Cattle were money, and justices of the peace and police officers could be bribed. Cattle were allowed to escape under the eyes of men assigned to hold them. The law specified that a justice of the peace could order impounded cattle destroyed if a drover failed to comply with a court order. If such an order were issued, the person appointed to kill the animals was to be compensated at the rate of one dollar a head, to be paid by either the Texas owner, if he was available, or by the county. Any deputy who failed to execute the order of the justice of the peace was to forfeit a sum equal to the amount of the fee he would have received had he carried out his duty.

This was a loophole in the law as large as the country gates used to take advantage of it. One dollar a head was a bargain price for even poor Texas cattle.

Once more the Missouri farmers organized, took the problem into their own hands, and began to stop the Texas herds with force of arms at the State border. The war against Texas fever continued until 1861, when a new and stronger statute against diseased cattle was passed. It, too, was ineffective, for no law devised by man which did not provide for the total exclusion of Texas cattle could have brought control of the scourge.

Under the 1861 statute, every Missouri township was given the right to appoint a board which would have the authority to inspect all stock entering its jurisdiction. Any cattle found to be afflicted with Texas fever were to be driven out of the State by the route they had entered. Diseased animals owned by a drover who failed to remove them could be destroyed.

It was of no avail. The fever continued to rage. Texas cattle that appeared healthy left devastation and ruin in their wake. Not law, not inspection, not shootings and bloodshed, but violence of a greater and more terrible kind saved the northern farmers. The Civil War brought traffic on the cattle trails to the north to a standstill.

5

Kansas had not escaped from the ravages of Texas fever. It had struck there in 1858, and the story was the same as it had been in Missouri. Passage of a law copied after that of Missouri was openly violated by the Texas drovers in 1859 and 1860, with the result that countless thousands of native cattle died while the Texas longhorns were being bought by eastern buyers. Gun battles between the Texans and the angry Kansans failed to solve the problem. Only the advent of the Civil War interrupted the flow of Texas trail herds to Kansas.

Then, for reasons easily ascertainable, the attitudes of the Kansas cattlemen, farmers and merchants underwent a drastic change. The cessation of the Texas cattle drives had brought a sharp decline in business, and rising demands for beef, engendered by the hostilities, had sent prices soaring.

Immediately south of Kansas were the rich rolling grasslands of the Indian Territory, and on them were countless thousands of cattle. The opportunity was obvious and the prospect of success both extremely enticing and promising. At best, law enforcement in the new State of Kansas had been feeble, and it might be expected to become weaker under the unsettled conditions brought by the war.

During the years 1862 to 1864, more than three hundred thousand cattle were stolen by organized Kansas raiders in the Indian Territory and the northern perimeter of Texas. The herds were driven to towns in eastern Kansas and openly sold on the market. The profits were high, for the cattle cost nothing, and the chief expenses of the ventures were the time and money, an extremely small outlay of cash, expended in going after the stock and driving them to points of sale.

It was not considered a crime to steal from the Texas rebels, but the main victims of the wholesale thefts were Indians, who were not participants in the white man's war. The tribes that suffered the largest losses were the Cherokee, Creek, Choctaw, Seminole and Chickasaw. The buffalo which had been so vital to their existence had been virtually exterminated in this area. Loss of the cattle on which they depended meant deprivation and hunger. Even in times of peace, government supplies often failed to reach them on schedule, if at all. The disruptions brought by the war to commerce and all government operations made even more unlikely the receipt of relief from any source except their own agricultural production.

Nor was stealing from Indians looked upon as a criminal act. They were fair game. Their powers of retaliation were nothing to be feared. In the uproar and confusion of the war, their complaints would go unheeded. Moreover, they had no rights in State and few in Federal courts. At this time they were not Americans, but foreign nations.

If the riders who committed the actual thefts were for the most part white, red and black renegades, their employers were not. Among them were not only Kansas cattlemen and farmers, but business and political leaders, officers of the Union Army, provost marshals, Federal Indian agents, Indian traders and other "prominent" citizens who were pillars in their respective churches. The mayor of Leavenworth was duly exposed as one of the most active community leaders participating in the rustling. The illegal cattle trade was a spur to business, and town officials and merchants did not permit either law or conscience to interfere with it.

The approaching defeat of the Confederacy threw a new light on the situation. The voices of individuals who had condemned the thievery—largely poor misguided persons such as ministers, priests, honest officials and law-abiding citizens who thought that even an Indian should get a fair shake—began to be heeded, but if they were influential they were not the weight that tipped the scales of justice. That resulted from much more practical reasoning. The end of the war would mean a resumption of legal cattle trade with Texas drovers. It would also mean that the Congress would be in a position to give more of its time to other matters.

Facing the pleasant prospect of even greater business conducted through legitimate channels, and the unpleasant one of a crackdown from Federal authorities, the leading lights of various towns advocated that the stealing be halted. At various council meetings and public gatherings the argument was asserted, as if it had only recently been discovered, that the rustling violated the Kansas law of 1861, which forbade the importation of infected cattle. The State Legislature duly responded to petitions calling for suppression of the "nefarious traffic." In February, 1865, a new law was enacted which forbade all persons, except emigrants, from driving cattle into Kansas from either Texas or the Indian Territory. That the

Federal Government was alert to the problem was indicated in March of the same year when Congress passed a law making interstate cattle stealing a felony.

Neither statute was effective. Quite to the contrary, they marked the beginning of the era in which the western cattle trade, both legal and illegal, enjoyed its greatest expansion, the decade immediately following the stillness at Appomattox.

6

In 1865, Texas, especially the gigantic odd-shaped triangle between the Trinity, the Rio Grande and San Antonio, swarmed with cows, probably in excess of six million animals. Blockades by Union forces of the Gulf coast and the Mississippi River had halted the delivery of Texas beef on the hoof to the Confederates, and cattle trails to the north had been closed to Texas cattlemen not only by the adverse conditions resulting from the conflict but by laws of the Confederacy which forbade traffic with the enemy.

Neither military engagements, statutes nor patriotism affected the breeding habits of the cattle, and with decimation at a minimum they increased with unprecedented rapidity. Texas soldiers returned home to find plains and valleys overrun with wild stock, much of which—probably most of which—was unmarked by an owner's brand.

The only possible market for them was the industrial North and its greater population. Looking hopefully in that direction, the impoverished Texan saw a land of golden opportunity. Cattle could be stolen in Texas for nothing, but even if one preferred the more orthodox system of purchasing them, the price was only three dollars a head. The same animal would bring thirty to forty dollars a head in the northern market.

It did not take an expert mathematician to figure out that a herd of three thousand Texas cattle, legally purchased at three dollars each, would bring a profit of approximately a hundred thousand dollars in a Kansas stockyard, after deduction of expenses. Needless to say, stolen or captured wild cattle, of course, would bring a greater return.

This was the theory. Drawbacks unseen at the time arose to reveal the extent of its impracticality, and in hundreds of cases prevented even partial fulfillment of the great dream. Yet, the fact is indisputable that in the following fifteen years, the Texans did deliver to the north some five million cattle.

As the railroads pushed their thin veins of steel steadily westward across the great northern plains, shipping points for the Texas herds were established, and the Texans set their courses for them. The cowtowns that gave so much color to the Cattle Kingdom were born.

The post-war reopening of the gate to the northern markets, in 1866, brought feverish activity on the cattle ranges of Texas, and the conditions there offered unprecedented opportunities to the dishonest cattleman as well as the legal owner of stock. Cattle stealing was an occupation in which many Texans were adept, but even a novice at it needed little instruction under the circumstances existing as the great trail drives got underway.

Under normal procedure, the ownership of a young animal was determined by the brand of its mother. This system could be effectively pursued on ranges which were controlled or regularly patrolled by cowboys. That was not always the case during the sixties in Texas. Cattle wandered over vast areas not only unguarded but unseen. Ownership was not only difficult but often impossible to prove.

It was a generally accepted custom, a law in some districts, that cowboys coming upon an unmarked animal which was at least a year old, on the open range, were entitled to burn the brand of their employer on it. They were not required to make any investigation in an effort to identify its real owner.

The facetious assertion that all a man needed to get into the cattle business was a good horse, a long rope and a branding iron is not without an element of truth. This becomes all the more apparent with further consideration of the factors involved, and slight changes provide a foundation in fact. All a man needed to become a trail driver was a band of capable cowboys, well mounted and well armed, and a few branding irons. Numerical strength gave assurance of success.

The word "maverick" came into the language to mean an unbranded range animal. It was the cognomen of a San Antonio lawyer, Samuel Augustus Maverick, who paid more attention to his legal practice than the cattle in which he had invested. Attended only by a lone lazy Negro cowboy, the stock ran wild, both cows and calves remaining unbranded.

Maverick at last sold his cattle interests, and the buyer proceeded to place his own brand on every unmarked animal he encountered in the area, purportedly believing them to be "mavericks."

The upright editor of a San Antonio newspaper took type in hand in 1867 to condemn the practice of maverick branding, declaring, "The term maverick which was formerly applied to unbranded yearlings is now applied to every calf which can be separated from its mother cow—the consequence is, the fastest branders are accumulating the largest stocks."

8

In the first postwar year, some two hundred and sixty thousand head of Texas cattle crossed the Red River and pushed toward various northern destinations. The old trouble of Texas fever again arose, and epidemics swept through Kansas and Missouri farm herds.

The businessmen of these States were not as eager to halt the drives as were the farmers, and conflicts over new laws arose in the legislatures. Kansas merchants were instrumental in securing repeal of the 1865 law, which closed the State borders to cattle from Texas, but other laws remained on the books. They were amended until the body of applicable statutes became a hodgepodge. Some laws prohibited Texas cattle from entering certain counties. Some permitted herds to enter at certain times of the year. Others permitted inspected herds to proceed to markets.

Missouri courts had appointed boards of cattle inspectors, and they found their job easiest by simply turning back all herds. Corruption often defeated the laws, however, as it had done before the war. Moreover, there were too many Texas cattle pouring up the trails to be stopped by any force less than an army. The Texans followed little used roads through mountainous, unsettled areas, and many of them reached points along the Pacific Railroad east of Sedalia. Some drove their stock all the way to St. Louis. Many were wounded and killed in gunfights with irate Missouri farmers and law enforcement officers. It was altogether an unprofitable enterprise.

In both eastern Kansas and western Missouri, a new and forceful element appeared in the drama—strong bands of cattle thieves. Under the pretext that they were aiding in preventing the introduction of Texas fever, these lawless groups stole entire herds, and took them to market, disposing of them with counterfeit bills of sale, when such legal instruments were requested.

The impetus of the northern cattle drives was too great to be stopped by either law or outlaw. On the herds came, the drovers desperately seeking ways through to a market, and suffering severe losses and, in countless cases, reverses from which they could not recover.

A new Kansas law provided that herds might pass into the State only between November 1 and April 1, and a great reservoir of Texas cattle at once began to accumulate just south of the southern border of the State. In the fall of 1866, more than a hundred thousand head were grazing on the Cherokee Strip alone as drovers awaited the date on which they could legally proceed to Kansas destinations. The plan brought little business to Kansas merchants and disaster to many of the Texas cattlemen. Blizzards swept down from the north, and herds were moved with great difficulty or not at all. Those which reached buyers during the winter and early spring were in such emaciated condition that they brought low prices or had to be sold at a loss.

Business leaders and politicians, envisioning the swift disappearance of the great potential dollar bonanza which had appeared on the horizon, early in 1867, concocted another cattle law. One of its provisions permitted the entrance of Texas herds at any season of the year "west of the sixth principal meridian."*

This decree and the advancement of rails across the plains were the factors which provided a foundation of practicality for proposals to build shipping points which drovers might reach unmolested by legal restrictions and at which both sellers and buyers might conduct transactions under advantageous circumstances. Most railroad officials failed to see the idea in this light, considering it visionary and chimerical. The Kansas Pacific, which was building southwestward from Kansas City, was the first to agree to try it out, but the president remained unenthusiastic and deemed it dangerously speculative.

One leading promotor was laughed at and ordered out of the Missouri Pacific's head office when he sought an agreement from that line to pick up stock cars from the Kansas Pacific and haul them to St. Louis. The smaller Hannibal and St. Joe Railroad, however, offered to take the cattle trains eastward from Kansas City, and, by way of its connections with other lines, deliver them to Chicago. The rejection of the plan by the Missouri Pacific was chiefly responsible for preventing St. Louis from becoming the largest cattle slaughtering center in the nation. The distinction went to Chicago.

The little village of Abilene, which was destined to become the first and the greatest, if not the wildest, of all western cowtowns, stood virtually on the border of the territory Texas herds were forbidden to enter. In 1867, when the first shipping yards were constructed there, it consisted of a dozen log huts. There was a small general store and post office, a

* The meridian crossed the southern Kansas border just east of the present town of Hunnewell, Sumner County.

blacksmith shop, a six-room hotel, and a saloon whose proprietor augmented his income by raising prairie dogs which he sold to travelers.

When the news that Abilene had been established reached drovers on the Texas trail it was too late in the year for many cattle to reach it. Yet before winter halted the trail herds, more than thirty-five thousand longhorns had passed through the Abilene shipping pens.

Some seventy-five thousand cattle were driven north to Abilene in its first full year of operation, 1868, and in the next year the number jumped to more than 350,000. Abilene's greatest year was 1871, when an estimated 700,000 Texas cattle passed through it. After that the number rapidly declined. Settlers were beginning to fill the surrounding territory, destroying the grasslands, and the cattlemen were forced to move their trails westward. Other railroads were building out across the plains, and these and new cowtowns were competing for the trade. Ellsworth, Newton and Dodge City each enjoyed their day as the mecca of the trail drivers and their turn to claim the dubious distinction of being the wickedest town on earth.

During the greatest years of the trail herds, however, the steady westward shift of the Texas trails was not the only important change which occurred in the cattle trade. A far more significant transition involving the entire western United States gradually took place—the establishment of that borderless, unnatural and illegal world within a world, euphemistically called the *Cattle Kingdom.*

9

The long cattle drives from Texas to the North may have been romantic, but they were, from beginning to end, economically unsound. Innumerable factors, geographical, climatic, social, commercial, legal, political in character, weighed against their success. Any one of them was damaging; in combination they brought disaster. The great dream of fortunes to be made by selling longhorns for a thousand per cent increase, which so many Texas drovers harbored, did not, except in a very few instances, come true. Trail drivers who went home with a profit in one year, lost it the next. For not a few the end of the trail was a lonely prairie grave.

The epidemics of Texas fever the tick-infested longhorns caused brought violent retaliations against them by force of law and gun.

Stampedes caused by outlaws, Indians, lightning or simply by unidentifiable ghosts—the wild cattle spooked easily—resulted in deaths, injuries and lost animals.

Cattle were stolen by rustlers and dishonest officers of the law.

Storms and prairie fires took a toll.

The drive itself, as long as fifteen hundred miles, kept the weight of cattle down to such an extent that few animals reaching northern markets could be sold for top prices, most of them going as feeders to be fattened on Iowa or Illinois grain.

Towns, counties and States inflicted "trail and transportation taxes" and impounded herds on charges that they had caused damage to property. While these were generally without foundation and were trumped up by grafting officials, the cattlemen had no alternative but to pay the assessed fines.

Tribes of the Indian Territory, standing on an old treaty provision which forbade traffic across their lands without written permission, levied charges against the drovers. To refuse to pay them was to invite the Indians to fire the grass or stampede the cattle.

Even when the cattle market was strong, buyers forced drovers to sell at low prices or face the possibility of attempting to hold their stock through the winter. A poor corn crop wiped out demands for feeders, and prices dropped accordingly. The national panic of 1873 ruined countless trail drivers.

Settlement closed immense areas, forcing the trails to move westward and increasing the length of the drives, as well as the costs of railroad shipping, which was reflected in the prices paid drovers.

In the latter years of the great trail driving period, northern cattlemen turned against their Texas brothers, assertedly because of danger from Texas fever, but more truthfully because they wanted to halt the intrusions on the ranges they controlled. On innumerable occasions a northern rancher, backed by armed cowboys, prevented a trail herd from crossing his domain, or forced its owner to sell out at a ridiculously low price.

No railroad could make money hauling only cattle, and as the lines extended across the plains to the high mountains they established towns, advertised for homesteaders and sold land cheap to settlers. They wanted the revenues that a growing population would bring; indeed, they needed them to exist.

The development of the Cattle Kingdom of the great plains and mountain valleys was a natural evolution, but the rapidity with which it spread remains one of the greatest phenomena in American history. In less than fifteen years after the end of the Civil War, enormous cattle ranges had been established in Kansas, Colorado, New Mexico, the Panhandle of Texas, Arizona, California, Nebraska, Wyoming, Idaho, Montana and the Dakotas. In that period as many Texas cattle went onto northern ranges as were shipped to market from the roaring cowtowns of Kansas and Nebraska.

During the expansion period of the Cattle Kingdom which might be said to have ended by 1880, and for somewhat more than a decade thereafter, the Cattle Barons remained in supreme control of virtually the entire western and southwestern United States. This condition prevailed despite the fact that from the beginning of the Cattle Kingdom the social and economic forces created and unleashed by the American industrial revolution worked against it, constantly modifying and eventually destroying it.

10

If one uses the appellation *Cattle Kingdom* reluctantly, knowing it to be a gross misnomer, one is obliged to recognize the improbability of finding any title that would be both accurate and suitable. Its geographical size alone is enough to dissuade one from making the attempt, not to mention the variations of the life within it, the contrasts of its operations, its history. Moreover, one is fully aware of the futility of trying to supplant a term so firmly entrenched in national thought patterns through constant usage and universal acceptance.

Cattle Kingdom it must be, but this does not alter the truths which lie beneath the haze of fancy that popular conceptions have woven over it. If it was *the* Cattle Kingdom, it did not produce many cattle.

The general conception of the Cattle Kingdom includes the immense territory lying between the Missouri River and the Rocky Mountains, the southern border of Kansas and the northern border of Montana, in other words, the great northern plains. Within these boundaries were the present States of Kansas, Nebraska, South Dakota, North Dakota, Montana, Wyoming and Colorado, comprising an area of some 422,000,000 acres.

In 1880, the Cattle Kingdom was enjoying its greatest days. At that period, these seven States (some were then territories) had some six million cattle grazing on their ranges, approximately one animal for each seventy acres. It may be remarked, incidentally, that this ratio meant they were being seriously over-grazed, for immense parts of these United States were poor grasslands, and large sections of them were under cultivation.

In 1880, the entire United States contained some forty million head of cattle. Therefore, these Great Plains States with the finest grazing grounds on the continent, had approximately 15 per cent of the national total.

If the Cattle Kingdom is enlarged to include all the sixteen western States and Territories,* an area of approximately 1,149,000,000 acres, it will be found they contained some thirteen million cattle, or only about 33 per cent of the national total.

In the face of these incontrovertible figures, especially those applying to the northern plains States, one may wonder why the West came to be known as the Cattle Kingdom. The

* Kansas, Nebraska, South Dakota, North Dakota, Montana, Wyoming, Idaho, Colorado, Utah, New Mexico, Texas, Arizona, California, Oregon, Washington, Nevada. Oklahoma is not included, as in 1880, it was Indian Territory.

explanation is not to be found in its production but in its way of life.

In Illinois, Indiana or Ohio, ten thousand eighty-acre farms might have some two hundred thousand head of cattle in their pastures and barnyards, and the fact would be largely unnoticed, except by government census takers and tax assessors. In the Cattle Kingdom, in Wyoming or Montana or Colorado, a Cattle Baron might own no more than ten thousand head, graze them over a range as large as the ten thousand midwestern farms, some 800,000 acres, and be a subject of national interest, a hero of song and story and legend.

In one case, the production of two hundred thousand head of cattle was an incident of agriculture. In the other case, the production of ten thousand head was a stirring drama, a colorful pageant, filled with galloping riders, bellowing herds, the smell of burning hair, the shooting of guns, dust and space and great sweeps of hills and plains, emptiness, discomfort, danger and lurking death.

Two worlds were involved, divided by the ninety-eighth meridian. East of that line an immense stock-raising industry was conducted quietly, unostentatiously and for the most part in compliance with the law. West of that line a comparatively small cattle industry was carried on with great noise and wild behavior under men who recognized no law but that which could be carried in a holster.

11

No thief, invader or man of conquest in history ever knew more idyllic conditions for the perpetration of his schemes, whatever they might have been, than the cattlemen who trailed the first herds onto the magnificent rolling grass seas of the northern plains.

In the beginning room was not a problem. Grass reached to the horizons. The Indians were being driven onto reservations, and the great buffalo herds were being wantonly slaughtered for their hides. A man's first and chief concern was to select an advantageous location, and that could hardly be called difficult to accomplish.

Only Texas knew large-scale cattle ranching. North and west of the Indian Territory it was a new industry. There it had no antecedents, no precedents, no laws specifically written to govern it. Neither Territorial, State nor Federal statutes contained provisions for controlling the actions of the plains cattle rancher by identity and provided no controls, no licensing procedures, no range or water rules, nothing that might confine him, direct his operations or place upon him any civic, social or legal responsibility whatsoever. He was the freest man in the world. Only morals and conscience were possible restraints upon his conduct, and the record shows that he was burdened little by obligations of this nature.

There being no duly constituted authorities to assume the task for them, the cattlemen made their own laws. The paper on which they were inscribed was memory. The ink used was a unique composition of experience, need, functional advantage and desire. The penalties ordained were elastic, but never mild. Infliction of them remained with the man injured; he was judge, jury and executioner. Enforcement was not rested upon officer or court, but delegated to forces less susceptible to either corrupt influence or the persuasiveness of justice—the Colt, the Winchester and the rope.

The Code of the Range was not a body of laws designed to

preserve the equality of man, to guarantee fair treatment, to punish the wicked and to protect the innocent. It was a feudal law. It recognized and endorsed suzerainty, and it condemned and disavowed commonalty.

It was not law, for it was not sired by constitutional right and born of legislation. It was a congeries of bastard pronouncements, shaped by the few to benefit the few, and its provisions were outnumbered by its exceptions.

It held cattle stealing to be a crime, but the shooting or hanging of the thieves by cattlemen was not. The taking of a homestead on a range illegally claimed by a cattleman was an intrusion on personal rights, but the burning of the homesteader's cabin, the destruction of his crops, injuring him or even killing him were not. Self-defense was the justification for a multitude of sins, and might was right.

It was the public domain the cattleman used, but he rejected the legal definition of the term. His interpretation of the word *public* was cattleman, and *domain* meant grazing ground to be used exclusively by him. He recognized Federal laws only so far as they benefitted him, and those which would have restrained him were not considered to exist. The public had no rights.

The system under which he operated was simple. Its basic factors were three in number: water, grass and the physical contour of the land. Inasmuch as men, as well as cattle, must have live and dependable water, headquarters camp inevitably was established beside a stream and preferably near the center of the range to be utilized. Isolation was an advantage, and the search for it was instrumental in increasing the speed with which the cattlemen spread over the plains.

12

The claim of a range was made not only on the basis of need. Probably no cattleman set an arbitrary limit on his own capabilities. The extent of his range rights was governed by the distribution of water more than by anything else. Cattle would walk only so far to drink, no more than two to two and a half miles. Thus, the locations and courses of the streams determined the size and shape of the range chosen. The dividing line between range rights was usually delineated by a watershed.

Like any other animal, creatures of environment, range cattle were motivated in their movements by inherent instincts. They drifted, sometimes for reasons known only to themselves, but generally their migrations could be explained. Invariably natural factors and forces were involved. Yet, on occasions, the cause was not easily identified.

As a youth I was employed one summer as a horse-wrangler on a large cow outfit in south central Montana. In June, some four hundred three year old steers were unloaded at a railroad siding on the Yellowstone River and driven sixty miles to a fine summer range in mountainous country. Two weeks later almost all of them had vanished. (The incident took place, needless to say, in a day when range rights were legally awarded under law, yet it serves as an appropriate illustration here.)

There were few fences in the Federal forest reserve area in which the four hundred steers were released, but the lushness and profuseness of the meadowlands prompted the belief that little drifting would occur, and that periodic observations by line riders would be sufficient. When only a few of the steers could be located, an intensive hunt for them was begun. Some of them were found grazing with cattle of other brands in hills thirty miles to the east. In time, ranchers an even greater distance away, in plains country, reported finding the strays among their own cattle.

The mystery was solved at last by an old cowboy who himself drifted in the following spring to work for my employer.

After hearing the story, he asked quietly: "Where'd them steers come from?" When informed they had been purchased in the Texas Panhandle and shipped north, he nodded knowingly. "Wal, that ain't much of a problem to explain. They was flatland cattle. Down where they growed for three years, you can see a piss ant eatin' his supper a hundred miles off. If you can't see him, you can hear him chawin'. At least, you know what he is and what's makin' the noise. Up there in them mountains, those cattle couldn't see nothin', and they didn't understand the sounds. They kept agoin' over the mountains to find flat country. They was uneasy and scar't. I don't blame 'em. I don't care much for this up and down country, neither. Just like a prairie critter, a man from the plains has got to see out to know he's all right."

The district roundup was the natural solution to the problem of mixed brands. If it was devised for practical reasons, however, it soon became a powerful instrument of another kind. It was the nucleus of organization. It was the genesis of the associations with which the Cattle Barons affiliated themselves, thereby uniting to create power, which for more than two decades made them supreme.

13

There are no agricultural census figures for the year 1867, when the cattlemen began to carve out their domains on the northern plains, nor any for the year 1878, by which time large-scale cattle ranching had reached the farthest ranges of the plains Cattle Kingdom. There are authoritative figures for the years 1860 and 1880, and they will serve to show the rapidity of the expansion.

In 1860, it was reported that in Kansas there were 93,455 head of cattle on ranches, and in Nebraska there were 37,197. These ranches, actually farms on which fodder was or could be grown, were in the eastern parts of these States. In the same census year, there were no established cattle ranges in Colorado, Montana, Wyoming or Dakota.

In 1880, cattle on ranches in these areas numbered:

Kansas	1,533,133	Nebraska	1,113,247
Colorado	791,492	Wyoming	521,213
Montana	428,279	Dakota	140,815

A gain of almost four and a half million head had occurred in twenty years.

The cattlemen had not only established their domains, but they had successfully maintained and held them. Hundreds of settlers had paid a high price for being foolish enough to believe they could intrude on these vast grass sanctums. They could, if they were stupid and brazen enough, seek redress in the courts, but even if they won there, the victories were meaningless. Their homes were destroyed, their fields ruined and the cattlemen still held the homestead lands. A sheriff, no matter how brave he might be or how honest, had no hope of protecting homesteaders or recovering damages for them. Few sheriffs were foolhardy enough even to consider such a thing.

The story of law enforcement in the Cattle Kingdom is an endless record of injustices condoned and even perpetrated by law enforcement officers. In most places a sheriff held office only through the sufferance of the cattlemen. He was their tool, or he was not sheriff. There are cases on record in which settlers defending their homes were arrested as lawbreakers and turned over to bands of cattlemen and cowboys to be punished. Cattle thieves with a price on their heads were captured by officers and delivered to the cattlemen offering the rewards to be hanged. Homesteaders who had dared to shoot at cowboys when under attack not only paid with their lives, but their bodies were saturated with coal oil and fired.

14

The cattlemen condemned and blasphemed the Preemption and the Homestead Acts, and at the same time made good use of them. In a typical situation, a rancher would preempt 160 acres and file a homestead claim along a stream. Perhaps his partners, his financial backers, his brothers, sisters, sons, daughters, cousins, aunts, uncles or other relatives would file on adjoining homesteads. The lands claimed might be along one side of a stream or along both sides of it, depending on the quality of the grass, the physical nature of the area, and the range it was desired to control. Thus far, the cattleman could not be charged with breaking the law, for the wish of his kin to be neighbors could hardly be construed as criminal conspiracy.

Not all cattlemen had large families, of course, but those who were unattached were not precluded from participating in the swindles. They could emulate their fraternal brothers who used relatives to good advantage by inducing cowboys whom they believed could be trusted to take out homesteads for them. Indeed, all cattlemen could, and most of them did, do this. They would pay the filing fees and guarantee to purchase the land at a nominal price when the claimant obtained a deed. Often the security of a job during the time he was proving the claim was enough reward for a cowboy. Meanwhile, his employer had the use of the land for five years at practically no cost.

Not only relatives and employees were used by cattlemen to strengthen their range rights in this illegal manner. Waitresses, prostitutes and bartenders in the cowtowns were enlisted, and for small bribes appended their names to the necessary papers.

Whosoever controlled access to water controlled the range in the surrounding watershed.

It was not extraordinary for a cattleman to control twenty or thirty miles of a stream through false homestead entries.

Self-government and absolute control of the range were the ultimate goals of the cattlemen. Besides the Preemption and Homestead Acts, Congress, quite unintentionally, passed another measure which helped them. The desirability of having trees on the plains was indisputable. In 1873, the Timber Culture Act was enacted. It provided that any homesteader could apply for an additional 160 acres, which would be deeded to him at the end of eight years, if he planted forty acres of it in trees.

A new wave of land frauds swept across the West. Along

the extreme eastern edge of the plains, where there was sufficient moisture to grow some kinds of trees, bona fide farmers were enabled to increase and improve their holdings by the Timber Culture Act. It benefitted them, but it also benefitted the cattlemen of the drier and higher regions. They and their dummy entrymen filed thousands of timber claims, and, thereby, they augmented their control of water and grass. It was not their fault if trees would not grow in the shortgrass plains country.

The Cattle Barons now were able to obtain land dishonestly by three Federal acts, none of which had been passed for their benefit. Next they devised another scheme by which they might increase their fraudulent practices.

By 1877, they were able to present a strong front through stockmen's associations, working in cooperation with each other. A bill called the Desert Land Act was introduced, and lobbyists were sent to Washington, armed with generous expense accounts, to secure its passage.

No law in history was more deceitful, nor more specifically designed to aid the vested interests of the Cattle Kingdom. The cattlemen's lobby, assisted by several members of Congress who were cattle raisers and had illegally secured control of vast areas of public lands, threw up a smokescreen which effectively obscured the true nature of the bill. It was maintained that the Desert Land Act would allow a settler to obtain enough western acreage on which to make a living. Here, at last, was the legislative instrument that would open the way to western settlement by the little man.

The Desert Land Act provided that anyone over twenty-one years of age could secure a right to 640 acres with an initial payment of twenty-five cents an acre. The claimant was required to irrigate a portion of his section—that is, to construct some kind of a gravity system by which water could be brought to it—within three years. Then, by the payment of an additional dollar an acre, he would be awarded a deed.

The word *desert* was not included in the title by accident. The old conception of the West as a desert region was still harbored in the minds of many persons, even numerous members of Congress. Had this not been the case, undoubtedly there would not have been so much bungling and stupidity in writing the land laws, and the cattlemen would not have secured the enactment of the Desert Land Act with such ease.

The cattlemen were fully aware that only comparatively small portions of the whole western United States were not adaptable to some extent for the grazing of cattle. If the general public retained the erroneous conception that it was mainly a desert, so much the better for them. The word *desert* might serve to discourage persons with ambitions to settle west of the hundredth meridian.

The act as passed applied to the entire States and Territories of New Mexico, Colorado, Wyoming, Montana, Idaho, Utah and Nevada, approximately to the eastern halves of Washington and Oregon, California south of San Francisco, and the western half of Dakota. As far as geography and climate were concerned, the western thirds of Kansas and Nebraska might have been included, but these States had succeeded in escaping from the "desert" category.

The Desert Land Act received no fewer plaudits than had the Homestead Act from the public, the press, the pulpit and on the floor of Congress. Not all the senators and representatives who spoke strongly in favor of the measure, however, were tools of the cattlemen's lobby. Far from it. Many of them were deceived by the lofty purposes it ostensibly proffered, as was the public, which had no means of looking behind its attractive disguise.

The cornerstone of the law's deception was not to be found

in anything it said, but in what it did not say. It contained no provision requiring an entryman to occupy the section of land on which he filed. The cattlemen had made certain of that omission.

Thousands of square miles of fine grazing land came into their ranges through dummy entries. For twenty-five cents an acre, they held tentative title to these immense segments of the public domain for at least three years, during which time no one had to live on them, and at the end of that period all they had to do was to show that they had brought water for cultivation to small portions of it, pay an additional dollar an acre, and obtain permanent title.

The irrigation provision was easily circumvented. It was no trouble to obtain witnesses to swear they had seen water on the land. What they had seen, of course, were a few buckets of water spilled on the grass. Water was water.

Claims for more than 9,100,000 acres were filed under the Desert Land Act. Most of the claimants gave up the fight at the end of three years, and perhaps six million acres reverted to the public domain. This was all to the advantage of the cattlemen. They had known all along that a man with a few dollars could not build an efficient irrigation system, even if he could obtain the water for it. In countless thousands of cases the claimants found they could obtain no water. Meanwhile, the cattlemen had quietly secured title to some three million acres of valuable range, for by far the largest part of this acreage was adjacent to or on streams in the finest shortgrass grazing areas of the high plains.

Complete concealment of such an immense number of land thefts was impossible, and as newspapers began to rail against the practice and demanded that the stealing be stopped, official inquiries were ordered. They were feeble breaths against the strong western winds. The Federal Land Office was a sink of corruption. Agents could be bribed to issue land patents to cattlemen who obviously had not obeyed any of the statutes.

The inquiries bore little fruit. Repeal of the four major land laws would have been the only means of halting the violations, and, at last, a report made to Congress recommended this drastic legal surgery. It pointed out that the ease with which frauds could be perpetrated under existing laws and the immunity offered by a hasty issue of patents encouraged the making of fictitious and fraudulent entries. Fraud would inevitably exist so long as the opportunity for fraud was preserved in the laws. With repeal of the Preemption, Homestead, Timber Culture and Desert Land Acts, the report said the illegal appropriation of the remaining public lands would be reduced to a minimum.

In the jargon of the atomic age, it might be said that the Cattle Barons had a lot going for them. *Congress:* Most of the members came from east of the Mississippi River and were woefully ignorant of the West. Not a few of the western members were cattlemen, or needed the support of cattlemen to be elected. *General Land Office:* Corruption was unbridled in it. Bribery was rampant. Little effort was made to verify the statements of any claimant, none at all in the cases of cattlemen with rolls of greenbacks. *Local Law Enforcement:* It was too weak in practically every State, Territory and community to oppose the armed bands of cowboy raiders and murderers employed by cattlemen. *Local Courts:* Witnesses were intimidated and threatened. Even in cases where evidence against cattlemen was incontrovertible, judges and justices of the peace were hesitant to endanger their own health by inflicting penalties. They permitted delays and dismissed cases on the slightest technicalities, or on none at all.

State Legislatures: Cattlemen controlled key votes in them, usually through bribery, and prevented the passage of laws that would assist or protect settlers.

Still the Cattle Barons were not satisfied.

15

Fraudulent filings under the land acts, great as they were, did not provide the protection which cattlemen needed to guarantee continuance of their illegal operations. There were in the Cattle Kingdom countless thousands of miles of running water, rivers, creeks, tiny brooks and springs—far too much to be guarded and controlled by lawful means. The extra-legal system of range rights, devised by the cattlemen themselves, had to be recognized and maintained. It was.

The system was simple. A cattleman "appropriated" water, that is, stream frontage, and this gave him control of the range lying back of it. His nearest neighbor might be twenty to fifty miles away, but the division of their individual range claims was understood and recognized. Often boundary lines were represented by natural divides between creeks. Disputes were not infrequent, of course, and sometimes resulted in shooting frays, but as a general rule cattlemen were careful to respect the "range rights" of adjoining outfits. The cattle were less circumspect in this regard—grass was grass, and they were not interested in ownership—but during the spring roundup, when calves were earmarked and their sexual futures settled, and in the early fall roundup, when beeves to be marketed were selected, wandering animals were restored to their proper ranges. During the balance of the year, line riders "drifted" strays back to their home grounds, and this was considered a neighborly act.

By 1880, the Cattle Kingdom had been fairly well divided. Between western Kansas and the mountains, the Texas Panhandle and Canada, range rights had been established. Ranches of a hundred thousand acres were commonplace; they were the small outfits. Half a million acres wasn't considered a really big range. One of a million acres was respectable but nothing at which to marvel. Individual cattlemen and companies claimed "range rights" over four, five and six million acres, some over territory as large as Massachusetts and Delaware combined—more than six and a half million acres.

"Within the cattle region," said a Senate report, "it is notorious that actual settlements are generally prevented and made practically impossible outside the proximity of towns, through the unlawful control of the country, maintained by cattle companies."

Yet, "actual settlements" were occurring, and they were not all close to towns. Homesteaders were locating on meadowlands along streams. Men with a few thousand, perhaps only a few hundred, dollars were registering their brands and turning out small bunches of cattle to propagate.

Pressures of frightening proportions were beginning to be felt, and some clear-sighted cattlemen expressed doubts that violence alone could dissipate them. They did not advocate dispensing with such efficient measures as destroying the property of the intruders, or even killing them, but they also looked about for another powerful weapon, preferably one which could be used openly, with which to strengthen and safeguard their range rights.

They found it in organization.

16

The rise of the Cattle Kingdom, its gunfights, roundups, vast ranges, immense herds, its wild life and wilder men and women, supplied the material out of which innumerable plays, novels, poems and songs were woven, with far less regard for fact than for fancy. They attracted enormous audiences in both America and Europe.

But there was another type of story about the West, solemnly represented to be factual, which, if it drew a smaller audience, thrilled its readers no less than the lurid romances and melodramas. It was the story of how cattlemen were reaping great fortunes, the text burdened with figures and percentages and dollar signs purporting to prove how insignificant investments brought unbelievable returns.

It was the purest of all fiction written in the 1870s and the 1880s, and if cattlemen were not the actual authors they were its source, and they did not expose its fallacies. In not a few cases they aided in spreading it, with dishonest intent.

Books, articles and pamphlets recounting the experiences of men who became rich virtually overnight by turning a few mangy cows loose on the range appeared in floods. Newspapers publicized the "cattle boom," the "beef bonanza." The ears of English, Scotch and eastern capitalists stood up. Reputable publications dedicated to agriculture, stock breeding and financial subjects swallowed the propaganda. Said one:

"A good sized steer when it is fit for the butcher market will bring from $45.00 to $60.00. The same animal at its birth was worth but $5.00. He has run on the plains and cropped the grass from the public domain for four or five years, and now, with scarcely any expense to its owner, is worth forty dollars more than when he started on his pilgrimage. A thousand of these animals are kept nearly as cheaply as a single one, so with a thousand as a starter and an investment of but $5,000 in the start, in four years the stock has made from $40,000 to $45,000. Allow $5,000 for his current expenses which he has been going on and he still has $35,000 and even $45,000 for a net profit. That is all there is to the problem. . . ."

That was not quite all. Nothing was said about calf losses from spring blizzards, wolves and accidents, or of the loss of grown animals from stampedes, prairie fires, diseases, injuries and to rustlers.

Swindlers, among them prominent cattlemen, also heard the entrancing song of the western Lorelei. Beautiful prospectuses and gold-lettered stock certificates began to appear from companies that existed only on paper. Fabulous success tales were broadcast by every medium available. An Irish servant girl accepted cows valued at $150 in lieu of wages due her. They were permitted to graze on her employer's range with her own brand on them. In ten years she sold out to him for $25,000. A lawyer took a hundred head of steers as a fee, forgot about them, and a few years later discovered he was rich. No explanation was made as to how the steers multiplied so rapidly, but that didn't matter. Men in the eastern banking houses and British drawing rooms didn't know the difference between a steer and a cow. Many people thought the word *steer* meant a good grade of beef. The capitalists were not interested in the sexual life of bovines, only in the results of it.

"Three years ago a guileless tenderfoot came into Wyoming, leading a single Texas steer and carrying a branding iron; now he is the opulent possessor of six hundred head of fine cattle—the ostensible progeny of that one steer," wrote a western humorist. Even as they fought nesters and rustlers who carelessly employed branding irons, the cattlemen got a laugh out of the story, but it was soberly repeated in the East by hysterical investors.

Some suspicious investigators began to appear in the Cattle Kingdom. The cattlemen and their bankers were ready for them. They went home convinced that El Dorado had been found.

In London, Edinburgh, New York, Philadelphia, Boston, companies and syndicates took shape. Money poured into them. How could one lose? The answer was to be found in financial journals: One couldn't lose. The journals printed the story of a Massachusetts man who took his family's fortune and bought some range rights and some 12,000 cattle in Wyoming for $230,000. In six months he sold the prime beeves and 6,000 other animals for $180,000. He still owned 6,000 cattle, including the year's calf crop, worth as much or more than his original investment.

Another easterner, according to the newspapers, had to go west for his health. Having nothing to do, he began to dabble in cattle, investing about $100,000—a small outfit. In four years he refused $300,000 for his ranch.

One of the first and largest companies financed by British funds reported that it was raising calves into beeves at a cost of only three shillings each, and announced a dividend of forty-two per cent for its stockholders.

There were a few financial advisers who advocated caution and a thorough investigation of a proposal before an investment was made, but their voices were drowned out by the noise of the gold dropping into new cattle syndicates. A leading British business paper suggested that it might be unwise to accept at face value the assertion that enormous dividends came out of actual profits. It was quite possible, and more likely, they came out of inflated and unfounded values placed on the cattle. A decline in the market could result in serious consequences, the paper warned.

A skeptical Scottish correspondent dared to remind his readers that in buying American range rights they were actually getting nothing of tangible or real value. Cattle grazed on the public domain on sufferance of the Federal Government. It could put them off at any time.

Other killjoys mentioned that in buying cattle by book count, rather than range count, the actual number purchased was not known. Estimates of annual increases were that and nothing more, and therefore, not to be relied upon.

Not only the public ignored such warnings, but supposedly hardheaded and shrewd capitalists also did. Admittedly they knew nothing of the cattle business, except what they read in the papers, but that problem could be easily solved. They simply went into business with experienced American cattlemen and retained their services through amalgamations and partnerships. Thus, veteran captains always stood at the helm. Clever, eh?

Not very clever. The cattlemen willingly entered into the agreements, banking the outside money or establishing new outfits for themselves. They sold range rights for millions of dollars, rights which were legally worthless. They sold the public domain. They sold cattle by book count—so many cows would have so many calves. When some cattlemen at a western bar complained that the winter was taking a heavy toll of their cattle, the bartender sagely reminded them that book counts did not freeze.

Some of the eastern and European companies, operated by American cattlemen shareholders, were incredibly large.

Not a few claimed range rights to three or four thousand square miles. In a span of five years, 1880–1884, an estimated twenty-one million acres were controlled by foreign syndicates, perhaps as many more acres by new companies organized in Boston and New York.

Few of them had title to much land. All of them operated for the most part on Federal ranges and grasslands leased from railroads. In the year 1883, twenty cattle companies, capitalized at more than $12 million were formed to operate in Wyoming alone.

The formula employed was simple. Typical of the procedure was one Wyoming corporation. It raised nearly $4 million by selling stock shares, bought three large ranches, took the owners in as partners to manage the enterprise, and claimed rights to a range one hundred and thirty miles long by fifty miles wide along the Laramie River. The book showed that they owned 130,000 cattle. In 1882, ten British-American companies were launched in this way and on a similar scale.

The plunging and the absentee ownership opened the gates to immense frauds. American cattlemen, company managers and partners swindled their angels. It was no trouble for them to put their own brands on calves and build up herds for themselves. The lords and bankers sipping wines in drawing rooms thousands of miles away would never know how they were cheated. A few of the Britishers and New Englanders who did come out to participate in the adventurous life of the wild west, however, were not above doing a bit of swindling themselves. If prospects for good returns appeared unfavorable, the means for brightening the outlook was always at hand. Inasmuch as the investors did not actually know how many cattle a company owned, the ravages of winter and other losses could be concealed by shipping a larger number of cattle to market. That may have adversely affected the entire operation, but the shareholders didn't know that, either. A dividend was all they wanted.

It couldn't last. Storm clouds mounted on the horizon and grew steadily darker, and not all of them were a figure of speech. Nature was getting ready to take a hand in the situation.

There were protests in the press about domination of the public domain by a few cattle kings. Cries that western legislatures were controlled by foreign money rang out. Cattlemen who were not involved with foreign and eastern investors warned that the ranges, immense as they were, were overstocked and becoming seriously overgrazed. The Secretary of the Interior ordered an investigation, as if he did not really know what was happening, and the cattlemen welcomed the snooping as they would an epidemic of Texas fever. Then someone in the White House decided that leases of land by cattlemen in the Indian Territory were both a source of the red man's discontent and unprofitable to him. It wasn't good for Indians who were starving to be surrounded by thousands of fine beef animals. A Presidential order forced the cattlemen to remove more than two hundred thousand head from the Indian Territory. There was no place for them to go, except the already overcrowded ranges to the west and north.

In 1882, at the height of the boom, prime beef sold in the Chicago stockyards for $9.35 a hundred pounds. It was an almost unbelievable price, but the profits to be made—at least on paper—were even more unbelievable. Cattle could be bought for $35 a head in Texas and sold in Wyoming for $60. So great was the demand for range stock that the number of cattle shipped westward and northward equaled the number sent to market. Cattlemen who had bought young stock three years earlier were reaping a profit of three hundred per cent on them.

Then, as one ranch manager put it, "over-production put us out of our saddles and took over." In 1884, prices began a sharp downward trend. Big packers, fully understanding the conditions in the Cattle Kingdom, contributed their muscle to pushing them lower.

In the spring of 1885, the highest quotation at Chicago was $5 a hundred. By early fall it was $3. By late fall it was $1.80. The railroads, seeing the desperate plight of the cattlemen, maintained the freight rates charged when prices were at a peak.

A Senate committee would get around to looking into the situation, after it was too late to do any good, of course. It would get a clear picture from a cattleman who operated in both Texas and Wyoming. He would relate how prices rose steadily for several years, and it became the policy of cattle raisers "to take better care of she-cattle and to hold onto them as cattle grew higher in price. Hence, for a few years, along from 1881 to 1885, heifers would cost more than steers of like ages—which in a few years gave us an immense supply of cattle.

"During those years, too, a great deal of money was sent out from the East and from Europe to invest in cattle, and in numbers of cases cattle were bought at very high prices and at book account by men who did not know what they were doing, they representing large capitalists, syndicates. Therefore, I claim that in many instances where Texas cattle were bought at $20, they paid $40 on the book account. The same thing held in Wyoming. . . .

"I do not think I ever saw a business that was as prosperous as the cattle business up to 1884 and 1885 that went down as quick and fast, with no confidence left in it at all."

The sources of foreign and eastern capital dried up, leaving ugly financial scars in the Cattle Kingdom. The boom ended. "If you have any steers to shed, prepare to shed them now," said a farm paper. The cattlemen shed what they could. Often freight costs were more than they received from the commission houses of Chicago.

The Cattle Kingdom was staggered by the blows, and more equally as vicious were to come, but some years would pass before its final fall. No matter what else they were—swindlers, frauds, thieves, murderers—the Cattle Barons were not weaklings, not cowards. It would take more than economic adversity, more than investigations and exposures, more than laws, more than public opinion, to dethrone them.

17

The cattlemen's associations were the illegal governments of the Cattle Kingdom. Their power even reached into the national Congress through the representatives and senators they supported, financed and elected. It was representation out of all proportion to reality, out of all keeping with democratic principles, for the cattlemen were few in number. The associations "owned" senators and congressmen, just as they "owned" members of State Legislatures.

Stockmen began to form what they thought of as mutual protective groups with the establishment of the cowtown shipping points along the first railroad to reach the western plains. Drovers moving herds northward and westward with the intention of founding ranches on the open ranges appeared to be afflicted with a peculiar inability to read brands. They picked up cattle as they moved along the trail, and frequently reached their destinations pleasantly surprised to find that their herds had increased without benefit of natural progeny, and in spite of losses suffered during the long drive.

The organized stockmen, in addition to patrolling their ranges, found it beneficial to employ stock detectives to observe trail herds and watch shipping pens, but if their motives in these respects may be considered justifiable, they were soon transformed into disguises for unjustifiable and wholly illegal activities.

The reasoning process which underlay the evolution of the diabolical plotting offered no mysteries. In organization there was strength—not only physical power but financial, social and political power. Rustlers could be effectively dealt with at the scene of capture. It was not unusual to come upon bodies swinging from trees, often with notes, such as *Rustlers Beware* or *Doom To Thieves,* fastened to them. The identities of the executioners were not difficult for a sheriff to discover, but arraignment and conviction presented other problems. Most sheriffs, understandably, left the bodies for the vultures and kept their own silence.

Homesteaders and small stockmen, if not actually cattle thieves were, nevertheless, considered intruders. They could be driven out by armed force, their homes and fields could be destroyed, and cattlemen could send cowboys to steal their livestock. Or they might be made the victims of trickery concealed in legal dress. The usual method was to inform the sheriff that a settler or small rancher was stealing stock. Incriminating evidence was planted. The investigating officer had no difficulty finding it; it was pointed out to him. Usually the evidence was a lone animal slipped among the stock of the man to be accused. In a nearby gully would be hides of butchered steers upon which was the brand of a cattleman in the area. This was an efficient but an annoying method, for it might necessitate a trial and perhaps require the appearance of witnesses. A much more direct and conclusive method was to shoot a settler from ambush as he drove along a road, and leave his body, his dead horses and his burned wagon in an adjacent gulch.

Most of the means that the Cattle Barons used against the helpless invaders of their domains were effective. Interference from law enforcement authorities was seldom encountered. If range rights had no standing under law, they were recognized and respected by officers of the law and by local courts, and legislatures were seldom successful in overriding them, even though repeated attempts were made by a few misguided legislators who considered it their responsibility to serve the best interests of all their constituents.

Yet, violence, conspiracy, murder did not rid the cattlemen of the irritating human thorns. New settlers appeared as fast as others were driven out or slain. There were always some damfool flatfeet who insisted on the rights theoretically awarded them by Federal statutes—even the right to starve and the opportunity to fail on a Government claim.

The cattlemen sought to improve their public image by the false charge that they were being infested by swarms of small rustlers in the guise of legitimate homesteaders. Their herds were being decimated by hordes of one-horse "maverickers." Meat markets and packers far and wide were conspiring with nestors to buy stolen cattle. Settlers banded together to drive hundreds of animals at a time to secluded places, or even out of a county, burn over brands—really a thing easily accomplished, for there were few brands that could not be changed by adding letters, bars or figures—and hold them to mature into prime beef or to drop calves. Fraudulent bills of sale were furnished by the thieves to buyers. Moreover, professional rustlers were being harbored by homesteaders and helped to escape.

It is to be noted that the cattlemen's associations disseminating this propaganda were careful not to demand that the legally constituted law enforcement authorities take steps to halt the depredations. That would have been in contravention of their purpose, and the last thing they wanted to happen.

Their complaints, cries of outrage and pleas for sympathetic public understanding duly registered and publicized, the united cattlemen swiftly took the next steps of their premeditated plan to obtain and maintain absolute control of their ranges. In doing so, they quickly put to shame the most talented professional rustlers and the most daring and accomplished outlaws who ever rode the trails of the West.

18

By the late 1870s, the larger part of the Great Plains was under the domination of cattlemen's associations. State and Territorial Governments were under their shadow, if not their complete control. They made their own laws and took it upon themselves to enforce them.

The actions of the big Wyoming association typify those of other groups in Colorado, Nebraska, Kansas, Montana and Idaho, most of which were modeled from it and adopted its methods of operation. The most powerful in the Cattle

Kingdom, the corruptive influence of the Wyoming association was not only incomparably strong in the Wyoming Legislature and State Government, but extended beyond the State boundaries. Numerous county commissioners, law officers and judges were its pawns; acceded to its demands; did its dirty work and delivered verdicts it requested.

For years it retained on its payroll notorious outlaws and killers. Called stock detectives, they rode through the country arresting suspected cattle thieves—most of them innocent homesteaders—and hailing them before cooperative judges on trumped up charges. Those who resisted were shot on their own doorsteps. Settlers, for good reasons, feared the association's representatives far more than bona fide outlaws and bandits.

The Wyoming association inaugurated a system of general roundups, over which it exercised strict supervision, and which were held at specified times in the spring and fall in western Nebraska, the Black Hills, Montana, Wyoming and northern Colorado. Any roundups held by others would not have its official sanction and, therefore, would be suspect and subject to investigation. Other decrees, approved, of course, by a majority of members and in accordance with standard rules of order, increased the association's control over virtually every phase of the cattle business.

It had happened that numerous cowhands wanted to improve their positions in life and accepted their wages in cows instead of dollars. To these they affixed their brands and turned them out to propagate on the range. It was the view of some cattlemen that this system was a means of retaining good men, and they used it. The association saw the matter in a different light. Too often cowboys had not been above mavericking or altering brands in their own interest. The association members were induced to pledge themselves not to employ any cowboy who owned stock, who would accept cattle in lieu of wages or who expressed a desire to lift himself above the status of a bunkhouse resident. A blacklist was prepared, and on it went the names of the honest cowboys whose only crime was that they wanted to get ahead in the world, as well as the names of suspected or known mavericker and rustlers.

This ruling, naturally, did not prevent in any way the association members from carrying on the mavericking and stealing in which so many of them had long indulged. Indeed, it was designed to eliminate the small fry. A cattleman was still free to hire his own personal stock thieves, to augment the wages of his cowboys with $2 to $5 for every maverick they branded, every brand they altered or every critter they could steal from a homesteader or small rancher.

No blacklisted cowboy or rancher whose brand was not duly recorded and accepted by the association was permitted to participate in a roundup. Foremen were required to post a bond of $3,000, which would be forfeited if they violated the edict. It was a powerful means of keeping newcomers from starting ranches, and any cattleman who was not an association member was prevented from safeguarding his own interests in the roundups. Numerous newspapers condemned the blacklists, but the association not only ignored the protests, but adopted even more stringent methods to strengthen its control.

Inspectors and detectives were placed at railroad shipping pens, at Indian agencies, military installations and packing plants. All cattle to be shipped or sold at these places which did not bear the brand of an association member were declared to be mavericks and were confiscated, by force of arms when necessary. The association then proceeded to sell the animals, the money received going into its own bank account.

This was unqualified theft. It was the system used by the association to seize the cattle of not only known rustlers but of honest settlers and small ranchers. No effective recourse was open to the victims, no matter how reputable they were, for not only would a lawsuit have been dragged out interminably at great expense, but defying the association was a risk few men were foolhardy enough to take.

Association attorneys advised that so-called cattle king laws would have no standing in a Federal court and counseled against their passage by State legislatures. The "cattle king laws" which the associations sought would have permitted their members to define range boundaries and rights, and would have prohibited all intrusions upon them. Such statutes, said the attorneys, even if upheld by corrupt State courts, would have been taken before the United States Supreme Court by the Federal Government, and would have been ruled unconstitutional. After all, the public domain was involved in the question. The cattlemen could take the attitude that it should be turned over to them, but that did not give them a legal claim to it. There was doubt that the august justices in far-off Washington would be impressed by the argument that grass placed upright by the hand of God should not be disturbed by the plow.

Discouraged but not defeated by such sound legal advice, the cattlemen took what they saw as their only alternative. They proceeded without benefit of "cattle king laws" to do exactly what they had intended to do from the beginning.

Announcements and advertisements, placed by both associations and individuals, began to appear in newspapers. The general tenor of them was this:

The undersigned refuse to allow any person, or any person's

herd, on the range. We refuse the use of our corrals. No party will be allowed to join in any roundup on our range after this date.

Many advertisements similar to the following were printed:

The undersigned hereby notifies the public that he claims the range beginning at the mouth of Double Cross Creek and continuing down the Crazy Horse Valley thirty-six miles to Rabbit Ear Butte, and the entire valley east and west between the Sundown Mountains and the Blue Bonnet Hills.

(Signed) Fred R. Smith
Rocking Chair Brand

The Cattle Barons delineated the boundaries of their respective kingdoms. They claimed exclusive rights to immense areas of the public domain. The advertisements gave no more legal standing to their claims than they had previous to publication of them—which was none at all. Yet, the advertisements were clear warnings. The lines of combat had been drawn. Crossing them was to invite serious trouble, if not death. Even Federal land agents, map makers and surveyors were not safe. They were shot at, their equipment was stolen and the markers they erected were destroyed. In western Nebraska one assistant to a government surveyor was wantonly murdered. There were no arrests, not even an investigation.

There were two ways found most effective in stifling protests against the high-handed methods of the associations—control of State and county political machinery and gun law. Both were used.

The Wyoming association, for example, got members elected, or appointed, at various times as United States attorney, receiver of the Federal Land Office, governor, attorney general, treasurer, State legislators, congressmen, senators and to numerous lesser posts, including the State Livestock Commission.

A notorious Texas gunman and outlaw was hired by the association as its chief range inspector. He soon proved his worth by murdering several homesteaders and owners of small outfits—all rustlers, of course—and was rewarded by being made sheriff of a county. His chief assistant was a former Nebraska law enforcement officer whose most distinguished accomplishment had been to win a large reward by capturing two homesteaders suspected of rustling and delivering them to a mob of cattlemen to be hanged.

When he applied for a job with the association as a range detective, one professional killer and former Pinkerton man boasted, "Killing men is my specialty." He was put on the payroll, and became a close friend of the Wyoming association's president. One of the assignments given him was to organize an efficient killing machine. He was sent to Dakota to hire experienced gunmen at $150 a month—three times what a top cowhand received—and guarantee them a bonus of $500 for every settler they killed.

Soon afterward the number of murders sharply increased. Most of them were ambushes or dry-gulch killings, the victims being shot in the back. Others were carried out in broad daylight by men who did not wear masks. It was not long until homesteaders were living in constant fear in all the vast territory between Colorado and Montana, the plains of Nebraska and western Wyoming. No settler could feel secure in his bed; indeed, some were dragged from their cabins in the middle of the night and hanged, and others were shot to death while they slept. A rumor that the association's raiders were approaching an area would cause people to dash for the protection of a settlement.

Still they came west—the young tenderfoot with great dreams of becoming a cowboy or cattleman, the flatfoot farmer from the Middle West, the young clerk from the city—all blinded by the false stories which made of the Cattle Kingdom a land of golden opportunity, adventure and romance.

The association's expenses steadily increased. Each member was assessed one cent a head on the cattle he owned, but it was not enough to meet current obligations and maintain a reserve. Strangely, a cattleman who boasted in saloons of the great herds bearing his brand, owned a much smaller number of cattle when he appeared at the association meeting.

Additional ways and means had to be found to pay the increasing number of detectives, professional murderers, inspectors and roundup foremen, and to dispense the necessary bribes to courts, legislators and law officers.

In 1884, the association forced passage of legislation, which it termed a Maverick Bill. The act made the branding of any maverick a felony. It was sought under the pretense that it would help to curb not only known rustlers but homesteaders who were careless with branding irons and who thought they were entitled to feed their families with any steer that frequented their corn patch or pasture. The excuse looked good in the newspapers, but it was thoroughly dishonest.

A careful reading of the bill would have disclosed that all mavericks were to be sold by the association to pay the salaries of its cattle inspectors. It defined mavericks not only in the usual way, that is, as unbranded animals, but as all cattle bearing the brands of "unknown" owners.

Thus, the thievery of the association was legalized. In its eyes an "unknown owner" was a rancher or settler who was not a member. The association's inspectors were the sole judges in every case. In reality, the Maverick Bill meant that anyone the association chose to call a rustler could be driven out of the cattle business.

The Maverick Bill brought in some money—every settler was considered a rustler—but not enough. To ease the situation, the association conceived a scheme for stealing from the Wyoming State Treasury. It pressured the legislature into creating a Board of Livestock Commissioners. The board would pay the wages of inspectors and detectives, most of whom had criminal records, supervise all roundups and handle the sale of mavericks. Only association officials would be eligible for membership on the board.

Control of the range, declared the association, was now in legally constituted hands, and that was true. It was also true that the State of Wyoming was condoning, directing and executing the stealing of cattle, waging war on settlers, approving shootings, lynchings and the destruction of private property, and employing gunmen and killers.

In a single period of ten months, during which the Maverick Law was rigidly enforced by the inspectors of the Board of Livestock Commissioners, more than sixteen thousand head of cattle were confiscated at shipping points. The charge registered was that the animals carried "unacceptable" brands. That meant brands not owned by an association member.

Most of the confiscated cattle were the property of small ranchers, men to whom two or three hundred head of stock represented a year's income. Their only hope of redress—generously proffered to them by the commissioners—was to appear before the board and prove that they had acquired their stock honestly and that they were not rustlers. No small rancher in Wyoming could have done that to the satisfaction of the association members who sat in the chairs of the commissioners. Few of them tried to do it.

The sixteen thousand head of cattle confiscated had a market value of $35 to $45 a head. They were sold by the Board of Livestock Commissioners at an average price of less than $3 a head—to association members.

19

A frail and sickly young man took a homestead and started a small store in the Sweetwater country. Near him, a strong and vivacious young woman also filed on a claim and built a stout log house. It was rumored that she was the young man's wife, but was using her maiden name so she and her husband could acquire more land. The young man owned no cattle, but he made the mistake of writing some letters to newspapers protesting the illegal occupation of the public domain by the Cattle Barons. The young woman did acquire some stock, and it was said in bunkhouse conversations that she got it by favoring cowboys with her womanly charms.

One day both the young man and the young woman were taken from their homes at gunpoint and hanged. The lynchings were witnessed by several settlers concealed in an adjacent gulley. The lynchers were identified. No charge was brought against them. The association controlled all officers of the county.

20

A group of small ranchers had settled in a remote mountain valley, taken up homesteads and formed a loosely knit association under which they conducted a community roundup and otherwise assisted each other. A Cattle Baron who was a member in good standing of THE association decided he needed the valley for his own range. Shortly after he had made his desire known to his colleagues in Cheyenne, a killer was sent into the valley. He unceremoniously shot to death the leader of the small ranchers. The others concluded that it would be wise to abandon their enterprise and move out.

21

Near Newcastle, a homesteader of German descent established a small horse ranch. He imported a number of blooded animals and was meeting with success. Four riders appeared at his house one evening, announced that they were deputies with a warrant for his arrest and took him away. A week later his body was found. The murderers made no effort to conceal their identities. They were a former United States marshal in the pay of the association, the foreman of another horse ranch and two cattlemen. The ex-marshal publicly boasted that he had been the leader and declared that the homesteader had "looked" guilty of stealing stock. The real sheriff confiscated a thousand horses in the German's pastures, but he had to return them to his widow. The sheriff was unable to prove that a single animal had been stolen.

22

Two brothers, both experienced cowpunchers, migrated from Nebraska to Johnson County, Wyoming. Sober, honest and ambitious young men, they rode the range for five years, saved their wages, bought some heifers and took out homesteads. One of them became engaged and went to Buffalo to buy lumber for a house to which he would take his new wife. As he was driving home, he was shot to death by a killer concealed beneath a bridge.

On a cold December day, another homesteader was driving to his home, which was sixty miles south of Buffalo. In his wagon were winter supplies and Christmas presents for his family. Before he left Buffalo, a friend had warned him that his life was in danger. An association gunman, an ex-sheriff, had been overheard telling the foreman of a big cattle outfit that he would "take care of that rustler." The homesteader had considered delaying his lonely journey until he could acquire companions, but the thought of his wife and three small children alone in their cabin brought the decision to go. He held a shotgun across his knees as he drove along the road.

A few miles south of Buffalo he was shot to death. A rider who happened to be nearby heard the shots and saw the former sheriff dash out of a culvert. Upon investigation, the rider found the homesteader shot in the back, his horses killed in their harness. The Christmas toys were covered in blood.

23

Sitting before the grate fires in the plush cattlemen's club in Cheyenne, the association members could take satisfaction in the way things were going. A report had been sent in by the president, a Scot whose syndicate controlled some three million acres of public lands, owned a hundred and fifty thousand head of cattle and who was a partner in one of the largest commission houses in Chicago, that homesteaders were fleeing into towns in fear of their lives. Buffalo was crowded with settlers and their families, who had come as far as a hundred miles. They had abandoned their cabins and corn patches. If they ever returned—and the report expressed the opinion that few of them would—they would find their homes burned, their fields destroyed, their stock, even their chickens and pigs, killed or stolen.

The public relations phases of the association's reign of terror had not been neglected. The two Wyoming Senators in Washington, both Cattle Barons and both members of the association, had seen to that. Eastern and midwestern newspapers were carrying stories that told of the cattlemen's courageous fight against rustlers. One Washington paper, getting the news right out of the Senators' own mouths, branded all residents of one Wyoming county as rustlers—except the big cattlemen there, of course.

Things were looking pretty good. Yet, there were a few troublesome signs that could not be completely ignored.

Not all newspaper stories were sympathetic to the cattlemen. Letters written to the Government by settlers who had been injured or driven from their homes had found their way somehow into the hands of editors.

Editorials condemning the lynchings and dry-gulch killings, the cattle thefts and the destruction of homesteads began to appear, some of them in the leading Wyoming papers. The association forced merchants to cancel advertising, but the papers came out with blank pages, which had been sold to advertisers who cancelled copy, and continued their denunciations of the association's tactics and the political corruption it spawned.

There was another kind of trouble. In several places, homesteaders had taken a leaf out of the association's book, formed groups of vigilantes, and fought for their rights. Two known association murderers, one a British cattleman, would have fallen into the hands of a settlers' posse and undoubtedly would have been lynched had not a sheriff helped them to escape capture and to flee across the State line into Nebraska.

Things were looking pretty good, but there was a tenseness in the air, and incidents were occurring that made some association members shake their heads in concern.

24

A few lines from a sketch, allegorical in nature, which I wrote as a romantic young man, may not be inappropriate here.

In a Cheyenne saloon that was crowded with cattlemen appeared one day a quiet little man who seemed to be lost in a maze of studious thoughts. He wore a speckled, tweedy suit and a large derby hat. In the opening of a soiled, ironed collar bobbed a large Adam's apple. His eyes were friendly, but they seemed to be gazing far beyond the bar, perhaps even beyond the plains that surrounded the town. He took several whiskies neat, and presently fell into conversation with some of the men about him. He talked easily and in a soft voice that held the attention of his listeners. Soon there was a crowd around him, and cowmen strained to hear his words, as if mysteriously attracted to them.

"I am the greatest changer in all the plains country," the little stranger said. "Whatever a territory may be, I can change it almost overnight into something else. I am not speaking only of conditions on the surface of the earth. When I get through with a place, the life in it also has changed—its people, its customs, its commerce, even its government. There are very few things I cannot change.

"I am, as well, an inventor who has contributed greatly to progress and development. I make it possible for a man to dwell in private. I can hold a man in prison, but I can also keep him out. I make it possible for a man to guard against trespassers, to isolate himself, to create his own domain, to build as he wishes. I give him protection that is not dependent upon laws or words or promises. Perhaps most important of all, I give men the power to create a country's destiny and to mold it to suit themselves."

This man must think he's God, the bartender told himself, and sent for the sheriff.

"Now, I don't do all these things for nothing," the little stranger went on. "I ask money for my services. In one way they may seem expensive, but considered in another way they are cheap. I've studied the situation in the Cattle Kingdom, in all the West, and I am prepared to offer a solution for its troubles—at least a long step toward a solution.

"I am the greatest friend a homesteader ever had. But, before you shoot me, consider also that I am the greatest friend the cattlemen ever had. I cannot keep from helping the homesteader, but I can also help you to help yourself.

"There are only a few great inventors in the world, and I

am one of them. But to achieve this exalted position, one also has to be the emissary of a new age, a scientist, a businessman, and possess the ability to make the materials of the earth serve in new and undreamed-of ways. Indeed, one must be a master magician, but not one dealing only in illusions. One has to be practical and precise, cold and logical. One has to upset and destroy old standards, force old customs into discard, change laws and traditions that have long been accepted. Change. . . ."

The sheriff pushed his way through the crowd. "Who are you?" he demanded. "What's your business?"

The little stranger looked at him with placid eyes. "I am the inventor of the barbed wire fence," he replied.

25

"It is beginning to be seen," said a Government report in 1871, "that our fence laws are inequitable in a greater degree than is required by the principle of yielding something of personal right, when necessary, for the general good. When a score of young farmers go west, with strong hands and little cash, but a munificent promise to each of a homestead worth $200 now, and $2,000 in the future, for less than $20 in land office fees, they often find that $1,000 will be required to fence scantily each farm, with little benefit to themselves, but mainly for mutual protection against a single stock grower, rich in cattle, and becoming richer by feeding them without cost on the unpurchased prairie. This little community of twenty families cannot see the justice of the requirement which compels the expenditure of $20,000 to protect their crops from injury from the nomadic cattle of their unsettled neighbor, which may not be worth $10,000 altogether."

The hopes, aspirations and hard work of more homesteaders were crushed and destroyed by range cattle than by any other cause. This did not occur only from cattle wandering of their own free will onto settlers' lands. Cattlemen took pleasure in driving herds through cultivated fields and pastures, leaving them cut into dust. Stockmen's associations publicly took the position that every man should be required to protect his own property.

It was a problem that began with the arrival in the north of the first trail herds from Texas, that is, from the creation of the Cattle Kingdom, and that became more acute with the passage of each year. Few, if any, plains homesteaders could afford to fence their land. Posts or rails could be obtained only at prohibitive costs from distant timbered regions. Brush and thickets, even if they could be grown, afforded little protection against wild range cattle. Prairie farms were dotted with the graves of settlers who attempted to defend their property by shooting stock, and not infrequently cowboys; the violence brought only tragedy.

Nothing, except the advent of the railroads, brought such drastic changes to both the surface of the Cattle Kingdom and the life within it as the barbed wire fence.

Barbed wire was invented in 1874. It was expensive, $20 a hundred pounds. Development of new processes and production machines steadily lowered the price. Within six years it was selling at $10, in 1890 at $3.45, and in 1897 at $1.80. Purchases in carload lots could be made at much lower figures.

Use of barbed wire spread with phenominal rapidity: 10,000 pounds in 1874; 600,000 in 1875; 2,840,000 in 1876; 12,863,000 in 1877; 26,655,000 in 1878; 50,377,000 in 1879 and

80,500,000 in 1880. Three years later one factory in Illinois was producing more than six hundred miles of fencing every ten hours.

Armed with a protective weapon they could afford, farmers swarmed onto the western plains. Drovers soon found their way blocked by an impassable tangle of dangerous wire. The trails to the north were forced westward, into the higher and drier shortgrass country. Even there the menace spread like a contagious disease. Homesteaders cut up the range, often using a common fence to enclose a dozen or more claims. They erected fences along streams and around waterholes, in some cases isolating whole valleys.

The Cattle Barons found themselves faced with a powerful enemy of not only their business but their way of life. They failed at first to see any possible advantage to themselves in the barbed wire—perhaps they were too stubborn to admit there could be an advantage—and they fought it in the manner in which they were most proficient—violent retaliation.

A new kind of outlawry appeared in the Cattle Kingdom, a new weapon was added to the customary six-gun, rifle and rope—the wire cutter.

Newspapers began to print stories about the wire-cutting war in the West. A Chicago paper told how cattlemen had cut more than five hundred miles of barbed wire fencing in one county. After making an investigation, a law enforcement officer, whose sympathies obviously were with the settlers, reported that the cattlemen in his area were "thieves as well as fence cutters." He told how farmers "have had their fence cut from around their little horse pasture . . . and around their cultivated lands. . . . Small pastures that would not support but milk cows and work horses for a very small farm have been cut time and again until the owners have not the means to put up the wire any more and now all pastures are down and this is called the free range country. . . . The fence cutters themselves have told me that while a man was putting up his fence one day in a hollow a crowd of wire cutters was cutting it behind him in another hollow back over a hill. They delight in telling all such things and most of it is true also. The good citizens hold the wire-cutters in dread for they know they would not hesitate a moment to murder them."

Reports of this type were duplicated countless times throughout the Cattle Kingdom. The fears of the homesteaders were fully justified. Murders occurred with increasing frequency.

The threat barbed wire made to their suzerainty and their control of the grass was the basis of the Cattle Barons' hatred of it, but in public they presented other reasons in justification of their violent reaction to it. "The first thing that especially aroused the indignation of the stockmen relative to barbed wire," wrote one of them, "was the terrible destruction to stock caused by being torn first on the wire, and the screwworm doing the rest—this was especially the case with horses. When the first barbed wire fences were made, the cattle, never having had experience with it, would run full tilt right into it, and many of them got badly hurt. Some men would come into a range, where the stock had regular rounds and beaten ways, and fence up several hundred acres right across the range and thus endanger thousands of cattle and horses. After the first three years of wire fences, I have seen horses and cattle that you could hardly drive between two posts, and if there was a line of posts (without wire on them) running across the prairie, I have seen a bunch of range horses follow the line out to the end and then turn."

The range stock soon came to look upon barbed wire as

they would a grass fire, a thing to be avoided, if possible, and never to be challenged. The cattlemen took an opposite view, yet reasoning made apparent the futility of a direct attack. The production of barbed wire could not be halted any more than the homestead laws could be expunged from the books, and a wire cutter was a feeble tool with which to engage such formidable antagonists. Moreover, newspapers were continuing their crusade against wire cutters; the public was becoming aroused; alert politicians, and even some conscientious Federal authorities, were talking of taking steps to halt the outlawry. Several States passed laws making wire cutting a felony.

The cattlemen did not stop their attack, but they began to adopt new tactics. They bought barbed wire by the carload, by the train load, and they sent out large crews to build fences. They fenced the public domain. They posted guards and signs warning trespassers against entering the vast areas they claimed under the old range rights, rights that had no more legality than the hundreds of miles of wire they strung throughout the Cattle Kingdom.

They did not enclose only their ranges. They enclosed homesteaders. A settler suddenly would discover that he was surrounded by a barbed wire fence that had no gates. His only means of egress from his own land was a wire cutter, and he well understood there was no quicker way to bring disaster down upon his own head than to use one. The fence around him was an unmistakable warning to leave the country. Hundreds of settlers, facing such a dilemma, abandoned their claims.

Quickly cattlemen arranged with "dummies" to file on the deserted homesteads. Not infrequently house guests from the East were persuaded to take out a homestead as a favor to their host. Invariably the guests found papers prepared for them. All that was needed was a bona fide name and address. Hundreds of easterners went home from a trip to the wild west during the eighties and nineties laughingly boasting that they had become ranchers and announcing that their land was being cared for by their old friend, the Cattle Baron. They had not committed a Federal crime, at least they hadn't meant to, for the whole thing was done in fun, just a joke.

Some Panhandle cattlemen built a wire fence from the Indian Territory to New Mexico. In Colorado, Wyoming, Montana, it was not uncommon to find cattlemen with half a million acres under fence, and some companies had put wire around a million acres. Public roads were barricaded, settlements were surrounded, and the barbed strands made hundreds of miles of rivers and creeks private property. Not only the public domain was fenced, but also railroad lands, millions of acres of them. A United States Senator from Wyoming had four hundred thousand acres of Federal lands under his fences, and other members of the Congress from the West had put their wire illegally around enormous areas of the public domain. In some regions, "drift" fences reached for miles across the range, isolating entire watersheds.

The tide of protests rose until it was washing the White House steps and the bastions of Capitol Hill. The Government at last saw the necessity of building dikes to hold it back. The main bulwark erected came in the form of a Presidential order for the fences to come down. The Cattle Barons responded with a counter proposal. Into the congressional hopper went legislation proposing a kind of "lend-lease" system.

Under this scheme, for example, a group of cattlemen with adjoining ranges, perhaps as many as six million acres which they had fenced, would organize what they termed a "land district," to which they would be awarded exclusive grazing rights. They would contend that all good homesteads in the "land district" had been taken, and the balance was unsuitable for farming, that is, it was semi-arid land on which nothing could be grown but buffalo grass. They made no offer to pay for the use of this vast area of the public domain. Nothing would accrue to the Federal Treasury from the bill.

It was not an easy job, but the cattlemen's lobby and their confederates in Congress, got the "lend-lease" act passed. When the news of their success was flashed westward by telegraph, noisy celebrations were held in cowtown bistros. The headaches were no sooner gone, however, than gloom descended. The bill had been vetoed.

The fences, said a White House statement, had to come down. Moreover, to make sure that they did come down, and forthwith, a famous ex-Confederate cavalry raider had been assigned to the task.

Now it was the old raider and his men who used wire cutters, and used them legally. Not only did they sweep through the Cattle Kingdom demolishing fences on public lands, but they arrested cattlemen who had erected them. The fines inflicted were nominal, but the lesson was bitter. No charges were placed against the Senator from Wyoming and other Cattle Barons in Congress, of course. In addition to the loss of some wire, they suffered only a slight stain on their reputations, and that, considering its nature, instead of injuring them increased their prestige among their influential supporters in their respective home districts.

26

One wonders what course the history of the Cattle Barons might have taken, had not nature interfered in 1885 and 1886.

It is not inconceivable that the Federal Government might have been forced to intervene to halt a civil war between cattlemen and the rapidly growing number of settlers, two bitter enemies flexing their muscles and on the verge of a conflict that would have tinged the streams of the Cattle Kingdom with blood. As it turned out, a terrible conflict of this kind was prevented by weather so unusual and so severe that each faction thought less of fighting than of finding a means of staying alive.

Only a few widely separated areas in 1885 had a summer that was abnormally dry. The autumn, from northern Texas to Montana, was generally pleasant. Cowboys rode on the fall roundup through clear brisk days and mild starry nights. Even though prices were weak, most cattlemen were optimistic. Always before, the market had recovered from slumps.

The fine weather continued until late fall, and many cattlemen held back shipments, anticipating rising prices. December had come before any appreciable amount of snow fell. Then storms were brief, and bright sun and strong winds helped to keep the grass open. Generally, stock was holding both strength and beef.

As the new year began, light rains fell throughout most of the high plains. Gradually the downfalls turned to sleet. The Rocky Mountains were enveloped in an ominous dark curtain. As the thermometer continued to drop, the ground froze. Then down from Canada came howling gales, and on them rode one of the worst blizzards ever known in the Cattle Kingdom.

For days the storm raged. White hands of death reached far into Texas. For the first time in the memory of the oldest cowboys, range cattle, searching desperately for shelter as well as grass, invaded towns. The streets of such cattle country centers as Miles City, Cheyenne, Great Falls and Dodge City were filled with freezing starving animals. They dropped dead at the doors of stores, saloons, homes.

In their customary manner, the cattle drifted southward, their rumps to the storm. Some animals traveled as much as two and three hundred miles, only to die in arroyos and canyons or in the ice of rivers. Some streams were bridged by carcasses. The drift fences took the lives of thousands; the cattle piled up against them and froze to death. In places the crush became so great that fences were torn down for miles, and animals walked on over ice-hard bodies. It was estimated that more than ten thousand head were trapped and died along one drift fence in southern Kansas and the Texas Panhandle. A Nebraska company lost 100,000 head, and there were many losses of forty and fifty per cent.

In every State of the Cattle Kingdom, the human toll also was heavy. Families of settlers were found frozen to death in their cabins. Freighters died with their teams. The loss of life was variously estimated between three and four hundred persons, but it was probably much greater. Men vanished, and whether they had escaped or perished was never learned. For a number of years skeletons were found and believed to be casualties of the storm.

Before the great blizzard subsided in February, 1886, thermometer readings of fifty degrees below zero were commonplace, and there were several places in which the mercury sank to sixty below.

Some Cattle Barons, especially those who had borrowed heavily to expand, lost their holdings and went out of business. The majority, while badly hurt, found reasons to be hopeful. The grass was still there. It would come back. It always had. Nothing could kill the grass. There was money to be had for rebuilding, although bankers took advantage of the situation by boosting interest rates. The storm had been the worst ever known, but that might well be a good sign in itself. It was unlikely, they reasoned, that another anywhere near as severe would come again for years, if ever.

The snow was gone in March; the days grew warm and balmy; the spring wind had the feel of summer. The new grass started under favorable conditions, but needed rains failed to come. Drying prematurely, the grass remained short. An unusual number of prairie fires filled the days with smoke haze and lighted the nights with eerie red glares.

By midsummer, skies were like hot metal. Cottonwood leaves hung in yellow dryness, stirred only by scorching airs. When the wind did blow, it was a burning dehydrated breath that baked men's throats and made them fear suffocation. The calf crop had been small, another result of the previous winter's ravages. Now cowboys, their own bodies burned by heat and ashen dust, helplessly watched weak emaciated calves fall and die, under the sides of their mothers.

A vast land, in most summers an endless sea of rich amber grass, was becoming an uninhabitable desert. The little streams were vanishing, leaving in their places ugly scars, cracked and white where alkali remained after the last drop of water had been absorbed. The large streams were hardly more than trickles.

By early autumn, the tree leaves, having long before given up the fight to live, had curled and fallen, and bare limbs were raised as if in supplication to the hot azure sky. In high countries pine needles had turned red, cones were wizened and impotent, cedars were dying like bent and wrinkled old women.

The wild game had fled from natural haunts. There were no birds, except a few vultures and buzzards, for the waterholes were seared alkaline depressions and seeds and insects had been destroyed. These were signs which made old Indians shake their heads in warning.

First in the south, where the drought was worst, and then in the north, cattlemen attempted to get their herds to railroads. Some moved them into Canada, where the plains had suffered less damage, but most of them shipped their cattle to Omaha and Kansas City, St. Louis and Chicago. The bottom fell out of the market, which was glutted with poor-grade animals.

The fall was a procession of clear burning days. Like an immense ball of fire the sun rose, moved in a flaming path over the stricken earth, and dropped in a coppery conflagration behind deep purple mountains. The stars welled up in a dense brilliant silvery fog. There was no relief from the punishment, no change or interruption in a disastrous scheme of things. Orange heat waves rolled over the ranges. It was weather out of all reason, a phenomenon born of a conspiracy of the elements. In October it was as hot as midsummer, as if the cycle of seasons had been disrupted by some supernatural force.

So the second act of the great tragedy closed.

When the curtain rose again, completely different scenery was revealed. Seldom did deep snow come to the Cattle Kingdom before December, but now heavy snows fell in some sections in October, and throughout the West, storms and gales raged during November. The cattle, poor and weakened by the long drought, pawed desperately through the heavy white blanket for a few blades of grass.

The storms continued, following quickly one upon another. If none of them equaled the great blizzard of the previous year, their constancy had a devastating effect. In December violent winds came, and the mercury dropped.

Now, for the first time, cattlemen saw birds whose natural habitat was the Arctic.

The first weeks of 1887 found cattle losses greater than those of the previous year. The toll in human lives surpassed the previous record. Wolves ate the bodies, both those of human beings and cattle.

Long lines of animals staggered through the snow, instinctively drifting in search of a haven. Many of them were covered with frozen blood, their legs raw from ice cuts and their hooves torn off in mad attempts to paw through the solid sheath over the poor grass. Some which miraculously survived had ragged patches of hide hanging where wolves had eaten on them, but with so much meat available had not troubled to kill them.

On January 9, snow fell in Montana, an inch an hour, for sixteen hours and the mercury hovered at twenty below zero. In some sections of the Cattle Kingdom, the thermometer did not register above forty below for two weeks. Suddenly, late in January, a chinook came. Within a few hours the ranges were seas of slush, the streams roaring torrents. It was a respite that saved the lives of thousands of cattle.

Then as suddenly as if they had gained their second wind, the elements resumed their assault. The worst storm of the winter swept in from the northwest, and it was late in March before the flinty ice that covered the ranges began to melt in a normal spring thaw.

It was said that a man could walk from the Black Hills across the Powder River country to the Big Horn Mountains without stepping off dead cattle. If this was an exaggeration, the estimates of ninety per cent loss reported by many companies were not.

Blizzard, drought, blizzard, and then normal weather,

strong green grass, balmy days, bright new leaves—normal, that is, except for the smell of rotting carcasses, which could not be escaped. How many cattle were lost, no one knew. Reports of investigators ran between ten and twelve million.

From coast to coast, newspapers and agricultural journals cried that the range cattle business itself was dead. Angrily one western paper declared: "A man who turns out a lot of cattle on a barren plain without making provision for feeding them will not only suffer a financial loss but also the loss of the respect of the community in which he lives."

The editorial writers were wrong. The range cattle industry was badly crippled, but it was far from dead. There was money in the nation's banks, and there were cattle in south Texas, in every eastern and southern State, in California and Oregon and Washington, that could be purchased and used for restocking the high grass plains east of the big mountains. Methods would be changed. Alfalfa and timothy hay would be grown in immense irrigated fields or purchased in temperate zones and held in reserve in the West. Shelters would be built for prize bulls. Other measures for protecting animals would be taken.

The Cattle Kingdom had almost succumbed to the most vicious attack in its history, but in the spring and summer of 1887, the Cattle Barons were beginning their rebuilding. Indeed, they were making greater plans than they had ever done. The range cattle business, from their viewpoint, was on the road to certain recovery. They had no more thought of surrendering the public domain than they had of becoming hoemen in little patches of corn and alfalfa.

As if there had been no interruption, the association renewed its war on settlers. Cattle detectives again rode the ranges, burning cabins, committing murders. Similar tactics were used against sheepmen, who had begun to infiltrate many sections—a war within a war. Herders were ambushed, and the sheep either killed or left to the coyotes and wolves to finish off. But the main fight was against the settlers, and it was waged with unprecedented viciousness, without mercy or quarter being shown on any front.

The Cattle Kingdom was far from being destroyed.

27

The Grand Finale of that great western opera, *The Rise and Fall of the Cattle Barons*, was staged in Wyoming, a most appropriate locale, five years after the disastrous blizzards. The producer was the association. Leading roles were played by distinguished members, among them the State governor, the Board of Livestock commissioners, various other State officers, and at least two United States senators.

The script was thoughtfully prepared. Its theme was a concentrated campaign against rustlers—a pseudonym for settler, homesteader and small rancher. Instead of sneak attacks, ambushes and isolated hangings, the action was carried on by a powerful armed force. The plan called for it to sweep through the country in swift surprise maneuvers, ruthlessly shooting down hundreds of residents and destroying their property. The initial target would be a county in which homesteaders had won control of the local government, ousted the association's sheriff, and supplanted him with a man whose conception of justice was rigid and unbiased enforcement of the law. Incidentally, he was on a list of seventy persons especially marked for death by the association's plotters.

At one period the association could boast of a membership of nearly four hundred cattlemen operating in Wyoming, northern Colorado, western Nebraska, southern Montana and the Black Hills region of Dakota. The disasters of 1886–1887 had brought ruin to a number of them. Some of the biggest outfits financed by eastern and European capital had collapsed. In 1892, only a hard core of a hundred Cattle Barons remained, some of their companies owned or controlled by foreign money. Most of them, however, were supported by western and midwestern finances, or owned by men who had weathered the storms.

Ranges were no longer overcrowded, as they had been before the big killings and with normal weather and the cessation of overgrazing the grass where it was not destroyed by plows or sheep, had once again become plentiful.

The work of rebuilding had been slow and expensive but steady, and by 1892, the hundred members of the association had their brands on more than three million cattle. They were determined, relentless men, and if their numbers were smaller than in the past, they had lost none of their power. The association still controlled the State government.

The thoroughness with which the association's plan for its campaign was formulated was admirable. A "war chest" of $100,000 was pledged. The terms *press agent* or *public relations counselor* had not come into general usage, but the association engaged a *literary bureau* to win the approval of the nation for the wanton deeds it intended to commit. A flood of stories went out to newspapers and magazines from coast to coast. They pictured Wyoming as being overrun with rustlers and outlaws who were not only stealing countless thousands of cattle each year but were committing the most dastardly and heinous crimes upon honest farmers and ranchers. Reputable citizens were not safe in their own homes. Cattlemen were facing ruin because of the depredations carried on against them. Law enforcement agencies were unable to cope with the situation. Local juries composed of citizens who were themselves thieves refused to convict arrested rustlers. The cattlemen were forced to defend their lives and their property as best they could, but they were in danger of losing the struggle to superior numbers.

Under Wyoming law, judges, sheriffs or mayors could call out a company of the State militia in their respective jurisdictions in case of emergency. This might well have posed a danger to the war plans of the association and its outlaws. The association got the law changed. The Legislature obediently revised the statute, placing power to use the militia solely in the hands of the governor. This action was completed only a short time before the war was scheduled to start.

The governor made certain of the hobbles on the militia with a directive, issued through its commander. It said that militia officers "shall obey only such orders to assemble their commands as may be received from these headquarters, to assist the civil authorities in the preservation or enforcement of the laws of the State of Wyoming."*

An association cattle detective who had been indicted for murder but never tried was sent to Texas to recruit gunmen. They were to be brought north at no cost to themselves, furnished all food, lodging and weapons during the campaign, paid wages of $5 a day, a bonus of $50 for every settler—

* After the war had started, the governor informed newspapers that the militia "matter has not been brought to my attention officially," that he had heard of it only "through newspaper reports." These, he added with a smile, were somewhat conflicting. Therefore, not until he had "learned the facts" would he take "such steps as I may deem necessary."

rather, rustler—they killed and furnished with a $3,000 insurance policy. Other detectives were sent on similar recruiting missions to Nebraska, Montana and Dakota, but these were unfruitful. The Texas emissary, however, met with some success, and he returned to Cheyenne with twenty-six deadly men, among them several former United States marshals and peace officers.

The Texans had been assured that they would be joined in Wyoming by more than three hundred northern gunmen, but for various reasons this large force failed to materialize. Numerous cattlemen scheduled to go suddenly found they had other engagements. Several of them selected Denver, and made sure they were seen there by newspapermen. One of these dropouts was an ex-Wyoming governor in whose business office a large part of the war had been planned. When news that it had begun came over the wires, he told Denver reporters that the "sympathies of nine-tenths of the people of Wyoming are with the cattle owners. . . . I am willing to give all the assistance possible to any body of men which will attempt to exterminate the rustlers. The latter have terrorized whole communities for years and practically control the actions of officials in several counties of the State. . . . The courts have been appealed to time after time, in vain. . . . It is simply a battle for existence on the part of the cattle owners. . . . They must maintain their positions with rifles or let the robbers have full sway."

If the reporters had been able to reverse every one of these statements, they would have been close to the truth.

Another leading association member who had aided in financing and preparing the invasion, but who lost his nerve when it came to participating in it, took a slightly different view in Denver, declaring that he simply did not believe the reports about the war. "I think that all these dispatches are inspired by rustlers and their sympathizers," he said. "There are newspapers of Wyoming which have always advocated the cause of the thieves. . . . The rustlers have charge of the wires and I am waiting now for the time when our men can get hold of them." Then, as if realizing that he had not adhered to the propaganda line as decreed by the association, he added quickly that the cattlemen "were fighting for life, home and property, and I want to predict that the rustlers will be wiped out."

When the "Regulators," as the association elected to call its invaders, started north from Caspar on horses on a gray April day in 1892, the professional killers from Texas had been joined by only two score cattlemen, foremen and detectives. Two settlers were soon killed, but others escaped and sped north to alert authorities in Buffalo. Crowds of armed farmers and homesteaders gathered and were organized to repel the invaders. Storekeepers threw open their doors so that the defenders could help themselves to weapons, ammunition, food, blankets, medicines and other supplies. A small army of settlers set out southward, with the sheriff whom the association had marked for death in the lead.

Apprised of the approach of this rather formidable force, the Regulators took refuge in a ranch building, twenty-five miles south of Buffalo.

The war ended there.

When word that the invasion had failed and the Regulators were trapped reached Cheyenne, Governor A. W. Barber at once telegraphed President Benjamin Harrison a completely untruthful report, and pleaded for Federal assistance. The cattlemen had to be saved from a mob that was threatening them. "An insurrection exists," the governor told the President. "The legislature is not in session and cannot be convened in time to afford any relief. . . . Open hostilities exist and large bodies of armed men are engaged in battle. A company of militia is located at the city of Buffalo, near the scene of action, but its continued presence in that city [The population of Buffalo was one thousand men, women and children, and many of the men were with the posse attacking the Regulators.] is absolutely required for the purpose of protecting life and property therein. The scene of action is 125 miles from the nearest railroad point, from which other portions of the state militia could be sent. No relief can be afforded by state militia, and civil authorities are wholly unable to afford any relief whatever. United States troops are located at Fort McKinney, which is thirteen miles from the scene of action. . . . I apply to you on behalf of the State of Wyoming to direct the United States troops at Fort McKinney to assist in suppressing the insurrection. The lives of a large number of persons are in imminent danger."

Telegrams of a similar vein were sent by the governor to Wyoming's two senators, who were cattlemen. Fully understanding that the governor's communications were wholly dishonest and deceptive, they hurried to the White House. It was late at night when they got the President out of bed. The Chief Executive summoned the Secretary of War. Orders went out to the commander at Fort McKinney. At sunrise, three troops of cavalry were en route to rescue the besieged cattlemen and their outlaw cohorts.

The truth soon began to emerge through the pages of the nation's newspapers. It was made clear that there was no more rustling in Wyoming than in any other western State. Efficient law enforcement officers could easily stop it from increasing. All the cattle stolen in a year in Wyoming could have been held in a medium sized corral. There was no insurrection. Settlers had gathered to defend their lives against hired gunmen and cattlemen bent on destroying them.

The association was fully exposed, but it ignored the condemnation and set about exonerating the half hundred men who had taken part in the abortive campaign. That it had lost none of its influence and power was soon demonstrated.

Charged with murder and arson, the rescued Regulators were held prisoner less than a week. The governor then arranged to have them transferred to Fort Russell near Cheyenne. It was announced that they would be quartered there sixty days under military guard, after which they would be tried. If this order was issued to the commandant at Fort Russell, it was not obeyed. The Regulators were soon enjoying complete freedom, the cattlemen in their own homes, the Texas killers in the saloons and brothels of Cheyenne. The accused men did not hesitate to laugh about their troubles and to boast in public that they soon would be going back in force to finish the job they had started.

Meanwhile, the association was busy clearing the legal roads. Judges were given their instructions. Witnesses scheduled to appear against the Regulators were kidnapped and with the help of United States marshals, presumably acting on orders from Washington, taken to distant parts of the United States. If they agreed not to return, they were freed. If they were stubborn, they were charged with selling liquor to Indians, a Federal offense, and sent to jail. Other witnesses were intimidated into vanishing of their own accord.

These were not thought to be safeguards enough. In the interest of gaining public sympathy, as well as to open a gate for another plan it wanted to carry out, the association arranged to sacrifice one of its own.

A young cattleman who had helped to kidnap two witnesses to the killings and burnings of the Regulators had been advised to flee the country. He left for a time, then returned and took a job as manager of a ranch owned by an association member. The association thereupon had him appointed a Deputy United States Marshal and arranged to have him sent to the northern part of Wyoming to serve some legal papers. There he was ambushed. His body, a bullet hole in the back, was left in a culvert not far from Buffalo.

The murder was cited as proof that the country was still dominated by rustlers. Twenty of the largest cattle companies signed a petition calling upon the governor to place the entire area of north central Wyoming under martial law.

Their plea made good reading in the newspapers. It said that cattle thieves "have grown so bold . . . that they have notified persons who differ with them to leave the country, and have in many instances enforced their threats by acts of violence, and they further threaten to assassinate those who have fled if they return."

If one did not know that the petitioners were speaking of settlers, one might think they were identifying themselves.

"There now exists in that country," the petition continued, "an organized plan of driving the stockmen out, so that their property may become common property for the thieves; cattle are being wantonly and openly slaughtered in that section by the thieves. . . . The ranches and homes of the owners in that vicinity [that is, the association members] have many of them been plundered, and the personal effects and furniture there stolen or destroyed. . . . Even women and children at these ranches have received these threats of violence, and have been compelled to seek places of safety. Letters in the United States mails have been opened by thieves. . . .

"No effort of any kind whatever on behalf of the civil authorities in that vicinity is being made to suppress this stealing, or any of the acts of violence and intimidation, and in many instances the civil authorities are . . . working with the thieves and under their influence.

". . . there exists in the district named an armed combination to prevent the administration of law and justice . . . the country is in a feverish state of excitement and under a complete reign of terror. . . .

"We therefore, pray your excellency will place the district under martial law. . . ."

Carrying out the prearranged plan, the governor sent the petition to Wyoming's senators, and they waved it in the face of the President.

Action quickly followed. Newspapers carried a bulletin stating that six troops of Federal cavalry had been sent to northern Wyoming. Martial law was not declared, but Hotchkiss guns frowned from strategic positions in the sagebrush, and soldiers patrolled the ranges, frightening the cattle more than the settlers, who wanted nothing so much as peace.

Authorizing the maneuvers of the troops was a Presidential proclamation, which had been prepared by the Secretary of State, as if northern Wyoming were a foreign country. The proclamation commanded "all persons engaged in such resistance to the laws and processes of the courts of the United States to cease such opposition and resistance and to disperse and retire peaceably to their respective abodes. . . ."

This was not part of a comic opera. It was a deadly serious, diabolical plot in which the President and United States senators were participants. Under any possible construction of justice, the proclamation would have been directed to the members of the Wyoming association, not to the homesteaders and storekeepers who had fought for years to get the United States Government to enforce Federal laws. It was the settlers who needed protection, not the Cattle Barons, yet the President cooperated in casting a blanket indictment over the little people fighting to survive with the words:

"Whereas, By reasons of unlawful obstructions and assemblages of persons it has become impracticable, in my judgment, to enforce by the ordinary course of judicial proceedings the laws of the United States within the state and district of Wyoming, the United States marshal, after repeated efforts, being unable by his ordinary deputies, or by any civil posse which he is able to obtain, to execute the processes of the United States courts. . . ."

This was not only untrue, it was ridiculous. The association, the governor and the Wyoming senators had done their job well. Fortunately, in the long run it availed them nothing.

The accused Regulators were found not guilty by dishonest judges in farcical proceedings, but they did not return to resume their war on the settlers.

The war was over. The powers of the association grew steadily weaker as settlers continued to pour into the State. New administrations, men with different philosophies and devoid of a king complex, took over the political helm and created a diversified economy. By the turn of the century, the Cattle Kingdom was history.

Yet, bitterness and hatred did not die, but endured for years. As a youth I worked on a cattle ranch owned by an elderly man who had been a Regulator. As he was riding along the Buffalo road one afternoon, near the scene of murders in which he had participated, he was shot at and narrowly escaped death. The sheriff expressed the opinion that the assassin was an old homesteader who had suffered at the hands of the association twenty-five years before.

"Memories make some of these old boys steam under the collar, now and then," he said, and advised my employer not to ride alone. The advice was heeded.

28

The meeting of the association which was held early in 1892, at which the final plan for the war on the homesteaders had been completed, had taken place behind closed doors. No minutes had been kept, no spoken words had been recorded, indeed, nothing had been written on paper. The members had departed without leaving a shred of evidence to show that they intended to murder, pillage and burn.

The meeting held by the association in the spring a year later was open to the public. The words spoken by the association president revealed clearly that no feeling of guilt existed, that regrets were not colored by remorse.

The president said:

"Not content with the imposition of financial and climatic troubles another burden had to be added to our lot. After a long period of forebearance and patience from range depredations, both petty and wholesale, the trouble culminated a year ago and the so-called invasion took place, which ended unfortunately and gave rise to an almost interminable amount of bad blood, politically and socially.

"While the invasion is now consigned to history, it developed during its progress last spring and the long, weary summer months which followed a spirit of admiration from all classes of the men—the very flower of Wyoming's citizens—who had taken part in the expedition. Under the most trying circumstances they stood shoulder to shoulder, scarce a murmur escaping them. Gentlemen, I am not here to defend these parties. Technically, legally, they did wrong, but I consider it no mean privilege to stand in this prominent position today and say that I count every one of them a friend. Notwithstanding their errors of judgment, we respect them for their manliness, for the supreme courage under the adverse fire of calumny and the usual kicking a man gets when he is down. *There will be a day of retribution, and the traitors in the camp and in the field will be winnowed like wheat from the chaff.*"

These were the words of the leader of the cattlemen, the head of the association which had operated a syndicate for murder on the high plains of Wyoming. Later in his memoirs, he would write of the unconscionable war against the settlers: "Great reforms are brought about by revolutionary methods. The Boston Tea parties, the victories of Washington, were protests flung world-wide against a Teutonic dictator."

Until the year 1902, the association fought desperately and with every corruptive weapon it possessed to keep the fences of its members on the range, the public domain. In that year the last of the illegal barbed wire came down.

The Cattle Kingdom was gone.

Notes

The Red and the White

[1] Schellie; Colyer.
[2] Terrell (1966).
[3] Hoig.
[4] Kroeber; Terrell (1971).
[5] Young.
[6] Young; Underhill; Goodwin; Terrell (1970, 1972).
[7] Cohen; Jackson.
[8] *U.S. Statutes at Large* (Peters, preface, Vol. 7) in Jackson; McNickle; Cohen.
[9] "Institutes of International Law" (Gardner) in Jackson; McNickle; Cohen.
[10] American Bar (Walker) in Jackson; McNickle; Cohen.
[11] U.S. Supreme Court, *Johnson's and Graham's Lease vs. McIntosh.*
[12] U.S. Supreme Court, *Worcester vs. Georgia.*
[13] Annual message to Congress, 1828.
[14] Sept. 22, 1783; Thomas.
[15] *U.S. vs. Clark* (9 Peters).
[16] Act of March 26, 1804, dividing Territory of Louisiana acquired from France into two American political subdivisions.
[17] McNickle; Debo.
[18] U.S. Supreme Court, *Cherokee Nation vs. Georgia;* Billington; Thomas; Debo; McNickle.
[19] U.S. Supreme Court, *Worcester vs. Georgia*, and *Cherokee Na-*

tion vs. Georgia, Johnson's and Graham's Lease vs. McIntosh; Jackson; Billington; Thomas; Debo.

[20] Indian Bureau Annual Report, 1838.

[21] *Ibid.*

[22] Tocqueville.

[23] Terrell (1970).

[24] Hodge; Royce; Cohen; Keppler.

[25] Quoted in Jackson.

[26] Cohen.

[27] Jackson.

[28] Chittenden and Richardson; Terrell (1964).

[29] Ponca Treaty with U.S. of 1825.

[30] Indian Bureau Annual Reports, 1856, 1857.

[31] Indian Bureau Annual Report, 1876.

[32] Foreman; *Indian Magazine of History*, Vols. 18 and 21.

[33] *Ibid.*

[34] Foreman quoting Terre Haute *Courier*.

[35] Indian Bureau Annual Report, 1871.

[36] Interior Department Annual Report, 1862.

[37] Manypenny.

[38] *Ibid.*

The Fur Trade

[1] As the so-called Mountain Men opened most of the western United States, the fur trade is inseparably linked to western exploration. However, these notes have to do with only two phases of the early fur trade, namely, its relations with Indians and its economics.

[2] Chittenden.

[3] Richardson.

[4] Morse; Phillips; Chittenden; Terrell (1963); Myers; Peake.

[5] Chittenden.

[6] Phillips.

[7] Plan of Secretary of War Calhoun.

[8] Senator Benton (Exec. Doc. 39 supra); Porter.

[9] Morse.

[10] June, 1821; Porter.

[11] President Monroe to former President Madison, 1821; Porter.

[12] Col. J. Snelling to Secretary of War Barbour, Aug. 23, 1825.

[13] Phillips.

[14] *Ibid.*

[15] Chittenden and Richardson; Terrell (1964).

[16] *Ibid.*

[17] Governor Cass of Michigan.

[18] Ramsay Crooks to John Jacob Astor in Porter; Terrell (1963).

[19] *U.S. Senate Doc. 90, 22nd Cong., 1st Sess.*

[20] Major Willoughby Morgan, Prairie du Chien.

[21] *Senate Doc. 60* supra.

[22] Supt. of Indian Affairs Thomas L. McKenney to Secretary of War, Feb., 1826.

[23] *Senate Doc. 90* supra.

[24] William B. Astor, 1832.

[25] Hudson's Bay Company, 1832.

[26] John Jacob Astor to Ramsay Crooks, 1832; Porter; Terrell (1963).

[27] Kenneth McKenzie, Fort Union Partner, to Ramsay Crooks, 1832; Porter; Terrell (1963).

[28] Correspondence of American Fur Company, Western Dept., Missouri Historical Society, Detroit Public Library.

[29] *Senate Doc. 60* supra.

[30] *Senate Doc. 90* supra.

[31] *Ibid.*

[32] Thomas Forsythe to Secretary of War Cass; Myers.

[33] George Boyd to Indian Bureau, 1820.

[34] Chittenden.

[35] Porter.

[36] Myers.

[37] Phillips.

[38] Nathaniel Wyeth.

[39] Chittenden.

[40] William H. Ashley; Morgan.

[41] *Ibid.*

[42] E. Prevost.
[43] Terrell (1964).

The Cattle Barons

Instead of using superscript numerals to indicate sources, I think it is sufficient in the case of "The Cattle Barons" to refer the reader directly to the works cited in the Selected Bibliography, to some of which I have appended notes. These volumes, on which I have drawn heavily, provide comprehensive accounts of the cattle business on the western public domain. Anyone desirous of obtaining information in greater detail on this subject is advised to consult the bibliographies of these books, some of which are extensive.

Selected Bibliography

The Red and the White

Reports of Government departments and Congressional committees are by far the most valuable sources of the history of the tragic relations between Americans and Indians. No more damning evidence of the Federal Government's corruption and criminal negligence exists. The most informative reports are those of the Indian Bureau, issued each year between 1824 and 1900. While some of them are deceptive and untruthful, at least in part, the majority are honest and amazingly frank and revealing. Between 1824 and 1848, these reports were issued through the War Department, which in that period had jurisdiction over Indian affairs.

IMPORTANT GOVERNMENT DOCUMENTS:

American State Papers, Class II, Indian Affairs, Vols. 1 to 7.

House of Representatives:

Exec. Doc. No. 267, 48th Cong., 2nd Sess.; *Exec. Doc. No. 1*, 38th Cong., 2nd Sess.; *Exec. Doc., No. 1*, 39th Cong., 1st Sess.; *Exec. Doc. No. 38*, 35th Cong., 1st Sess.; *Report No. 271*, 27th Cong., 3rd Sess.; *Doc. No. 986*, 60th Cong., 1st Sess.

U.S. Senate:

Doc. No. 425, 34th Cong., 1st Sess.; *Misc. Docs.*, 36th Cong., 1st Sess.; *Doc. No. 134*, 49th Cong., 1st Sess.; *Report No. 829*, 51st Cong., 1st Sess.; *Misc. Docs.*, 35th Cong., 2nd Sess.

Report of the Commissioners of Agriculture, 1865–1867.

Bureau of American Ethnology Annual Report No. 46, 1930.

Bureau of American Ethnology Bulletin No. 137, 1946.

Court of Claims of the United States, Sioux vs. United States, Case No. C 53 (17), 1937.

U.S. Dept. of Agriculture, *Census of Agriculture*. 1880.

OTHER WORKS, MOST OF WHICH CONTAIN EXTENSIVE BIBLIOGRAPHIES:

Abel, Annie Heloise, (Editor), *The Official Correspondence of James S. Calhoun While Indian Agent at Santa Fe, and Superintendent of Indian Affairs in New Mexico*. Washington, 1915.

Billington, Ray Allen, *Westward Expansion*. New York, 1949.

Chittenden, Hiram Martin, and Albert Talbot Richardson, *The Life, Letters and Travels of Father Pierre Jean de Smet, S. J.* New York, 1905.

Cohen, Felix S., *Handbook of Indian Law*. Washington, 1945.

Colyer, Vincent, *Peace With the Apaches of Arizona and New Mexico*. Report of the Board of Indian Commissioners, Washington, 1872.

Debo, Angie, *And Still the Waters Run*. Princeton, 1940.

—— *The Road to Disappearance*. Norman, 1941.

Foreman, Grant, *The Last Trek of the Indians*. Chicago, 1946.

Harmon, George D., *Sixty Years of Indian Affairs, 1789–1850*. Chapel Hill, 1931.

Hodge, Frederick W., (Editor), *Handbook of Indians North of Mexico*. Washington, 1907. Reprinted, New York, 1960.

Hoig, Stan, *The Sand Creek Massacre*. Norman, 1961.

Jackson, Helen Hunt, *A Century of Dishonor*. Cambridge, 1885.

Keppler, Charles J., *Indian Laws and Treaties*. Washington, 1903.

Kroeber, A. L., *Handbook of the Indians of California*. Washington, 1925.

McNickle, D'Arcy, *They Came Here First*. New York, 1949.

Malin, James C., *Indian Policy and Westward Expansion*. Topeka, 1921.

Manypenny, George W., *Our Indian Wards*. Cincinnati, 1880.

Moher, Walter H., *Federal Indian Relations*. Philadelphia, 1933.

Morse, Jedediah, *Reports on Indian Affairs*. New Haven, 1822.

Richardson, James D., *Messages and Papers of the Presidents*. Washington, 1896.

Royce, Charles G., *Indian Land Cessions in the United States*. Washington, 1906.

Schellie, Don, *Vast Domain of Blood*. Los Angeles, 1968.

Schoolcraft, Henry R., *Thirty Years with the Indian Tribes*. Philadelphia, 1851.

Sonnichsen, C. L., *The Mescalero Apaches*. Norman, 1958.

Terrell, John Upton, *Black Robe*. New York, 1964.

——— *Faint the Trumpet Sounds*. New York, 1966.

——— *The Navajo*. New York, 1970.

——— *American Indian Almanac*. New York, 1971.

——— *Apache Chronicle*. New York, 1972.

Thomas, Cyrus, *The Indians of North America in Historic Times*. Philadelphia, 1903.

Tocqueville, Alexis de, *Democracy in America*. New York, 1898.

Underhill, Ruth M., *Red Man's Religion*. Chicago, 1965.

Wellman, Paul, *The Indian Wars of the West*. New York, 1947.

Young, Robert W., *The Navajo Yearbook*. Window Rock, Ariz., 1961.

The Fur Trade

AS IS THE CASE WITH THE INDIANS, A NUMBER OF FEDERAL GOVERNMENT DOCUMENTS ARE INVALUABLE AS FUR TRADE SOURCE MATERIAL. SEE THE FOLLOWING:

Report of Coleraine Factory. Bureau of Indian Affairs, 1820; *Reports of Indian Factory Office, 1806–1816*. Bureau of Indian Affairs; *Reports of Committees, Doc. No. 34*, Vol. 1., 2nd Sess., 16th Cong.; *Reports of Committees, Doc. No. 5*, 2nd Sess., 22nd Cong.; *Reports of Committees*, 1st Sess., 24th Cong.

U.S. Senate:

Exec. Doc. No. 67. 20th Cong., 2nd Sess. (Report on fur trade by Senator Thomas H. Benton).; *Exec. Doc. No. 39*. 21st Cong., 1st Sess. (Message from President Jackson); *Doc. No. 60*. 1st Sess., 17th Cong.;

Doc. No. 58. 1st Sess., 19th Cong.; *Doc. No. 90.* 1st Sess., 22nd Cong.; *Doc. No. 1.* 2nd Sess., 35th Cong.; *Exec. Doc. No. 11.* 1st Sess., 35th Cong.; *Doc. No. 10.* 2nd Sess., 17th Cong.

For early background of the fur trade, as well as its history following the acquisition of Louisiana Territory by the United States, see these works:

Bigger, H. P., *The Early Trading Companies of New France.* Toronto, 1901.

Brebner, John Bartlet, *The Explorers of North America.* 1492–1806, London, 1933.

Campbell, Marjorie W., *The North West Company.* New York, 1957.

Champlain, Samuel D., *The Works of Samuel D. Champlain.* Toronto, 1922.

Chittenden, Hiram Martin, *History of the American Fur Trade in the Far West.* New York, 1902.

Johnson, William, *The Papers of Sir William Johnson.* 12 vols., Albany, 1921–1957.

Larpenteur, Charles, *Forty Years a Fur Trader on the Upper Missouri.* New York, 1898.

Leonard, Zenas, *Narrative of Adventures.* Cleveland, 1904.

Morgan, Dale L., *The West of William Henry Ashley.* Denver, 1964.

Myers, Gustavus, *History of the Great American Fortunes.* New York, 1936.

Peake, Ora B., *A History of the Indian Factory System.* Denver, 1954.

Parkman, Francis, *La Salle and the Discovery of the Great West.* Boston, 1879.

Phillips, Paul Chrisler, *The Fur Trade.* Norman, 1961.

Porter, Kenneth Wiggins, *John Jacob Astor, Business Man.* Cambridge, 1931.

Ross, Alexander, *Fur Hunters of the Far West.* London, 1855. Reprinted Norman, 1956.

Ruxton, George Frederick, *Life in the Far West.* Norman, 1951.

Terrell, John Upton, *Furs by Astor.* New York, 1963.

——, *La Salle: The Life and Times of an Explorer.* New York, 1968.

The Cattle Barons

Baber, D. F., *The Longest Rope: The Truth About the Johnson County Cattle War*. Caldwell, Ida., 1940.

Brisbin, James S., *Beef Bonanza: Or How to Get Rich on the Plains*. Philadelphia, 1881.

Bronson, E. B., *Reminiscences of a Ranchman*. Chicago, 1910.

Burlingame, Merrill C., *The Montana Frontier*. Helena, 1932.

Clay, John, *My Life on the Range*. Chicago, 1924. A dishonest book by a despicable character. Clay condoned the murders of homesteaders by cattlemen, of which he was one. He was a president of the Wyoming Stockgrowers Association, and helped to plan the organization's war on settlers.

Clemen, Rudolph Alexander, *The American Livestock and Meat Industry*. New York, 1923.

Cox, James, *The Cattle Industry of Texas and Adjacent Territory*. St. Louis, 1895.

Donaldson, Thomas, *The Public Domain: Its History*. Washington, 1884.

Dale, E. E., *The Range Cattle Industry*. Norman, 1930.

Dobie, J. Frank, *A Vaquero of the Brush Country*. Dallas, 1929.

——, *The Longhorns*. Boston, 1941.

Frantz, Joe B. and Julian E. Choate, Jr., *The American Cowboy: The Myth and the Reality*. Norman, 1955.

Frink, Maurice, *Cow Country Cavalcade: Eighty Years of the Wyoming Stockgrowers Associations*. Denver, 1954.

Gard, Wayne, *The Chisholm Trail*. Norman, 1954.

Greenberg, Dan W., *The Cattle Industry in Wyoming*. Cheyenne, 1932.

Hastings, Frank S., *A Ranchman's Recollections*. Chicago, 1921.

Hayter, Earl W., *Barbed Wire Fencing—A Prairie Invention: Its Rise and Influence in the Western States*. Chicago, 1939.

Hunter, J. Martin, *The Trail Drivers of Texas*. Nashville, 1925.

Jackson, W. Turrentine, *Railroad Relations of the Wyoming Stock Growers' Association*. Annals of Wyoming, Vol. XIX, 1947.

McCoy, Joseph G., *Historic Sketches of the Cattle Trade*. Kansas City, 1874. An extremely valuable book by the man who built the first shipping point on the western plains for Texas trail herds, the town of Abilene.

Maverick, Mary A., *Memoirs*. Rena Maverick Green, editor, San Antonio, 1921. Mrs. Maverick was the widow of the Texas lawyer-cattleman whose name became a noun in the English language.

Mercer, A. S., *The Banditti of the Plains*. Cheyenne, 1894. The history of the Johnson County War, which the Wyoming Stock Growers Association launched to drive out homesteaders. When the book appeared, Wyoming courts, under the influence of cattlemen, ordered it suppressed as "obscene" and ordered the destruction of all copies. Even the copyright copies were stolen from the Library of Congress. The printer who printed the book was driven out of business. However, a few original copies were smuggled out of Wyoming by men who were pursued by gunmen. A number of reprints have appeared. A classic of western Americana.

NEWSPAPERS WHICH CONTAIN MATERIAL ON THE ERA OF THE CATTLE BARONS:

Abilene Chronicle, 1867; Belton, Texas, *Weekly Independent*, 1865; Boonville, Missouri, *Weekly Observer*, 1860; *Cheyenne Daily Leader*, 1891–1893; *Cheyenne Daily Tribune*, 1890–1893; *Cheyenne Sun*, 1891–1892; *Chicago Daily Inter-Ocean*, 1891; *Chicago Daily Journal*, 1893; *Chicago Daily Press and Tribune*, 1890; *Dallas Herald*, 1860; *Fort Scott Democrat*, 1867; *Galveston Weekly News*, 1866; *Illinois Daily Journal*, 1859; Junction City, Kansas, *Weekly Union*, 1868; *Kansas City Daily Journal of Commerce*, 1870; *Kansas City Star*, 1870; *Kansas City Commonwealth*, 1871; *Kansas Daily Tribune*, 1867; *Leavenworth Daily Conservative*, 1871; *Lawrence Tribune*, 1872; *Lawrence Republican*, 1871; *New Orleans Times*, 1863; *New York Herald*, 1869; *New York Daily Times*, 1871; *New York Daily Tribune*, 1871; *Rocky Mountain News*, 1892; *Fort Worth Livestock Journal*, 1875; *Wichita City Eagle*, 1869.

Osgood, E. S., *The Day of the Cattleman*. Minneapolis, 1929.

Peake, C. B., *The Colorado Range Cattle Industry*. Glendale, 1939.

Pelzer, Louis, *The Cattleman's Frontier*. Glendale, 1936.

Rollins, Philip Ashton, *The Cowboy*. New York, 1906.

Sandoz, Marie, *The Cattlemen,* New York, 1958. Authoritative and dramatic by a first rate western historian.

Shannon, Fred A., *The Farmer's Last Frontier.* New York, 1945.

Streeter, Floyd Benjamin, *Prairie Trails and Cow Towns.* Boston, 1936.

Tait, J. S., *The Cattle-Fields of the Far West.* Edinburgh, 1884.

Treat, Payson J., *The National Land System.* New York, 1910.

Von Richthofen, Baron Walter, *Cattle Raising on the Plains of North America.* New York, 1885.

Webb, Walter Prescott, *The Great Plains.* Boston, 1931. A basic source book on the subject, and still outstanding in its field.